The Production and Consumption of Music in the Digital Age

The economic geography of music is evolving as new digital technologies, organizational forms, market dynamics, and consumer behavior continue to restructure the industry. This book is an international collection of case studies examining the spatial dynamics of today's music industry. Drawing on research from a diverse range of cities such as Santiago, Toronto, Paris, New York, Amsterdam, London, and Berlin, this volume helps readers understand how the production and consumption of music is changing at multiple scales—from global firms to local entrepreneurs; and, in multiple settings—from established clusters to burgeoning scenes. The volume is divided into interrelated sections and offers an engaging and immersive look at today's central players, processes, and spaces of music production and consumption. Academic students and researchers across the social sciences, including human geography, sociology, economics, and cultural studies, will find this volume helpful in answering questions about how and where music is financed, produced, marketed, distributed, curated, and consumed in the digital age.

Brian J. Hracs is a lecturer in human geography at the University of Southampton.

Michael Seman is a senior research associate at the University of North Texas Economics Research Group.

Tarek E. Virani is a post-doctoral research associate at Queen Mary University of London.

Routledge Studies in Human Geography

For a full list of titles in this series, please visit www.routledge.com

This series provides a forum for innovative, vibrant, and critical debate within Human Geography. Titles will reflect the wealth of research which is taking place in this diverse and ever-expanding field. Contributions will be drawn from the main sub-disciplines and from innovative areas of work which have no particular sub-disciplinary allegiances.

50 Intergenerational Space
Edited by Robert Vanderbeck and Nancy Worth

51 Performativity, Politics, and the Production of Social Space
Edited by Michael R. Glass and Reuben Rose-Redwood

52 Knowledge and the City
Concepts, applications and trends of knowledge-based urban development
Francisco Javier Carrillo, Tan Yigitcanlar, Blanca García and Antti Lönnqvist

53 Migration, Risk and Uncertainty
Allan M. Williams and Vladimír Baláž

54 Transport, Mobility, and the Production of Urban Space
Edited by Julie Cidell and David Prytherch

55 International Perspectives on Age-Friendly Cities
Edited by Kelly G. Fitzgerald and Francis G. Caro

56 Ageing Resource Communities
New frontiers of rural population change, community development and voluntarism
Edited by Mark Skinner and Neil Hanlon

57 Access, Property and American Urban Space
M. Gordon Brown

58 The Production and Consumption of Music in the Digital Age
Edited by Brian J. Hracs, Michael Seman and Tarek E. Virani

The Production and Consumption of Music in the Digital Age

Edited by
Brian J. Hracs,
Michael Seman and
Tarek E. Virani

NEW YORK AND LONDON

First published 2016
by Routledge
711 Third Avenue, New York, NY 10017

and by Routledge
2 Park Square, Milton Park, Abingdon, Oxon OX14 4RN

Routledge is an imprint of the Taylor & Francis Group, an informa business

Library of Congress Cataloging-in-Publication Data
Names: Hracs, Brian J. | Seman, Michael. | Virani, Tarek E.
Title: The production and consumption of music in the digital age / edited by Brian J. Hracs, Michael Seman and Tarek E. Virani.
Description: New York, NY : Routledge, 2017. | Series: Routledge studies in human geography ; 58 | Includes bibliographical references and index.
Identifiers: LCCN 2016007644 | ISBN 9781138851658
Subjects: LCSH: Music—Social aspects. | Musicians—Economic conditions. | Music trade. | Dissemination of music. | Music and the Internet. | Music and geography.
Classification: LCC ML3916 .P63 2017 | DDC 338.4/778—dc23
LC record available at http://lccn.loc.gov/2016007644

ISBN: 978-1-138-85165-8 (hbk)
ISBN: 978-1-315-72400-3 (ebk)

Typeset in Sabon
by Apex CoVantage, LLC

Contents

Figures

Tables

Acknowledgments

The origin of this edited collection lies in a series of conference sessions entitled "'This Must Be the Place': The Evolving Economic Geography of Music" that took place at the 2013 Association of American Geographers Annual Conference held in Los Angeles, California. We would like to thank all of the presenters and those in the audience for contributing to a stimulating day of discussion.

We would also like to thank those who contributed chapters to this book for their efforts in meeting deadlines and responding to editorial requests.

Finally, we would like to extend our thanks to the following people, who in various ways have made this collection possible: Andrea Hracs, Max Novick, Morag Shiach, Jennifer Koshatka Seman, Kerri Virani, and the faculty and staff of SMU-in-Taos.

Part I

Introduction

1 Introduction

The Evolving Economic Geography of Music

Brian J. Hracs, Michael Seman, and Tarek E. Virani

Although geographers have demonstrated a sustained empirical interest in music-related topics, the economic geography of music continues to evolve as new digital technologies and practices are introduced and adopted (Connell and Gibson 2003; Hracs 2012; Leyshon 2014). Indeed, new technologies, organizational forms, market dynamics, and consumer behavior continue to restructure the industry at multiple scales (from global firms to local entrepreneurs) and in multiple spatial settings (from established clusters and burgeoning scenes to online environments). Record labels and intermediaries are reinventing themselves while independent musicians are negotiating a range of new opportunities and challenges. Against this backdrop, a new interconnected sonic ecosystem of cities, scenes, venues, festivals, record shops, and online communities is emerging.

In the late 1990s and early 2000s the MP3 file format and file sharing networks such as Napster and Kazaa emerged as transformative forces. Together, the digitization and illegal downloading of music catalyzed a "structural shock" within the industry that fundamentally altered its spatial dynamics and business models (Hracs 2012). The change has been so dynamic and widespread that a framework for studying the global music landscape is emerging that views related activities in terms of pre- and post- "MP3 Crisis" (Hracs 2012).

In the contemporary era, change is constant and pervasive and it is difficult to measure or predict the impacts of digital technologies. For example, the rise of streaming services such as Spotify and Apple Music, the refusals of artists like Taylor Swift and Neil Young to allow their music to be streamed, and the near collapse of streaming companies like Jay Z's Tidal remind us that the effect of digitization on music is not only far from straightforward, but far from over. Given the restless dynamism associated with the contemporary marketplace for music, this volume gathers cutting-edge research that nuances our understanding of the digital revolution and raises new questions for further music-related research in geography.

Together, the scholars in this volume provide an analytical snapshot of how and why several important and interrelated processes in the music industry are evolving. The chapters are diverse in terms of theoretical framework, methods, and empirical focus, but they are unified by a common approach which emphasizes the geographic analysis of music, or "the examination of music and how it interacts with the people, economy, built environment, and technology that comprises a certain space or place" (Paquette 2014). Although nascent within the broader discipline, much like the analysis of food and other cultural phenomena, applying a geographic lens to music can offer considerable "insight into how landscapes develop and how they might continue to do so in the future" (Paquette 2014).

This volume acknowledges and builds upon relatively recent works, including Connell and Gibson's (2003) *Sound Tracks: Popular Music, Identity, and Place*, Bennett and Peterson's (2004) *Music Scenes: Local, Translocal, and Virtual*, Adam Krims' (2007) *Music and Urban Geography*, and Johansson and Bell's (2009) *Sound, Society and the Geography of Popular Music*. These books examine the geography of music holistically, but do not focus on the influence of digital technologies. The explicit focus on economic geography in this volume complements *Sonic Synergies: Music, Identity, Technology and Community* edited by Bloustien et al. (2008), which offers an excellent collection of essays about the influence of digital technologies from the perspectives of anthropology and cultural studies. Ultimately, this volume seeks to continue the lineage of geographers examining music by addressing the topic in terms of economics and digital technology—two aspects of the discipline that are still underutilized to analyze the production, distribution, and consumption of music.

The majority of the contributors to this volume are geographers by training, but the disciplines of urban planning, public policy, business, political science, cultural studies, and sociology are also represented. While many are established scholars who have chronicled developments in the music industry over time, others are emerging scholars with fresh perspectives and cutting-edge insights. It should also be noted that many of the contributors are not only music researchers and consumers but musicians in their own right. Together, the contributors address a range of questions related to music, digital technologies, and economic geography from a wide geographic spectrum that includes cities such as Santiago, Toronto, Paris, New York, Amsterdam, London, and Berlin among others.

This volume is structured to illustrate how digital technologies are altering every facet of the global music landscape. The reader is guided from the production of music, including the recording of songs, to the consumption of music which may occur in the home, at a festival, or online. The chapters are organized in sections to highlight the process from start to finish.

In the first section, "Recording," Watson (Chapter 2, this volume) and Arditi (Chapter 3, this volume) offer insight into how digital technologies have given musicians the financial and spatial freedom to eschew large studios (often controlled or owned outright by major labels) and record more affordably in their homes or project studios elsewhere, adhering to a time schedule they develop. However, this freedom is a double-edged sword.

Digital recording has blurred boundaries forcing everyone from recording engineers to interns looking to break into the music industry to be available 24/7. This availability often results in precarious work practices that exploit studio labor—a practice that ultimately benefits major labels.

In the second section, "Working," consideration is paid to how the digitally driven double-edged sword of freedom extends to musicians in all facets of their career and has also impacted those working at major labels. Digital technologies are continuing to allow music to be acquired free of charge or at a price point that is disadvantageous to musicians (e.g., through illegal downloading or low-paying streaming platforms). This loss in revenue and the retreat of label support is forcing musicians to exchange a specialized division of labor for a DIY approach. As Hracs notes in Chapter 4, this volume, it is not uncommon for indie musicians in Toronto to take on roles such as manager, promoter, booking agent, and merchandising expert. Yet, digital technologies also afford musicians spatial freedom from the established centers of music production. As a result, Hracs demonstrates that musicians are leaving Toronto's bohemian downtown core for more affordable and creative spaces in the suburbs. In Chapter 5, of this volume, Speers notes a similar multitasking trend amongst hip-hop artists in London. This trend proves problematic for two reasons. First, the new role of cultural entrepreneur causes some hip-hop artists internal friction as they struggle to balance art and commerce in their careers. Other artists find it difficult to master the digitally-driven skill sets required to be a cultural entrepreneur which results in the marginalization of their art in the commercial marketplace. Haijen (Chapter 6, this volume) focuses on this trend amongst Dutch hip-hop artists noting that although digital technology has lowered the barrier of entry for artists in the scene, increased competition places a heavier importance on artists being more entrepreneurial in nature. She found that having access to social and financial capital, a savvy business strategy, and retaining an authenticity were needed to survive in a crowded marketplace. Juggling these dynamics finds musicians engaging in business pursuits both online and in-person outside of the traditional locations of venues or recording studios while also underscoring the increasing need to network socially and professionally. Frenette (Chapter 7, this volume) examines working conditions at record companies during the digital age and finds that these employees face similar challenges to musicians. For example, as revenues continue to plummet, major label employees must learn how to fill multiple roles in order to remain viable as companies continue to restructure and shed employees in the digital age.

The steps taken to record music and the actions necessary to ensure that one can operate as a musician are often the backstory to what many interpret as the primary role of the musician . . . performer. Digital technologies have disrupted all facets of the music industry, with live performances being no exception. The core of a live performance is still a performer playing a song for an audience, but the instruments and equipment used in the process of that performance, the promoting of it, methods of selling tickets for it, and how it might be streamed globally or captured for fans to hear later are all areas affected by the digital revolution. Live performance is an important area to consider in the post-MP3 Crisis era, for although consumers may be buying less music, they are still going to see musicians play live.

Virani (Chapter 8, this volume) introduces the section, "Playing" with a case study of a London venue specializing in eclectic music programing that leans towards free improvisation. Virani details how the venue continues to act as a physical hub for the surrounding scene while leveraging digital technologies to archive what are generally one-time only performances. This archiving helps elevate the venue's brand globally, attracting interest and acts from far beyond its physical location and the scene it anchors. Johansson, Gripshover, and Bell (Chapter 9, this volume) shift the focus from London to Pittsburgh and Nashville where venues, including bars and clubs, have embraced digital technologies like social media to help promote shows and navigate ticket purchases. The authors suggest that the advent of the Internet has been advantageous to all venues, but continuing corporatization of larger venues and changing dynamics in ticketing, marketing, and booking may marginalize some smaller venues if they are not nimble in embracing a rapidly evolving set of digital tools. At the same time as revenues from recordings continue to fall, the popularity and prevalence of festivals has risen dramatically, giving a much-needed economic boost to musicians who tour. However, these festivals are shifting in mode in the digital age. Wynn and Dominguez-Villegas (Chapter 10, this volume) consider the "Newport Effect" and illustrate how a festival appearance, in this case at the storied Newport Folk Festival, ascends from being a live performance opportunity to a tool increasing one's brand cache on touring circuits. In Chapter 11, this volume, Jansson and Nilsson show how the changing structure of the music industry in the digital age is forcing musicians in Sweden to be more entrepreneurial. This results in festivals becoming interconnected, critical networking spaces for performers to gain more work—on tour and off.

Fans always want a final product that captures the performances of their favorite musicians. The "Distributing" section looks at how digital technologies have altered this step after recording, working, and playing that historically resulted in a physical product one purchased to enjoy at their own discretion. In Chapter 12, this volume, Bürkner notes how many in Berlin's thriving electronic dance music (EDM) scene take a cue from the previous "Working" and "Playing" sections and see the physical or digital product as a calling card to gain better shows at venues. For example, these scene participants release tracks on their own labels expecting low monetary returns, but increased name recognition for booking live shows. Brandellero and Kloosterman (Chapter 13, this volume) then shift the focus to the internationally recognized world music scene in Paris arguing that, much like music scenes around the globe, sales of physical products continue to decline while live performances have emerged as an important revenue stream. Scene actors respond to the effects of digitization by leveraging it for global promotion and communication concerning recordings and live shows, while also investing in the production of elaborately packaged physical products to differentiate product in the market. In Chapter 14, this volume, Sonnichsen explores another vital site of distribution—vinyl record stores. It is suggested that the success of these stores is partially due to their ability to create hybrid places incorporating both a physical and online presence which mirrors, to a degree, the business acumen of participants in the Parisian world music scene. Looking to the future, Pratt (Chapter 15, this volume) considers the global dynamics of copyright law and argues that the future of global music consumption rests on the interaction between the continuing development of digital technologies and copyright issues, and how that interaction is interpreted in countries with very different laws and moral perspectives regarding the subject.

The final section, "Promoting and Consuming" explores how digital technologies have changed the relationships amongst musicians, intermediaries, fans, and the spatial arenas where interactions take place. In Chapter 16, this volume, Arriagada considers the activities of several bloggers living in Santiago who focus on creating and disseminating content online about their local music scene while also acting as funnels for information concerning music scenes abroad for readers in Santiago. The practice encompasses aesthetic preferences, design, and technical acumen to create a "digital habitus" imbuing the bloggers with competitive cultural capital exceeding that afforded to those who only operate in a journalistic space. Lange (Chapter 17, this volume) then addresses the enduring value of professional tastemakers such as music journalists, suggesting that it is increasingly tenuous as digital technologies have opened the door for passionate amateur scribes like the bloggers in Santiago and elsewhere to gain international followings. In addition, Lange outlines the growing importance of digital music service algorithms which are designed to curate personal playlists based on past selections. Finally, Chapter 18, this volume, examines the viability of digitally-driven crowdsourcing options in the music industry. Leyshon, Thrift, Crewe, French, and Webb detail how crowdsourcing technology has made it easier for bands to connect with fans directly. This connection allows the creation of an album to be an immersive experience wherein fans can track its progress and fund it while it is still in the developmental stages. The authors note that while crowdsourcing is currently met with enthusiasm, it alone is not a significant enough force to reverse the course of the music industry's overall economic struggles and places an additional burden and risk on artists employing the process.

The chapters contained in this volume are a snapshot of an industry in transition. This volume is meant to inform, engage, and encourage readers to push the discourse presented further through their own research and writing. Digital technologies have disrupted the majority of the music industry and have brought entirely new economic and spatial dimensions to those who create music and those who listen to it. As the industry continues to search for ways to adjust to this disruption and fans encounter and embrace new ways of enjoying music, it is important to continue documenting and analyzing this transition through a geographic lens. After all, there will always be someone ready to sing a song and someone ready to listen—it is our hope that this research will help to facilitate that connection, wherever it may take place.

REFERENCES

Bennett, Andy, and Richard, A. Peterson. *Music Scenes: Local, Translocal, and Virtual*. Nashville: Vanderbilt University Press, 2004.

Bloustien, Gerry, Margaret Peters, and Susan Luckman. *Sonic Synergies: Music, Identity, Technology and Community*. Burlington: Ashgate Press, 2008.

Connell, John, and Chris Gibson. *Sound Tracks: Popular Music, Identity, and Place*. London: Routledge, 2003.

Hracs, Brian J. "A Creative Industry in Transition: The Rise of Digitally Driven Independent Music Production." *Growth and Change* 43, no. 3 (2012): 442–461.

Johansson, Ola, and Thomas L. Bell. *Sound, Society and the Geography of Popular Music*. Burlington: Ashgate Press, 2009.

Krims, Adam. *Music and Urban Geography*. New York: Routledge, 2007.

Leyshon, Andrew. *Reformatted: Code, Networks and the Transformation of the Music Industry*. Oxford: Oxford University Press, 2014.

Paquette, Danielle. (2014, September 8). "Meet the Man Who Studies Indie Music Economies." Accessed September 8, 2014. http://www.washingtonpost.com/news/storyline/wp/2014/09/08/meet-the-man-who-studies-indie-musics-economic-impact-yes-hes-in-a-band-too/

Part II
Recording

2 Laptops, Pro Tools, and File Transfer Protocols

On the Intensification and Extensification of Recording Work in the Digital Age

Allan Watson

Cultural and creative workers, it has been argued, symbolize the contemporary transformations of work perhaps more than any other type of worker (see Gill and Pratt 2008). Such an argument stems from the pervasive effects of neoliberalization in the cultural industries, which has seen these industries become marked by an expanding workforce comprising freelance, casualized, and project-linked persons (McRobbie 2002). Indeed, for Jones (1996), cultural and creative workers are "exemplars" of the move away from stable notions of career to more informal, insecure, and discontinuous employment. The music industry is no exception. Over the past decade, a significant body of literature has emerged concerned with this "precarity," which characterizes cultural and creative work (see, for example, Arditi, this volume; Frenette, this volume; Gill and Pratt 2008; Hracs and Leslie 2014; Murdock 2003; Neilson and Rossiter 2005; Ross 2008; Watson 2013). Providing critical perspectives on the politics of cultural work, such work has been concerned with revealing the subjective experiences of cultural and creative workers who are subject to precarious working lives, long hours, and self-exploitation.

Yet, although the nature of creative work has received significant attention from this particular angle, little research has been undertaken on subjective experiences of performing the work *itself*. Elsewhere, in literature concerned with communication- and information-rich service sector jobs, a growing body of literature has been concerned with how a combination of flexible working practices and new technologies for working and communicating are resulting in not only the *intensification* of work, but also its *extensification*—that is to say, the exporting of work across different spaces/scales and times—and the impact of this on individual workers and their families/households. Given the flexible and often technological nature of creative work, it is somewhat surprising that such concerns have rarely been focused towards the creative industries. One area of exception in this respect is research into working lives in new media (see, for example: Henninger and Gottschall 2007; Jarvis and Pratt 2006; Perrons 2003).

This chapter focuses on one particular sector of the creative economy—the recording sector of the music industry (for a more in-depth appraisal of this sector, see Watson 2014). The recording sector is an appropriate one to focus on when considering the working lives of creative workers, given the freelance and flexible, yet increasingly precarious, nature of work in the sector (see Arditi, this volume; Watson 2013). It is also a sector in which working relations between freelance labor and firms are highly complex and ephemeral. As the knowledge base required to produce a recorded musical product is largely external to the record company, recording projects are carried out mainly in the market, in order that record companies can draw on essential competencies as individual projects require. As such, "market-based" projects transcend the boundaries of firms (Lorenzen and Frederickson 2005).

The main focus of this chapter, building on the above research, is on the way in which new technologies—including laptop Digital Audio Workstations (DAWs), mobile phones, stem-mixing, and networking technologies such as File Transfer Protocols (FTP)—are changing the spatial and temporal nature of recording work, and the subjective experiences of these changes amongst recording engineers. The chapter seeks to demonstrate how developments in digital recording technologies—in particular recording software running on laptop computers—are enabling increased forms of flexibility in terms of work locations and times, yet at the same time are resulting in the increased overflowing of work into the home environment and the heightening of a culture of long and unsociable working hours. The chapter begins with a brief review of recent literature on the nature of creative work, which in particular highlights its flexible yet precarious nature. Following this, the chapter outlines developments in recording software technology and the ways in which these developments have fundamentally altered the nature of music production, in particular emphasizing the mobility that has been enabled by digital recording platforms. Building from this discussion, the chapter then considers the extensification and intensification of work, emphasizing both the role of technology in the spatial and temporal overflowing of work, in particular into the home environment.

The discussion presented in this chapter is based on empirical data from 20 semi-structured interviews undertaken with record producers and recording engineers working in recording studios in the UK between June 2010 and August 2013. Interviewees were from a range of employment categories—freelance, contracted to a recording studio, or owner-operator of a studio (this chapter is in particular concerned with the experiences of freelance recording engineers). The majority of the interviews were undertaken at the recording studios in which the interviewees worked, ranging from very small project studios to large internationally renowned recording facilities. This provided important observational data on the types of workspaces in which producers and engineers were working in, the types of recording technologies they were typically using (for example, large analog consoles versus solely computer-based set-ups), and the range of recording activities these studios were able to provide. All interviews were undertaken using a common schedule of questions, but with flexibility to explore interesting issues that emerged in discussion. Interviews lasted between 30 minutes and 2 hours, resulting in a total of almost 19 hours of recorded data. All interviews were recorded and transcribed, and transcripts were subsequently analyzed using systematic coding and recoding based around key themes and common categories emerging from the data, considered in relation to the overall theoretical framework. Interview data is supplemented with insights gained from a large number of informal conversations with recording engineers via the Twitter social networking platform.

THE NATURE OF CREATIVE WORK

The creative industries are characterized, perhaps more than any other industrial sector, by project-based work (Christopherson 2004). As Gill and Pratt (2008) note, employment in project-based work is characterized by short tenure and constant employment uncertainty; that is to say, it is *precarious* employment (see also: Murdock 2003; Ross 2008). Here the terms "precarity" and "precariousness" (see Neilson and Rossiter 2005) are used to refer to all forms of insecure, contingent flexible work, from illegalized, casualized, temporary employment to homeworking, piecework, and freelancing. Gill and Pratt (2008) highlight how increasing numbers of workers in affluent societies are engaged in insecure, casualized, or irregular labor and note that while capitalist labor has always been characterized by intermittency for lower-paid and lower-skilled workers, the recent departure is the addition of well-paid and high-status workers into this group of "precarious workers," who have become subject to "structured job insecurity" (Blair et al. 2001, 174). Hesmondhalgh and Baker (2010) identify a number of features that apply to labor in the cultural industries, including irregular work, short-term contracts, little job protection, uncertain career prospects, and unequal earnings.

Further, there has developed in most sectors of the creative economy a new relationship between employee and employer, where employers no longer accept responsibility for the employment and development of the workforce, but rather have a relationship with the employee that is transactional, contractual, and short-term (du Gay et al. 1996). Recent research on the work and employment of record producers and recording engineers, for example, has demonstrated how new employment relations between producers/engineers and recording studios have shifted the pressure of obtaining work, and the financial risk of not doing so, on to individual producers and engineers (see: Arditi, this volume; Watson 2013). As such, risks have been passed to the workforce and away from firms (Dex et al. 2000), and individuals have a heightened level of responsibility for their individual destinies (Ekinsmyth 1999, 2002). Thus, Entwistle and Wissinger describe creative work as "unpredictable, erratic and precarious" making "considerable demands upon the individual in terms of their self-reliance and resourcefulness" (2006, 782).

Henninger and Gottschall note that one of the distinct features of freelance work is that "working conditions are flexible in terms of working hours, income, and place of work" (2007, 44). Neff et al. suggest that this is a "desired flexibility," that is to say, that flexibility is valued as part of the "postmodern work ethic" (2005, 330) in which workers can exercise individual choices regarding work and life arrangements. As such, "flexibility" and "work-life balance" are often construed as one and the same. However, while some scholars have suggested that this offers a rising potential for improvements in work-life balance, others have stressed that "work patterns demanding flexibility might decrease individual autonomy regarding workload and work organization and thus threaten the balance of work and life" (Henninger and Gottschall 2007, 45). For cultural and creative workers, job gratification can come at a heavy, sacrificial cost (Ross 2008). Gill and Pratt (2008), for example, argue that much research points to the extraordinarily long working hours of cultural workers, often considerably in excess of working-time agreements and exerting heavy costs on, or even prohibiting, personal relationships with friends, family, and partners outside work.

Gill and Pratt (2008) also note that research points to the significant disruption caused by "bulimic" patterns of working, in which "idle periods with no work can give way to periods that require intense activity, round-the-clock working, with its attendant impacts on sleep, diet, health and social life" (2008, 17). This has led to the development of productivist critiques that focus on the politics of cultural work and emphasize the exploitive nature of capital and the demands placed on workers by the commercial imperatives of the firm (see, for example, Banks 2007). It is argued in such critiques that a cultural worker's whole life and sense of self becomes bound up with their work (Blair 2001), effectively commercializing the entire context of their life (Pongratz and Voß 2003). Gregg (2011) terms this "presence bleed," in which boundaries between personal and professional identities no longer apply.

Related to this is an academic debate regarding the role of new technologies for working at distance (for example, laptop computers and mobile phones) in exacerbating the overflowing of work practices into private life, and especially into the home space (see Gregg 2011). Jarvis and Pratt (2006), for example, explore the extensification and overflowing of work and its impacts on individual workers and new media households in San Francisco. The process of extensification, they suggest, is one which involves the distribution or exporting of work across different spaces/scales and times, and is one which is experienced "both in terms of the *nature of work* (a temporal overflowing) and *the location of work* (spatial overflowing)" (2006, 337, emphasis in original). Many accounts view this temporal and spatial overflowing of work as being indicative of the deeply exploitive nature of creative work, with firms taking advantage of the fears of unemployment amongst workers in precarious industries to draw a benefit from "free" labor.

However, as Hesmondhalgh (2010) argues, the situation is much more complicated than one of simple exploitation. This free labor is "simultaneously voluntarily given and unwanted, enjoyed and exploited" (Terranova 2004, 74). As Gill and Pratt (2008) argue, while "long hours and the takeover of life by labor may be dictated by punishing schedules and oppressive deadlines, and may be experienced as intensely exploitive, but they may also be the outcome of passionate engagement, creativity and self-expression" (2008, 18). Indeed, the passionate engagement with, and attachment to, work in the creative industries means that many cultural and creative workers, as Gill and Pratt (2008) recognize, frequently make no distinction between "work time" and "other time," with the borders between work and life becoming more permeable or even dissolving entirely (c.f., Henninger and Gottschall 2007). Work, as paid employment, is not, therefore, separated out in a clear-cut way from other domains of life. Furthermore, for many cultural workers, self-exploitation and dispensability are seen as the price to be paid for a career that offers both autonomy and flexibility (Neff et al. 2005). The experience of cultural workers, and the meanings which cultural workers give to working practices, may then, therefore, not correlate with many productivist critiques.

THE LAPTOP DIGITAL AUDIO WORKSTATION AND THE MOBILITY OF RECORDING TECHNOLOGIES

This chapter focuses specifically on the impact of technological developments on the work of freelance recording studio engineers. The role of the engineer is both a technical and an artistic one, being skilled in operating the complex equipment of the recording studio, and in getting the required sound and effect from the equipment (Longhurst 1995; Negus 1992), transforming sound from performance to artifact (Tankel 1990). Their work is highly dependent upon a very particular set of technologies. It is the multitrack recording studio that is the basis for our contemporary notions of what a recording studio is, how it operates, and how music is made (see Théberge 2012). Now the most common technological method of recording popular music, multi-tracking is a method of sound recording that allows for the separate recording of multiple sound sources to create a cohesive whole. Musical instruments and vocals can be recorded, either one at a time or simultaneously, onto multiple tracks of audio that can be individually processed and manipulated, either during or post-recording, to produce the desired results. It was the development of in-line digital recording consoles in the late 1960s, led by the UK technology companies Solid State Logic (SSL) and Neve, which really defined the beginning of the era of multi-tracking. As Théberge (2004) notes, the entire development of multi-tracking, along with the practices associated with it, is inseparable from a simultaneous evolution in the design of recording and mixing consoles. The multi-track recording console would become the center-piece of almost every recording studio. Given their high cost and large physical size prevented their purchase or use outside the realms of the professional recording studio, the work of recording engineers was firmly located within the formalized space of the studio.

However, during the late 1980s and early 1990s, a new generation of computer software emerged for recording music. This new generation of software was enabled primarily by the increased level of processing power and storage capacity found in personal computers from the 1990s onwards (Théberge 2004). Writing in 2000, Berk suggested that:

> The future of music technology is likely to be centered on the desktop. Advances in desktop processor speeds and hard disk capacity have made it possible to run all the elements of a virtual electronic studio—multitrack recorder, signal processors, and sound sources—on a single machine
>
> (Berk 2000, 201).

In what are commonly now referred to as computer-based Digital Audio Workstations (DAWs), a computer both acts as a host for an audio interface and software and provides processing power for audio editing. The software controls all related hardware components and provides a user interface to allow for recording, editing, and playback. Prominent examples of software include Avid Technology's Pro Tools, Apple's Logic Pro, and Steinberg's Cubase. These software programs have enabled multi-track recording and mixing on a level only previously afforded by large expensive recording consoles, as well as incorporating inbuilt effects processors that were previously only available as expensive "outboard" units separate to the consoles. The shift to digital software-enabled recording has significantly reduced the cost of entry-level recording equipment, which has improved the quality and capacity of home recording (Arditi, this volume; Leyshon 2009). Therefore, the development of software DAWs has had a significant beneficial impact for smaller project and home studios. Théberge (2012), for example, reports data from the U.S. census that shows an increase both in the number of commercial studios and people involved in sound recording between 1997 and 2002.

With home computers becoming powerful enough to run audio-production software and affordable enough to become part of a home studio (Knowles and Hewitt 2012), the proliferation of DAWs has resulted in the home space becoming a space of production. DAWs have "enabled the un-tethering of professional and semi-professional production practices from the geographical confines of the large-scale recording studio" (Holland 2013, no pagination), and brought into the home those recording practices that were previously only possible in a formal recording studio. Yet, the idea of "home recording," much like the recording studio, suggests another spatial fixing of the recording process, i.e., recording software installed on a desktop computer fixed within a room. This is something that has been rendered outdated by developments in the performance of laptop computers which mean that many are now capable of running processor- and memory-intensive DAW software packages. This, combined with the portability of these devices, as Prior suggests, "opens up a series of possibilities for music that sends it beyond spatial anchorages such as the recording studio or domestic space" (2008, 916). This is a significant development in terms of the work of recording engineers, because for the first time it frees their work from fixed working environments; as Prior notes "the difference is . . . mobility" (2008, 915).

Take, for example, location recording, where recording techniques are employed outside the studio in a range of alternative spaces, for reasons that might include capturing particular acoustics (for example, recording in a church), recording in the home environment of an artist where they feel more productive or comfortable, or recording a live performance. This is something that has been possible since the 1950s, but due to the size and expense of studio-quality recording equipment required equipment to be either trucked to a particular venue or installed on a mobile recording truck. Contrast this with the situation today, where an engineer can arrive on location with equipment that fits into little more than two bags. Central to this is the laptop, which, as Prior (2008) argues, encapsulates technological convergence, in that with the right software it replaces the function of a host of hardware devices (see also Arditi, this volume). The laptop, combined with a selection of microphones, an audio interface, microphone preamplifier, and some material for baffling sound, constitutes a modern "rig" for location recording.

This makes location recording a much easier and feasible option for recording in the digital age. This is significant not only because it allows for (indeed, increases the demand for) the increased mobility of the recording engineer. It is significant with regards to the need for freelance engineers to win work because it allows an engineer to take work when, and wherever, it arises, while at the same time allowing for the client to avoid expensive studio fees during a time when recording budgets are small.

It is important to recognize that the work of the recording engineer goes beyond recording a moment of performance to include activities such as mixing which are most frequently undertaken without the client present. In this sense, the DAW-enabled laptop also frees the engineer from the studio space and opens up a range of other spaces of work for the recording engineer. Activities like mixing are frequently performed at home, in a coffee shop, or during a commute.

THE EXTENSIFICATION AND INTENSIFICATION OF RECORDING WORK

These technologies would seem to enable a high level of flexibility, allowing engineers to choose where and when they work on music-editing tasks.

Yet, the way in which work occurs in other times and other spaces than the formal recording studio is also undoubtedly reflective of the experience of many engineers that location and time of work become secondary considerations when faced with a long "to-do" list and a number of deadlines. Indeed, long hours have always been a part of recording studio work, with long days of 16–20 hours over a number of weeks typical on many recording projects. However, unlike in previous decades, in the contemporary industry these hours are not confined to the studio space. Long hours spent recording either inside the studio or on locations during the day are combined with long hours of audio editing in the evenings, mostly at home. Further, given the constant on-going development of new technologies and associated techniques for recording, editing, and mastering music, continuous learning becomes a crucial part of developing the "craft" of production and engineering. As one interviewee explained:

> Every time the software gets updated there are new sets of stuff to work. It gets more and more advanced and has more different features and different things you can do, so there's all those sort of things to learn. And then when it comes to mixing and things like that there's all sorts of techniques to learn as well as you're going along really
>
> (Interview 14, male engineer, thirties).

It is typical for many hours to be spent outside the studio on self-learning activities, which include the reading of "how to" books, websites, trade journals and magazines; engaging in online forums; as well as experimenting with software, plugins, effects, instruments, and recording and mixing equipment outside of the studio. The *intensification* of work thus becomes mirrored by the *extensification* of work. Clients who use recording services are wide and varied. Traditionally, the main clients for studios would have been record labels, but with falling recording budgets due to the "crisis of reproduction" in the music industry (see Leyshon 2009), other clients have become increasingly important. These include media companies involved in television, film, and computer games production, independent self-funded musicians, as well as a range of business clients looking for jingle/voice-over work for radio and advertising. The client base for any given freelance producer or engineer will depend upon areas of recording in which they may have gained a reputation (e.g., a particular genre of music, voice-over work, orchestral recording) as well as the reputation, size, facilities, and recording equipment of the recording studios in which they typically work. Whomever the clients, as in many other forms of service work, many engineers feel a sense of responsibility to their clients to make themselves ready and willing to work beyond their paid hours (see Gregg 2011).

Yet, long hours and the intrusion of work into private time is not just a product of an engineer's willingness to work. It is also driven by the precarious and freelance nature of employment in the sector, with the intensification of work a result of both the unpredictable nature and flow of work together with tight deadlines (Perrons 2003). For most freelance engineers, work cannot be turned down when it becomes available, and, further, due to the importance of repeat work to engineers, engineers are extremely careful not to do anything that might displease a client, such as not meeting a deadline or producing a product the client is happy with; as one interviewee noted, engineers "cannot turn work down . . . you're hamstrung; you've got no choice if you want to please the client, than to just do it in the time frame" (Interview 20, male recording engineer, twenties). Thus, engineers can potentially find themselves becoming slaves to the demands of clients. For the same interviewee, this resulted in the invasiveness of work into the home reaching new levels when the client asked to be present for the mixing of record. He described how "I did actually have the CEO and the chief A&R guy for [record label name omitted] in my bedroom looking over my shoulder while I was mixing something that they didn't want to pay the studio for," going on to note "that does happen more often than people like to admit I think." This anecdote is reflective of the seemingly growing expectation amongst clients that engineers will be on call as and when required for work. This is profoundly at odds with the "desired flexibility" (Neff et al. 2005) of freelance creative work, as described by another interviewee when explaining his reasons to become freelance rather than take a contracted position with a studio:

> I think with the whole freelance thing, not that I turned down much work, but the opportunity to turn down work, not burn out and not be expected to be on call permanently. It was quite a big factor in the decision
>
> (Interview 8, male engineer, twenties).

As is the case in other areas of the service economy, this expectation of engineers being "on-call" 24/7 is in part due to the "function creep" (Gregg 2011) of mobile devices which allow work communications to intrude into private time. As Jarvis and Pratt (2006) argue, rather than releasing workers from particular locational imperatives, new technologies often extend already long days by forcing additional business communication into the home and during the commute. Thus, the overflowing of work is being driven not only by changing behavioral dimensions but also by new *expectations* of communication.

Here, then, another set of technologies have been vital—networking technologies. As with other information sectors, the affordability of broadband in the home has facilitated home-working; however, in the recording sector high-speed broadband is particularly important given the size of the files often being received and sent for editing. Previously, only large studios had the internet infrastructure required for sending and receiving audio files, whereas superfast broadband connections are now available in many homes. This, along with the development of technologies for sharing digital music files between recording studios in geographically distant locations, such as File Transfer Protocol (FTP), allows large files to be sent and received even from the home studio. But yet again, the laptop is removing any physical fix to space—with its built-in connectivity the laptop can connect the user to the Internet through any one of the many networks available in public spaces and on public transport, making *almost* anywhere a globally-connected workspace for the recording engineer.

The commonality of these DAWs, means that not only can files be shared, but sent in a common format which allows files to be opened and worked on almost any computer with DAW software, before being saved and then transferred on. Further, another technological development, stem-mixing and stem-mastering—a method of mixing/mastering audio material based on creating groups of audio tracks and processing them separately—enables "sub mixes" or "subgroups" of audio files to be transferred and edited prior to combining them into a final master mix/master. Importantly in terms of obtaining work in a precarious sector, for recording engineers the ease of file transferring has opened up new avenues for obtaining work. It is now common for recording engineers to offer "online" mixing and mastering services to clients who they will not meet face-to-face. Yet, while these technologies would again seem to support flexibility in work, they are also resulting in an intensification of work and an increasing demand on the time of engineers. There exists an increasing awareness on the part of clients that engineers will have a software DAW on a computer which can recall, import, and export stems for editing. Thus, it is now commonplace for clients to call an engineer at any time of the day to request minor edits:

> You're on call all of the time . . . they'll send it back at half past one in the morning and say "Do you know what, can we have a tweak?" And you know that it is going to be mastered the next day . . . People just expect that now because they know you can just open up a laptop and the session is there with all the recall and everything else
>
> (Interview 20, male recording engineer, twenties).

Not only is this intrusive into the personal time of the engineer, but it often involves an intensification of work in the form of free labor, as often these tasks are asked for as a series of small "favors" or "tweaks." When or when not to provide this free labor to clients provides a dilemma for recording engineers, who often—despite efforts to provide clear expectations to clients regarding working hours on a project—find themselves undertaking free labor; as one engineer described via Twitter "I have an official line on mixing, stems, revisions, but that's all it is . . . an official line! Rarely sticks."

CONCLUSIONS

In this chapter, it has been argued that there has been a marked extensification and intensification of work for recording engineers in the digital age. It would seem that the technological developments in production and communication that in other parts of the music industry labor chain have proven to be positive—such as in allowing independent musicians to gain complete creative control over the production, direction, content, and marketing of their music and related products (see: Hracs 2012, this volume; Speers, this volume; Haijen, this volume)—have had a negative impact on the role and conditions of engineers. Based on interviews, as well as informal discussions with recording engineers via social media, this extensification and intensification seems to be attributed to two factors. First, the precarious nature of freelance working in the recording studio sector means that when work is available, it is not refused. This results in periods which are light on work being mirrored by periods of punishing overwork when work is plentiful. Such a "bulimic" pattern of work is common more widely across the creative industries. This periodic intensification of work is seen to be part and parcel of freelance work: it is an intensification which, despite frequently involving free labor, and despite its negative impacts on health and social life (see Watson 2013), is often accepted with little resistance in the face of continued job insecurity (see Campbell 2002).

Second, and related to the above, modern digital technologies for audio recording and editing, communication, and networking are allowing for the temporal and spatial "overflowing" of work (Jarvis and Pratt 2006) into the home, the commute, and a variety of other previously private spaces and times. Put simply, these technologies allow work to invade spaces and time that might have previously been less susceptible to its presence. Further, the purported convenience of mobile technologies can obscure the amount of additional work they demand (Gregg 2011). In particular, these technologies have led to an increased expectation from clients that engineers will be on call as and when required for work, whether or not it falls within agreed working hours or fees. Mirroring the economy more widely, then, it seems that while the adoption of flexible working is ostensibly about allowing the employees choice in terms of when and where to work, in practice this is not always the outcome (Higgins et al. 2000).

It is important, however, in closing this chapter, to recognize that while the extensification and intensification has largely here been presented in negative terms, it is not always experienced in a negative way. As Eikhof et al. (2007) have pointed out, it is typical of studies of work, and especially those considering work-life balance, to consider labor as a negative experience, overspills from which are to be contained. Such an assumption, they suggest, is contradictory to the fact that work can be satisfying, motivating, and self-fulfilling, and in itself be a sense of life satisfaction. One might argue this is especially the case with creative work, which, it is frequently suggested, is invariably more than a job but rather a labor of love. As Neff et al. argue, the desirable qualities of work in the creative industries have less to do with material rewards and more to do with the qualities of creative work, namely that it is "cool," "creative," and "autonomous" (2005, 330). This goes some way to explaining why recording is still very much a sought after career, despite high levels of employment uncertainty, exploitive and exhausting work regimes, and work overflowing into personal spaces and times. Furthermore, while it has been argued that particular technological developments are driving the extensification and intensification of work in the recording sector, these technologies are also central in facilitating the flexibility and autonomy that is a desired part of creative work.

REFERENCES

Banks, Mark. *The Politics of Cultural Work*. Basingstoke: Palgrave Macmillan, 2007.

Berk, Mike. "Analog Fetishes and Digital Futures." In *Modulations: A History of Electronic Music,*190–201. New York, NY: Caipirinha, 2000

Blair, Helen. 'You're Only as Good as Your Last Job": The Labor Process and Labor Market in the British Film Industry." *Work, Employment and Society* 15, no. 1 (2001): 149–169.

Blair, Helen, Susan Grey, and Keith Randle. "Working in Film: Employment in a Project Based Industry." *Personnel Review* 30, no. 2 (2001): 170–185.

Campbell, Iain. "Puzzles of Unpaid Overtime." In *Flexible Work Arrangements: Conceptualizations and International Experiences,* edited by Zeytinoglu, Isik U., 25–43. The Hague: Kluwer, 2002.

Christopherson, Susan. "The Divergent Worlds of New Media: How Policy Shapes Work in the Creative Economy" *Review of Policy Research* 21, no. 4 (2004): 543–558.

Dex, Shirley, Janet Willis, Richard Peterson, and Elaine Sheppard. "Freelance Workers and Contract Uncertainty: The Effects of Contractual Changes in the Television Industry." *Work, Employment and Society* 14, no. 2 (2000): 283–305.

du Gay, Paul, Graeme Salaman, and Bronwen Rees. "The Conduct of Management and the Management of Conduct: Contemporary Managerial Discourse and the Constitution of the 'Competent' Manager." *Journal of Management Studies* 33, no. 3 (1996): 263–282.

Eikhof, Doris Ruth, Chris Warhurst, and Axel Haunschild. "What Work? What Life? What Balance? Critical Reflections on the Work-Life Balance Debate" *Employee Relations* 29, no. 4 (2007): 325–333.

Ekinsmyth, Carol. "Professional Workers in a Risk Society." *Transactions of the Institute of British Geographers* 24, no. 3 (1999): 353–366.

Ekinsmyth, Carol. "Project Organization, Embeddedness and Risk in Magazine Publishing." *Regional Studies* 36, no. 3 (2002): 229–243.

Entwistle, Joanne, and Elizabeth Wissenger. "Keeping Up Appearances: Aesthetic Labor in the Fashion Modelling Industries of London and New York." *The Sociological Review* 54, no. 4 (2006): 774–794.

Gill, Rosalind, and Andy C. Pratt. "In the Social Factory? Immaterial Labor, Precariousness and Cultural Work." *Theory, Culture and Society* 25, no. 7–8 (2008): 1–30.

Gregg, Melissa. *Work's Intimacy*. Cambridge, UK: Polity, 2011.

Henninger, Annette, and Karin Gottschall. "Freelancers in Germany's Old and New Media Industry: Beyond Standard Patterns and Work and Life." *Critical Sociology* 33 (2007): 43–71.

Hesmondhalgh, David. "User-Generated Content, Free-Labor and the Cultural Industries." *Ephemera* 10, no. 3–4 (2010): 267–284.

Higgins, Christopher, Linda Duxbury, and Karen Lea Johnson. "Part-Time Work for Women: Does It Really Help Balance Work and Family?" *Human Resource Management* 39 (2000): 17–32.

Holland, Michael. "Rock Production and Staging in Non-Studio Spaces: Presentations of Space in Left or Right's Buzzy." *Journal of the Art of Record Production* no. 8 (2013). http://arpjournal.com.

Hracs, Brian J. "A Creative Industry in Transition: The Rise of Digitally Driven Independent Music Production" *Growth and Change* 43, no. 3 (2012): 442–461.

Hracs, Brian J., and Deborah Leslie. "Aesthetic Labour in Creative Industries: The Case of Independent Musicians in Toronto, Canada." *Area* 46, no. 1 (2014): 66–73.

Jarvis, Helen, and Andy C. Pratt. "Bringing It All Back Home: The Extensification and 'Overflowing' of Work. The Case of San Francisco's New Media Households." *Geoforum* 37 (2006): 331–339.

Jones, Candace. "Careers in Project Networks: The Case of the Film Industry." In *The Boundaryless Career: A New Employment Principle for a New Organizational Era,* edited by Arthur, Michael Bernard, and Denise M. Rousseau, 58–75. Oxford: Oxford University Press, 1996.

Knowles, Julian D., and Donna Hewitt. "Performance Recordivity: Studio Music in a Live Context." *Journal of the Art of Record Production*, no. 6 (2012). http://arpjournal.com/.

Leyshon, Andrew. "The Software Slump?: Digital Music, the Democratization of Technology, and the Decline of the Recording Studio Sector within the Musical Economy." *Environment and Planning A* 41 (2009): 1309–1331.

Longhurst, Brian. *Popular Music and Society*. Cambridge, UK: Polity Press, 1995.

Lorenzen, Mark, and Lars Frederiksen. "The Management of Projects and Product Experimentation: Examples from the Music Industry." *European Management Review* 2, no. 3 (2005): 198–211.

Neff, Gina, Elizabeth Wissinger, and Sharon Zukin. "Entrepreneurial Labor among Cultural Producers: 'Cool' Jobs in 'Hot' Industries." *Social Semiotics* 15, no. 3 (2005): 307–334.

Negus, Keith. *Producing Pop: Culture and Conflict in the Popular Music Industry.* London, UK: Edward Arnold, 1992.

Neilson, Brett, and Ned Rossiter. "From Precarity to Precariousness and Back Again: Labor, Life and Unstable Networks." *Fibreculture* 5 (2005): no pagination.

McRobbie, Angela. "Clubs to Companies: Notes on the Decline of Political Culture in Speeded Up Creative Worlds." *Cultural Studies* 16, no. 4 (2002): 516–531.

Murdock, Graham. "Back to Work: Cultural Labor in Altered Times." In *Cultural Work: Understanding the Cultural Industries,* edited by Beck, Andrew, 1– 12. London: Routledge, 2003.

Perrons, Dianne. "The New Economy and the Work Life Balance: A Case Study of the New Media Sector in Brighton and Hove." *Gender, Work and Organisation* 10, no. 1 (2003): 65–93.

Pongratz, Hans J., and Günter G. Voß. "From Employee to 'Entreployee': Towards a Self- Entrepreneurial Work Force?" *Concepts and Transformations* 8, no. 3 (2003): 239–254.

Prior, Nick. "OK Computer: Mobility, Software and the Laptop Musician." *Information, Communication and Society* 11, no. 7 (2012): 912–932.

Ross, Andrew. "The New Geography of Work: Power to the Precarious?" *Theory, Culture and Society* 25, no. 7–8 (2008): 31–49.

Tankel, Jonathan David. "The Practice of Recording Music: Remixing as Recoding." *Journal of Communication* 40, no. 3 (1990): 34–46.

Terranova, Tiziana. *Network Culture: Politics of the Information Age*. London, UK: Pluto Press, 2004.

Théberge, Paul. "The Network Studio: Historical and Technological Paths to a New Deal in Music Making." *Social Studies of Science* 34, no. 5 (2004): 759–781.

Théberge, Paul. "The End of the World As We Know It: The Changing Role of the Studio in the Internet Age." In *The Art of Record Production: An Introductory Reader for a New Academic Field,* edited by Frith, Simon, and Simon Zagorski-Thomas, 77–90. Farnham, UK: Ashgate, 2012.

Watson, Allan. "Running a Studio's a Silly Business: Work and Employment in the Contemporary Recording Studio Sector." *Area* 45, no. 3 (2013): 330–336.

Watson, Allan. *Cultural Production in and Beyond the Recording Studio*. New York, NY and London, UK: Routledge, 2014.

3 Disturbing Production

The Effects of Digital Music Production on Music Studios

David Arditi

In 2004, while living in Blacksburg, Virginia, some friends from Williamsburg, Virginia contacted me about meeting them in Nashville, Tennessee, to record an album. I played with this band, Ozone Patch, periodically for several years and needed very little practice to record the songs. My friends seemed very excited about the opportunity to make the pilgrimage to Nashville and record an album, so I packed my drums and made the 4-hour trek. During my drive, I imagined the recording studio with multiple rooms to record. I pictured a constant in-and-out flow of musicians as they used other studio space in the building. Perhaps I would see the next rising star of the Nashville music scene. To my surprise, we would not be going to a large multi-room professional studio. Instead, the friend that Ozone Patch knew in Nashville lived in a suburb of the city and we would be recording in his home.[1] The producer built a studio in his basement that included a control room, a studio room, and a waiting room. Over the course of the week, the waiting room was where we spent a lot of time watching the producer's kids—at one point we even helped the producer's wife move some furniture. In effect, besides paying this producer to record us, we were also doing labor around the house that he would have otherwise done. However, the studio had everything that it needed to create a great recording. What I observed on this trip to Nashville was the way that new project studios disturb production. As more producers record music in personal studios, the significance of cities known for recording music decreases.

This story highlights the decreased significance of recording studios. Bands no longer have to travel long distances to recording cities (i.e., Nashville, New York, Los Angeles, Austin) because the same level of professional quality recording is possible from the comfort of their own garage. However, the availability of Digital Audio Workstations (DAWs)—digital software that allows musicians and producers to record music on a computer—has a profound impact on the social relations of production in the studio. Much as digital music stores helped to close bricks-and-mortar music stores (Arditi 2014a), cheap DAWs deemphasized the importance of large record studios (see also Watson, this volume).

In effect, DAWs and small studios are *disturbing production* in two ways. First, DAWs disturb production by interfering, interrupting, or altering the basic function and position of professional major label studios. As more musicians and labels moved away from the large studio record production model, the social relations of production in the recording industry were disturbed. Second, the alteration to the social relations of production is disturbing in the sense that it is creating a deranged or unstable work environment for many of the workers who labor in recording studios. Studio production is dispersed through a number of smaller craft studios, which fundamentally changes the work environment for people working in studios. The prospect of full-time employment in large studios has always been a challenge, and studio workers are known to labor precariously to earn a living; however, digitization has rapidly increased this precariousness over the last several decades. Many of these workers live job-to-job or toil in part-time positions in other industries (retail, restaurants, etc.) hoping to catch a break with their music production career. We see in this new form of production a way for corporations to increase capital by cutting production budgets.

The disturbing disposition of the digital transition of recording studios is not the logical outcome of the progress of technology, but rather a product of the logic of capitalism. A raw technological determinism assumes that technology is devoid of ideology and that the creation of new technology can only mark progress that advances society and humanity. However, it is important to remember that technological development is embedded within a particular set of social relations. In *Noise, The Political Economy of Music* (1985), Jacques Attali postulates that the political economy of music predicts or foreshadows shifts in the economic system. With regard to record production, there is a remarkable similarity between the displacement of studio production from large label studios to small project (typically home) studios and the overall shift from large corporate-owned manufacturing plants to sub-contracted production in the global economy. A way to think about how the political economy of music foreshadows larger economic shifts is with regard to the buzzword "creative industries" and "creative workers" (Florida 2004). Yet, discussions about creativity obscure the social relations of production of workers, no matter their degree of creativity. Scholars in the critical and political economy tradition have discussed the Culture Industry (Horkheimer and Adorno 1972) and the cultural industries (Garnham 2000; Hesmondhalgh 2002; Miège 1989; Miège and Garnham 1979) for decades. The shift to discussing creative industries instead of cultural industries was part of a political project aimed at "reinvigorating post-industrial national economies" (Hesmondhalgh and Pratt 2005); this shift in terminologies, then, parallels the neoliberal shift to discussions of post-industrial, post-Fordist, and globalized economies. In effect, it "serves as a slogan, as a shorthand reference to, and thus mobilizes unreflectively, a range of supporting theoretical and political positions. This lack of reflexivity is essential to its ideological power" (Garnham 2005, 16). By using the term creative industries and deploying creativity to discuss cultural work, an ideological position is established based on romantic ideals such as autonomy, beauty, and flexibility. In reality, the ideology of creativity obscures the insecurity that creative labor experiences. In reality, this is "a world where flexibility is the mega-sign of affluence, and precariousness its flipside: one person's calculated risk is another's burden of labor, inequality is represented as the outcome of a moral test, and the young are supposed to regard insecurity as an opportunity rather than a constraint" (Miller 2010, 97). The insecurity associated with such flexible creativity means that workers are never quite sure how they will pay their bills (see also: Frenette, this volume; Haijen, this volume; Hracs, this volume; Speers, this volume; Watson, this volume).

This chapter traces changes to the recording studio, then interrogates these changes in terms of their effect on labor. It uses a cultural studies methodology that interrogates a cultural object (music studios) with the goal of illuminating the situatedness of that object within a broader social discourse. To do this, I employ the method of immanent critique as "a means of detecting the societal contradictions which offer the most determinate possibilities for emancipatory social change" (Antonio 1981, 330). My theoretical perspective is that of critical theory in the Frankfurt School tradition. What follows is a theorization of the effects of digital music production on the social relations of production in new studio spaces.

DISTURBING STUDIO SPACES

For decades, the culture industries have clustered in a few specific areas in a few cities. Allen Scott contends that this "clustering together of many different types of firms and specialized workers in one place provides all participants in the industry with a form of social insurance in the sense that clustering will almost always guarantee a relatively high probability of finding just the right kind of input within easy access at just the right time" (Scott 2000, 121). In other words, record labels and musicians cluster in New York, Los Angeles, and Nashville because there are already musicians in those locations.[2] The clustering allows easy access to a pool of qualified musicians, producers, engineers, Artist and Repertoire (A&R) staff, and composers, among other types of musical labor. With all of these different types of labor near each other, capitalism has an efficient system of production because little time and resources are lost seeking out the right types of labor. As a result, record labels built studios in these key cities to harness the cultural labor that existed in these locations. Large record label-owned or established studios allowed capital to expropriate labor at a large profit; however, DAWs are disturbing the structure and preeminence of these large studios in favor of smaller decentralized studios.

These large label-affiliated or established studios operated under a Fordist economic model. Their goal was to produce a large quantity of music with a minimal amount of costs. The most effective strategy to produce music was to develop an economy of scale. Berry Gordy perfected this model in the Detroit-based Motown Studios, 1959–1972, where composers/authors, musicians, engineers, producers, and directors worked under the same roof (Smith 2001). Gordy's model worked under a logic where the parts were interchangeable (Horkheimer and Adorno 1972); a song written by Holland-Dozier-Holland (a Motown songwriting team) could be recorded by Motown session musicians, vocals could be recorded by both Stevie Wonder and Marvin Gaye, then ultimately Motown management could decide which recording artist would have the song on their album. This was possible because of the location of various types of labor in one place.

This model was used across the recording industry. Again, this is based on an economy of scale. If we just consider janitorial services, one large studio that has the capacity to record multiple sessions at the same time could employ one janitor to clean the floors and bathrooms of a large studio, but if the studio were half the size and split into two locations, two janitors would be needed to keep the studio clean. I mention janitors because this is how deeply embedded labor is in these studios. On the production level, a team of sound engineers in a large studio allows an engineer to set-up a session in one room while recording is taking place in another room. Their labor is always necessary around the studio on a rotating basis to keep projects moving through the studio. While the clustering of labels in specific cities allowed for the grouping together of various types of labor across the recording industry (Scott 2000), these studios allowed for fewer workers on a larger scale.

Since recording equipment itself was so expensive, recording studios required a large capital investment to open; this meant that record labels were logical owners of studios. Recording studios have been the main element of the means of production in the recording industry. Therefore, record labels owned recording studios as a means to employ various types of labor to produce music. The reason why musicians recorded in these large studios was simple: musicians did not have the capital to own the means of production to record music. If musicians wanted to record and sell music, they had to pay for time in a studio. Ownership of the means of production is so important to capitalism because it is what allows capital to exploit labor. Since labor cannot afford to produce on their own, they need to work for capital. However, all of this changes with DAWs because of the diminution of the cost of recording equipment. This decline in the cost of recording equipment has led to the closing of recording studios.

For example, the closure of Room With a View studios illustrates the expense to run a high-end recording studio. *Billboard* closely followed the development of Room With a View studios going as far as to consider this small one-room facility "one of the top mixing facilities in the world" used by recording artists such as Dave Matthews Band, Ozzy Osbourne, Paula Cole and The Verve Pipe (Verna 1997). The excitement around the studio, which opened in 1994, stemmed from the studio's purchase of a Solid State Logic (SSL) 9000 J series console, a recording console that cost "hundreds of thousands of dollars" (Verna 1997). Slightly over a year later in 1998, Paul Verna reported a story about the closure of Room With a View. In this later story, former studio owner Alessandro Cecconi stated the following:

> When we got our 9000, there were three in town . . . [n]ow there are eight or nine, and SSL is dropping their prices, so the studios are dropping their rates. You can get an 80-channel board for $400,000. As a studio owner, you never win. You put in a 9000 and you sell your room for $2,000 a day. Then the next guy puts one in and charges $1,800 a day. Then the next guy charges $1,600.
>
> (Verna 1998a)

This illustrates the high cost of high-end recording studios. Cecconi attempted to create a high-end recording studio on a small-scale to compete with the large multi-room studios run by the major record labels. While Cecconi blames the cost of SSL for his studio's failure, a point that SSL vehemently denies (Verna 1998b), this episode exemplifies the barrier for small studios to purchase the means of production to compete on equal ground with the majors. For a major record label or an established multi-room studio, $400,000 for a piece of equipment is an investment in a business that can be made by reinvesting capital, whereas Room With a View undoubtedly received a loan to purchase the equipment that would ultimately have to be paid off with more expensive studio time. This initial difference in capital reflects the capacity for different types of studios to charge different daily rates; large concentrated firms will always be able to stifle the competition similar to the effects of Walmart on small businesses in the retail industry. And yet, it is an irony that Room With a View made an attempt to compete with large studios by purchasing an expensive recording console at a time when expensive recording equipment was quickly becoming unnecessary.

A transformation to this model of large recording studios began decades ago because studio equipment has become less expensive, smaller, and more portable. As the smaller and cheaper equipment has improved in quality, "the distinction between what can be considered a 'professional' or 'commercial' project studio and simply a 'personal' or 'home' studio has become increasingly difficult to make" (Théberge 2012, 83). Since high quality recording technology is available in the home that is indistinguishable from that available in expensive studios, there has been widespread adaptation of these technologies by musicians and producers. A report by *Billboard* about the closing of Hit Factory in New York City and Cello Studios in Los Angeles within five days in 2005 points to the fact that music can be "completed in small, inexpensive DAW-based suites, some of them personal or home studios" (Walsh 2005). The low cost of new recording technology has lowered the cost of the means of production displacing the importance of large studios in the recording process. Even Sony Studio, one of the last unionized studios in NYC was valued "more as real estate than any amount of financial gain, organization efficiency or corporate prestige" (Théberge 2012, 78). In other words, even the organizational efficiency and corporate inertia of large studios was no match for the increased efficiency of outsourcing studio work to independent producers. Susan Christopherson highlights a similar process in the film and television industries where "new technologies have also affected content production, making it less expensive and adapted to the demand for inexpensive programming. In particular, light-weight video, lighting and audio equipment have made it possible to reduce the number of people necessary for a 'shoot'" (Christopherson 2008, 79). Because cheaper production processes are available, film and television budgets have decreased, thereby forcing producers to produce content on smaller budgets using cheaper technologies; this is precisely the process taking place in the recording industry.

Large studios have been closing around the country. Mergers have been the source of some closures, such as the A&M Recording Studios complex, which closed as a result of Universal Music Group's purchasing of Polygram records in 1999 (Verna 1999). In New York City, Hit Factory, famous for recording artists from Paul Simon to Michael Jackson, closed its doors in 2005 and is now luxury condos (Rose 2009). As *Billboard* contends, "inexpensive, high-quality digital recording equipment has increasingly enabled musicians to take production into their own hands," a trend that the recording industry's trade journal claims to find "troubling" in places like Austin, Texas (Walsh 2003). I highlight the word troubling because it implies a degree of conscience on the part of *Billboard*; however, the overall thrust of the content in *Billboard* emphasizes the profitability of major record labels. To that end, the closing of studios in Austin, Texas, signals the reduced costs for major record labels to produce and sell albums. In fact, later in the same article (Walsh 2003), *Billboard* blames the closing of Austin's studios on the declining major label recording budgets; however, the article does not identify the availability of cheap recording equipment with the declining budgets.

What causes the decline of major record label recording budgets? The dominant narrative perpetuates the idea that declining budgets are a direct result of declining music sales. As an example, an article in the *Christian Science Monitor* relays the narrative that "following the downturn in music sales this decade, many studios are struggling or simply have closed their doors" (Guarino 2009). This articulation implies that studios are closing because of declining music sales. However, as I have demonstrated elsewhere (Arditi 2014a, 2014c), this argument is specious because the major record labels define this narrative. A critical analysis of the status of recording budgets points in a different direction: the decline of the cost of the means of production (in this instance, recording equipment and space) led to smaller budgets. Smaller budgets are a result of the logic of capitalism. Why would a label budget for a $2,000/day studio when it can budget for a studio that charges $500/day? Major record labels will not spend unnecessary money on the recording process. Because recording can be done on a small scale from small/boutique/producer-owned/home studios, there is no longer a need for record labels' budgets to support the overhead cost of running a large recording studio. The new low cost of the means of record production disturbed production by forcing the closure of large studios and changing the space of record production to decentralized small studios.

As a result of the shuttering of large studios in major recording cities, there has been a parallel shift that disturbs the importance of these cities. Austin, Texas, is an example of a burgeoning music studio scene that thrives on independent music. Musicians began recording in Austin specifically to avoid the large studios in Los Angeles, New York, and Nashville, which formed a recording scene of its own. However, even smaller studios in Austin struggle to stay open and remain relevant as recording has become a cottage industry (Guarino 2009; Walsh 2003). Not only can musicians avoid the cost of a large studio, now musicians can avoid the recording cities altogether. Digital technology allows musicians to record at home, register with ASCAP or BMI online, and even have musicians record tracks from distant locations. The hegemony of recording cities has been displaced by a cottage industry that allows small home studios to surface across the United States and the world.

Small home studios have become a prerequisite to a musician's identity. In an ethnography of the underground hip-hop music scene entitled "Get on the Mic: Recording Studios as Symbolic Spaces in Rap Music" (2014), Geoff Harkness investigates the role of studio space in rap music. In Harkness' illustration of the symbolic spaces in which emcees record and produce their music, I see two levels of craft production. First, Harkness describes the studio space of National Sound, a "professional studio with enough computer gear and digital paraphernalia to fill a small airplane hangar" (Harkness 2014, 82). Second, Harkness identifies the myriad varieties of home studio spaces. These spaces remove the centrality of capital in the recording process because they allow for the dispersal of recording sites. However, these new spaces more thoroughly point to the disturbing types of labor that are a quintessential part of the contemporary recording industry.

DISTURBING LABOR

Before the proliferation of DAWs and cheap recording equipment, musicians were the primary source of precarious casual labor in the recording industry. Many musicians have an ideology that to succeed in their craft, they need to sign a record contract, and as part of that ideology, they earn a living by not committing themselves to a stable career. Rather, musicians dedicate their lives to one day "making it" in the music business by playing gigs at night and working part-time jobs or teaching music lessons during the day. In doing so, these musicians accept whatever type of work can permit them the flexibility to set their own schedule. Since they see their primary source of work (i.e., being a musician) as flexible and casual, they are willing to accept other forms of flexible and casual employment to supplement their income (Arditi 2014b). This has been the labor model for musicians for the better part of a century. Attali's proclamation that the political economy of music foreshadows the broader political economic system is relevant here because the global economic system shifted to embrace the contingent nature of employment for musicians for all types of labor. "Capital-owners have won lavish returns from casualization—subcontracting, outsourcing and other modes of flexploitation—and increasingly expect the same in higher-skill sectors of the economy. As a result, we have seen the steady march of contingency into the lower and middle levels of the professional and high-wage service industries" (Ross 2008, 34). As Andrew Ross suggests, capital is instituting precarious labor at all levels and in all types of labor. This has been implemented through the language of creativity and creative workers under the argument that for workers to be the most productive and happiest, they must be given the space to have a flexible work environment. The non-musician labor in the recording industry is increasingly emulating the labor conditions of musicians. While some workers within the cultural industries have made considerable money from flexible outsourced label, far more make less money.

In large multi-room studios, there are a number of labor positions necessary for the everyday functioning of the studio. As discussed above, this labor includes everything from the janitorial staff to sound engineers. Large studios employ these workers on a full-time basis to ensure a smoothly operating studio. Therefore, these studios must pay employees for working full-time, which includes complying with required benefits such as health insurance. This is the "organizational efficiency" (Théberge 2012) discussed above; because record labels owned large studios, they already had labor within these studios. There was no need to locate workers and negotiate their wages because they were part of the studio; labor in these large studios was part of the means of production. Small studios work under a mode of production where the cost of the means of production is shifted to labor itself.

The political economy of this scenario is interesting because of the way the new model places the economic burden on subcontracted firms. As a hypothetical example, whereas an established studio may charge $1,500–2,000/day for the use of a studio, a small professional project studio may charge $50/hour (or $400 for an eight-hour day). The availability of cheap digital recording equipment is not enough to explain this decrease in price; it can only be described in terms of a parallel reduction in labor costs. As Susan Christopherson characterizes this process, "large media firms are paring down their production workforces to an essential core and using temporary workers and self-employed workers on an as-needed basis" (Christopherson 2008, 83). In other words, record labels reduce the cost to produce albums by relying on contingent labor that not only produces music at a lower cost, but also does this by employing fewer workers. Small project studios are operated generally by the owner who acts as owner/producer/engineer/janitor as is the case with Abe at National Sound (Harkness 2014). Even in instances where the producer has a big name, these relations of production require the producer to determine his/her studio's labor configuration to meet the demands of a budget. In other words, it is the producer's decision who to hire to help run the studio. Unfortunately, this has led to both a reduction in the number of employees necessary in a production studio and the amount that producers are willing to or required to (by law) pay employees; therefore, the proliferation of studios led to the increasingly precariousness of employment for workers in the recording industry; this is a particularly disturbing position to be in for recording industry labor.

The concept of "precariousness" used by many Autonomist Marxists and critical media theorists is relevant to this disturbing labor position. "Precariousness (in relation to work) refers to all forms of insecure, contingent, flexible work—from illegalized, casualized and temporary, to homeworking, piecework and freelancing" (Gill and Pratt 2008, 3). Whereas many economists promote creative labor as a model for all labor, Gill and Pratt argue that it is precisely the flexibility of so-called "creative workers" that puts them in an insecure position. For instance, the two types of new project studios, described by Harkness (2014), allow for endless tinkering on the part of musicians, and in the professional project studios, it overworks the staff of the studio for little pay. The musician's home tinkering is a form of homeworking that advances itself in perpetuity—a musician will spend all of his/her free time working on a track to "perfect" it, but there is no compensation for time-spent working. Meanwhile, producers who open their own studios must always work to find musicians to record sessions because their survival is contingent on a demand for studio space. If their studio business is struggling to remain open, the producer-owner must be willing to record whenever musicians would like to record. Whereas labor in a Fordist industrial model is guaranteed a wage as long as they remain employed, precarious employment is dependent on the whims of demand and the insecurity of the next project.

An illustrative fictional example of the lone-wolf record producer operating in his/her home studio can be seen in the television show *Nashville*. In the series the character Liam McGuinnis is a rock star turned producer who records music for fictional country musicians Rayna Jaymes and Scarlett O'Connor. Scriptwriters for *Nashville* promulgate McGuinnis as one of the hottest musicians and producers around and target him to try to tap some crossover success for the show's country acts. Two things are readily apparent about McGuinnis' position as a producer. First, he appears to work around the clock, whether that is Jaymes showing up at his home studio for unannounced late-night recording sessions or the marathon recording sessions that he does with O'Connor in which he ultimately gives her prescription drugs to keep recording music after long sessions. Second, no one else ever seems to work in McGuinnis' studio. This could be the product of it being a fictional television show; however, in other recording sessions on the show, there are always a number of background actors playing the roles of sound engineers. Rather, McGuinnis' long hours and solitary work environment demonstrate this move to single producers in home studios. And yet, McGuinnis' cultural capital as a rockstar and an in-demand producer apparently allow him to charge a significant rate to record.

However, recording a session as a singular owner-producer in a project studio can be difficult for even the most experienced producers. To help with the recording process, these owner-producers seek even more contingent/flexible/casual labor. Many project studios turn to interns to fill the labor gaps in their studios. Whereas the traditional studio model used apprentices to do much of the grunt work around the studio and paid sound engineers to facilitate the recording process, today's project studios focus on interns. In some instances, studios open "their doors to interns for a fee, thus generating income during periods when the studio would otherwise be unused" (Théberge 2012, 88). In other words, the precariousness of project studio employment encourages owner-producers to use further types of casualized labor and go as far as charging them for their exploitation. Alexandre Frenette (2013) reveals the precariousness of interns working for the major record labels. In a way, the interns who Frenette describes at the major record labels represent a privileged position compared to those working at project studios because the major labels, at least ostensibly, operate within the work standards of labor laws. Since project studios may operate without licenses, there may not be documentation that an individual interns at a project studio; this increases the precariousness of the intern's labor (see also Frenette, this volume).

By contracting studio work to small independent project studios, major record labels create disturbing labor practices that exploit the disempowered nature of small studio owner-producers (see also Watson, this volume). People that want to work in recording studios do so only in the most precarious of labor relations. Ultimately, the most practical way to make money working in a recording studio is for aspirant producers to build their own studios because their work is too contingent otherwise. However, opening one's own studio is also a quick route to bankruptcy because the lack of contracts and competition among producers makes owning a studio unstable. Major record labels continue to decrease recording budgets for their recording artists because they know how the system of outsourcing works to minimize costs. Recording artists seek out cheaper studios to make their recording budgets go further. As a result, there is a race to the bottom among project studio owners who are desperate to slash their rates to compete against the always-increasing number of project studios.

CONCLUSION

In moments of technological change, it is important to look beyond new technologies to understand the broader social, political, and economic changes that occur as a result of these changes. With the transition to digital production, cheap recording technology is not only disturbing the spaces of record production, but also disturbing the basic social relations of production in those spaces. An increasing number of people can enter the recording industry as record producers, but along with the increasing number of record producers is an increasing precarity among producers, even among those who used to work in large studios. Producers can work from project studios, but they do not know the next time they will get work. When they have a gig, any assistants need to be hired cheaply or as exploited intern labor. Musicians can spend countless hours in their home studios tinkering with their music, but that does not mean that anyone will ever purchase their music. In other words, there is a disturbing dearth of compensation for labor worked in a digital recording studio; rather than being paid an hourly wage, studio workers now depend on the completion of projects. What is happening with recording studio labor is similar to the labor situation that has been experienced by musicians over the past century; they are being asked to act as their own business. Furthermore, these shifts mirror broader shifts that are occurring in the global economy; production is increasingly outsourced to production sites that have no guarantee of future work because of their contracted position in relation to the corporations for which they produce—subcontractors bear all the risk.

While the availability of cheap recording equipment allows more musicians to record their music, it does not place those same musicians on equal footing with major record labels. Rather, the significance of the studio as the primary means of production in the recording industry has shifted. Now the major record labels administer their power through marketing and promotion; record labels utilize their connections to other cultural industries (movies, television, and games), which increases revenue based on the deployment of intellectual property rights and increased marketing budgets. Smaller recording budgets from record labels implement this shift.

While Digital Audio Workstations give musicians the tools to circumvent costly production processes, the availability of cheap recording equipment disturbs production. The contradiction of DAWs points to disturbing labor trends that precariatize recording studio labor. By paying fewer employees less money, the recording industry increases profits on the backs of its workers.

NOTES

1. Ironically, I had been in more professional studios in Blacksburg and Roanoke, Virginia, than this basement studio in Nashville. The waiting room was more like the part of the finished basement that was not part of the studio. Virginia Tech has a quality recording facility off campus and I had ample experience recording at the Downtown Music Lab in Roanoke, Virginia.
2. Of course, there are varying reasons why these cities became sites for the recording industry. For example, Los Angeles developed as musicians from across the United States migrated to be close to film recording (Zinn et al. 2002).

REFERENCES

Antonio, Robert J. "Immanent Critique as the Core of Critical Theory: Its Origins and Developments in Hegel, Marx and Contemporary Thought." *The British Journal of Sociology* 32, no. 3 (1981): 330–345.

Arditi, David. "Digital Downsizing: The Effects of Digital Music Production on Labor." *Journal of Popular Music Studies* 26, no. 4 (2014a): 503–520.

Arditi, David. *iTake-Over: The Recording Industry in the Digital Era*. Lanham, MD: Rowman and Littlefield Publishers, 2014b.

Arditi, David. "iTunes: Breaking Barriers and Building Walls." *Popular Music and Society* 37, no. 4 (2014c): 408–424.

Attali, Jacques. *Noise: The Political Economy of Music*. Theory and History of Literature. Minneapolis: University of Minnesota Press, 1985.

Christopherson, Susan. "Beyond the Self-Expressive Creative Worker: An Industry Perspective on Entertainment Media." *Theory, Culture and Society* 25, no. 7–8 (2008): 73–95.

Florida, Richard L. *The Rise of the Creative Class: And How It's Transforming Work, Leisure, Community and Everyday Life*. New York, NY: Basic Books, 2004.

Frenette, Alexandre. "Making the Intern Economy: Role and Career Challenges of the Music Industry Intern." *Work and Occupations* 40, no. 4 (2013): 364–397.

Garnham, Nicholas. *Emancipation, the Media, and Modernity: Arguments about the Media and Social Theory*. Oxford and New York: Oxford University Press, 2000.

Garnham, Nicholas. "From Cultural to Creative Industries." *International Journal of Cultural Policy* 11, no. 1 (2005): 15–29.

Gill, Rosalind, and Andy Pratt. "Precarity and Cultural Work: In the Social Factory? Immaterial Labour, Precariousness and Cultural Work." *Theory, Culture and Society* 25, no. 7–8 (2008): 1–30.

Guarino, Mark. "Could Home Recording Doom Professional Music Studios?" *Christian Science Monitor*, December 17, 2009. http://www.csmonitor.com/innovation/2009/1217/Could-home-recording-doom-professional-music-studios

Harkness, Geoff. "Get on the Mic: Recording Studios as Symbolic Spaces in Rap Music." *Journal of Popular Music Studies* 26, no. 1 (2014): 82–100.

Hesmondhalgh, David. *The Cultural Industries*. London and Thousand Oaks, CA: SAGE, 2002.

Hesmondhalgh, David, and Andy C. Pratt. "Cultural Industries and Cultural Policy." *International Journal of Cultural Policy* 11, no. 1 (2005): 1–13.

Horkheimer, Max, and Theodor W. Adorno. "The Culture Industry: Enlightenment as Mass Deception." In *Dialectic of Enlightenment*, xvii, 258 p. New York: Herder and Herder, 1972.

Miège, Bernard. *The Capitalization of Cultural Production*. New York: International General, 1989.

Miège, Bernard, and Nicholas Garnham. "The Cultural Commodity." *Media, Culture and Society* 1 (1979): 297–311.

Miller, Toby. "Culture+Labour=Precariat." *Communication & Critical/Cultural Studies* 7, no. 1 (March 2010): 96–99.

Rose, Joel. "Recording Studios Face Uncertain Future." *All Things Considered*, December 10, 2009. http://www.npr.org/2009/12/10/121304883/recording-studios-face-uncertain-future

Ross, Andrew. "The New Geography of Work Power to the Precarious?" *Theory, Culture and Society* 25, no. 7–8 (2008): 31–49.

Scott, Allen J. *The Cultural Economy of Cities: Essays on the Geography of Image-Producing Industries*. London and Thousand Oaks, CA: SAGE Publications, 2000.

Smith, Suzanne E. *Dancing in the Street: Motown and the Cultural Politics of Detroit*. Cambridge, MA: Harvard University Press, 2001.

Théberge, Paul. "The End of the World As We Know It: The Changing Role of the Studio in the Age of the Internet." In *The Art of Record Production: An Introductory Reader for a New Academic Field*, edited by Frith, Simon, and Simon Zagorski-Thomas, 77–90. Burlington, VT: Ashgate Publishing, Ltd., 2012.

Verna, Paul. "In N.Y., a Room with a View That Draws Top Mixers." *Billboard*, June 21, 1997.

Verna, Paul. "Room with a View's Closing Illustrates Harsh Realities." *Billboard*, October 24, 1998a.

Verna, Paul. "SSL and Others Sound Off on Room with a View's Closure." *Billboard*, October 31, 1998b.

Verna, Paul. "Universal Closes A&M Studios Complex." *Billboard*, October 9, 1999.

Walsh, Christopher. "DIY Recording Spells Tough Time for Austin's Studios." *Billboard*, March 15, 2003.

Walsh, Christopher. "Studio Closings Stun Audio World." *Billboard*, February 19, 2005.

Zinn, Howard, Robin D.G. Kelley, and Dana Frank. *Three Strikes: Miners, Musicians, Salesgirls, and the Fighting Spirit of Labor's Last Century*. Boston: Beacon Press, 2002.

Part III

Working

4 Working Harder and Working Smarter

The Survival Strategies of Contemporary Independent Musicians

Brian J. Hracs

"If you actually want to make a living as an indie musician, it is a tough go. You've got to pretty much do it yourself"

—Interview

Since the late-1990s, digital technologies and the rise of entertainment alternatives such as DVDs, video games, cell phones, and the Internet have radically altered the North American music industry. To date, geographers have examined the rise of file-sharing, the so-called "MP3 Crisis" and the implications for major record labels, music retailers, and recording studios (Connell and Gibson 2003; Fox 2005; Hracs 2012; Leyshon 2014; Power and Hallencreutz 2007; Watson 2014, this volume). However, less is known about the impact of industrial restructuring on the working lives of musicians. Consider, for example, that inexpensive computers, software, and equipment have democratized the production of music by allowing recording, editing, mixing, and mastering to be performed in home studios instead of capital-intensive recording studios (Arditi, this volume; Watson 2014, this volume; Young and Collins 2010). Digital technologies and online retail spaces have also allowed musicians to enter the world of marketing, fundraising, and distribution for the first time (see also: Brandellero and Kloosterman, this volume; Bürkner, this volume; Haijen, this volume; Leyshon et al., this volume; Speers, this volume). Using the Internet, independent musicians can cheaply and easily set up websites and social media platforms to engage with their fans/consumers directly and to promote and distribute digitally recorded music tracks in MP3 format. This has resulted in lower entry barriers and less dependence on major record labels and the established centers of music production such as Los Angeles, New York, and London. Beyond creating a new geography of music production, digital technologies have transformed the traditionally niche "Do It Yourself" (DIY) model from a punk-inspired alternative to the dominant organizational form for up-and-coming musicians (Hracs 2015; Spencer 2008). In Canada, for example, 95 percent of all musicians are not affiliated with either major or independent record labels (CIRAA 2010). Instead they operate as entrepreneurs who are individually responsible for the growing range of creative and non-creative tasks, including music writing and recording, but also fundraising, marketing, communication, and booking tours.

This transition has furnished musicians with unprecedented opportunities, freedom, and control over how and where they work. In practice, however, the demands of independent music production, the inefficiencies of the DIY model, and intense competition in the marketplace serve to constrain this freedom. As musicians de-specialize, multi-task, and spend less time making music, they suffer from what McRobbie (2002) has termed the "corrosion of creativity" (see also Frenette, this volume). This trend is exacerbated by the rising cost of space in many large cities and the declining value of music in the digital age which squeezes traditionally low incomes and increases the need to take on debt and multiple jobs (Hracs et al. 2011).

This chapter draws on a case study of independent musicians in Toronto to explore the interrelated spatial, organizational, and commercial strategies that some musicians are developing to overcome the inefficiencies of the DIY model and mediate the risks associated with the global and hyper-competitive marketplace. After outlining the research methods and situating

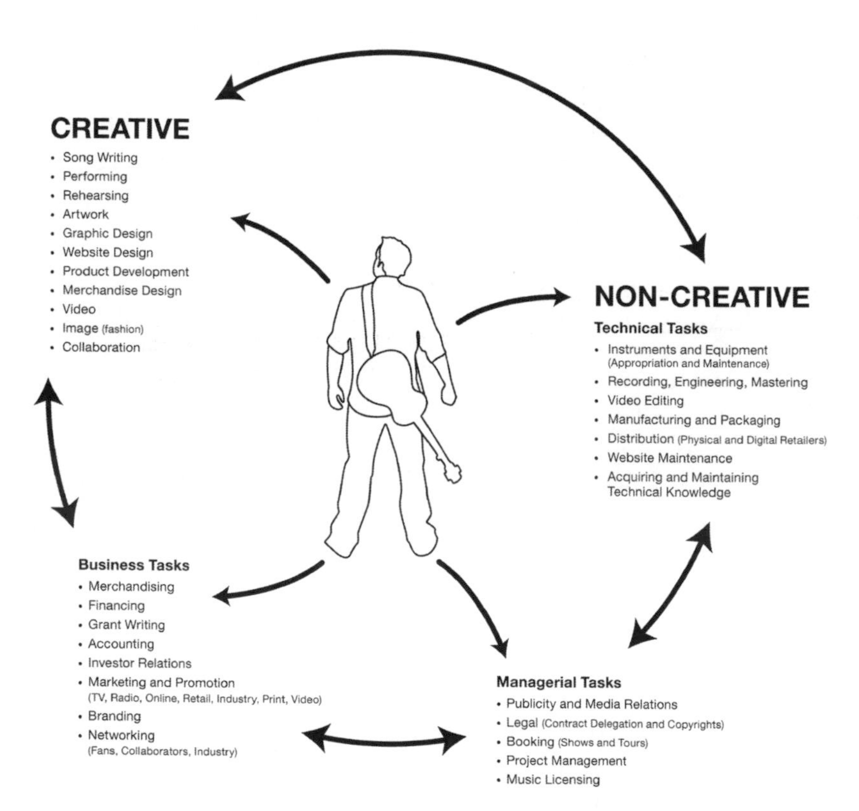

Figure 4.1 The Creative and Non-Creative Tasks of Independent Music Production

the case of Toronto, the chapter demonstrates that independent musicians are exchanging their bohemian identities and spatial preferences for professional personas and banal live/work spaces in Toronto's suburbs. Organizationally, it argues that musicians are shifting their networking practices from traditional social networking to what Grabher and Ibert (2006) call "connectivity" networking. This shift relates to the strategic decision by some musicians to move beyond the constraints of the DIY model by "getting help" from a range of skilled collaborators and intermediaries. The chapter also highlights how musicians are fusing sonic and visual styles and harnessing the construct of "exclusivity" to generate distinction, value, and loyalty in the crowded marketplace. Ultimately, this chapter contributes to existing literature on music, creative entrepreneurship, and geography in the digital age.

RESEARCH DESIGN

The analysis presented in this chapter is based on 65 interviews conducted in Toronto. Using a purposive sampling strategy, 51 independent musicians were asked about their employment experiences. The sample also includes 14 interviews with key informants who work in the Toronto music industry as educators, producers, studio owners, managers, union representatives, government employees, and executives at major and independent record labels. These individuals provided invaluable information about the broader context of industrial restructuring within the music industry and the challenges associated with contemporary independent music production. To get a broad cross-section of experiences and opinions, the respondents varied by age, gender, level of education, genre, and career stage. The location of these interviews included "third spaces" such as coffee shops, home studios, offices, performance venues, recording studios, and music stores. The diversity of these locations is noteworthy because it afforded the opportunity to observe the range of spatial environments where independent musicians live and work. The interviews, which lasted an average of 75 minutes, were recorded with the consent of the participants and coded thematically. Verbatim quotations are used throughout the chapter to demonstrate how participants expressed meanings and experiences in their own words.

PLACE MATTERS: PROFILING THE TORONTO CASE

Regardless of where musicians choose to live and work, the demands and challenges associated with independent music production are arguably universal. Yet, as the literature asserts, specific places are not mere containers of economic activities. Rather, local conditions shape the way work is rationalized, practiced, and experienced (Vinodrai 2013). This section provides some context about Toronto and highlights specific local conditions that influence the experiences and strategies of musicians.

Toronto has long been recognized as the largest and most diverse music center in Canada. The city is home to several important educational and performance institutions, all of the major Canadian record labels, and features the largest number of recording studios and performance venues in the country. Given its size and infrastructure, Toronto supports a diverse array of genres, including jazz, classical, blues, rock, pop, country, hip-hop, electronic, and punk (Berman 2009). Toronto has also developed a strong reputation as "the place to be" for established and aspiring musicians who continue to migrate from smaller regional centers across the country (Hracs et al. 2011). In Toronto, the specific contours of music-work are shaped by local conditions, including labor market dynamics, cost of living, and institutional supports. Although Toronto supports the country's largest number of music venues, live music competes for consumption dollars with the city's diverse range of other cultural and entertainment choices including theatre, restaurants, sports, and nightclubs. Toronto has a static number of performance venues and a steady inflow of ambitious musicians. The market has responded to the surplus labor by driving down the value of live music and the earning potential of musicians. At the same time, the cost of space in Toronto for living, rehearsing, and recording is increasing rapidly, especially in the city-center. In contrast to other large Canadian cities, such as Montreal where affordability for lower income students and "creatives" is regulated through strict rent controls, musicians are more likely to be priced out in Toronto (Cummins-Russell and Rantisi 2011). Moreover, whereas music in Halifax and Montreal enjoys strong government supports and policies, music in Toronto comes second to other more celebrated and unified sectors such as film and fashion. Thus, unlike Halifax and Montreal, where musicians tend to form strong local networks of collaboration and support, Toronto's expensive and highly competitive marketplace pits musicians against one another, individualizes the experience of risk, and exacerbates the difficulties of earning a living as an independent musician (Hracs et al. 2011).

MOVING BEYOND BOHEMIA: THE SPATIAL STRATEGIES OF INDEPENDENT MUSICIANS

> "You can make music from anywhere"
>
> —Interview

How do independent musicians in Toronto achieve their primary goal of making a sustainable living from music? My findings suggest that some musicians in Toronto are becoming more disciplined and professionalized (working harder) and becoming more strategic and specialized (working smarter) (Hracs 2015). As subsequent sections will demonstrate, professionalization entails abandoning bohemian practices, such as "hanging out" in cafes. It also means taking advantage of spatial freedom, optimizing locational choices according to a range of factors and literally moving beyond the bohemian spaces in Toronto's downtown core (Hracs 2009).

Despite the well-established body of literature which suggests that musicians, and other creatives, are attracted to a common set of urban aesthetics, some musicians in Toronto are becoming disenchanted with bohemian living (Bain 2003; Lloyd 2006). For these musicians, the allure of inhabiting decaying urban frontiers is wearing off—if it ever existed—and the grit, danger, and isolation of bohemian spaces are cited as "push" factors. As one musician explained: "I would rather live in a safer or nicer area than right where the scene is if it's really run down or dangerous." Musicians also reported that too much "buzz" was a hindrance to productivity and the creative process. In the era of digitally-driven independent music production the free time once available to experiment creatively and indulge in the "rock star" lifestyle has been lost. As a consequence, professionalizing musicians in Toronto spoke of the danger of being sucked into activities that, in such a competitive climate, might derail their career goals. As one musician, who saw his fledgling music career thwarted by a "rock-star fantasy" and cocaine addiction put it: "There is a partying lifestyle that comes with being a musician in a band . . . there is late night stuff, drinking, drugs . . . you can get sucked into the party atmosphere as an entertainer . . . I fell victim to it."

In addition to the negative externalities associated with local buzz, other factors including rising rents, overcrowding, competition, and changing preferences are pushing serious musicians out of Toronto's downtown core. As one musician explained: "When areas with lots of artists become vibrant, just like Queen Street (inner city bohemian quarter), they become popular and suddenly the artists can't afford it anymore because the prices go up." But their flight from these spaces is not random. Indeed, a range of "pull" factors including more affordable and music-friendly space, better employment opportunities, greater control over their work/life balance, and isolation from career sabotaging temptations are attracting musicians to banal spaces in the inner and outer suburbs of Toronto.

As many of my participants complained about the costs of independent production, finding cheap or even free space emerged as the most prominent pull factor for musicians. As one respondent put it: "Proximity is great, but it has to be economically feasible." Moreover, as some of these musicians leave Toronto on tour for long stretches during the year a further goal was to avoid paying high rents for unused space. The strategy of this musician was to move out of the bohemian inner city neighborhood of Queen West and relocate to Oakville, a suburban community within easy commuting range:

> I used to live in Queen West, but in January I moved home with my parents, because I spend most of January and February on the road. I'm going to be gone for most of May, so I need to save money and stuff like that. So I've been commuting back and forth from Toronto to Oakville.

Musicians also reported being attracted to suburban spaces because the built form is flexible and more conducive to the creative process. In addition to needing enough space to store their equipment and hold rehearsals, musicians also need to be able to make noise, often outside of the 9–5 work day. As one musician recalled: "In an urban environment there have been times where I practiced late at night out of necessity and I had neighbors and people knocking on my door complaining about the noise." Interestingly, musicians also require silence to create and recharge from their hectic schedules. For these reasons some musicians prefer larger more isolated spaces in the suburbs to small, crowded apartments in the city with sleeping neighbors next door. This musician moved to the outer suburbs to make noise and concentrate on the creative process in complete silence:

> In an ideal world I would have an apartment with a studio (in the downtown core) and I would practice in my pyjamas at 11:30 at night. But that is not possible in the city. But here is the twist. As a musician I make a lot of noise, which is bad enough, but I also need to live somewhere where there isn't a lot of noise, because I can't be creative with that noise. I need that silence to be effective and to focus on what I'm doing. I also need the peace and quiet just to rejuvenate myself from the stress of my working life . . . So where can I actually live to accommodate my needs? The only place is where I live now in the outer suburbs.

Perhaps even more important than the ability to facilitate the creative process and provide affordable and flexible space, Toronto's suburbs allow struggling musicians to sustain their creative passions by providing better employment opportunities. In Toronto's downtown core the oversupply of musicians drives down the value of live music and many musicians end up playing for free or worse, paying to get on stage. As this musician explained, however, playing shows in the outer suburbs and smaller towns in the periphery often generates better attendance and pay because the market is less saturated with musicians and entertainment alternatives:

> The music scene in the slightly less populated areas north of the city is getting to be really good . . . kids have less to do and there are fewer entertainment options for them. In Toronto there are a million things to do so if there is a live band those kids are gonna go and you can sell tickets easier. The highest turnouts to any of our shows have all been in Newmarket and Keswick (both outer suburbs of Toronto).

Another key finding is that "just-in-time" access to specific spaces (studios), activities (performing), and people (collaborators) is more important than permanent proximity. As this musician argued: "You can live wherever as long as you can get to things. I have lived in five different neighborhoods in Toronto and if I need to go to a specific space, I go to that space."

As independent musicians professionalize they become more strategic and rational about where they live and work. As this respondent asserted: "In a capitalist economy it is not a viable expectation for musicians to be able to expect to live in a subsidized environment where they don't have to deal with market forces." Based on their own unique criteria, musicians try to achieve the optimum balance between a range of factors including the affordability, accessibility, and music-friendliness of the physical space and crucially the availability of paid work.

COLLABORATING . . . WITH THE RIGHT PEOPLE: THE ORGANIZATIONAL STRATEGIES OF INDEPENDENT MUSICIANS

> "It is a full-time job but only about 10% actually involves music"
>
> —Interview

In Toronto, it is easy to form a band and dabble in basic tasks such as performing and recording music, but becoming a self-sufficient business entity requires mastering advanced functions such as financing, distribution, merchandising, public relations, marketing, and branding. During my fieldwork it became clear that digitally-driven DIY is an inefficient system that makes reaching a sustainable level of creative and economic success difficult. Beyond the sheer number of demands imposed on independent musicians, the typical work-day is chopped up into tasks which are often spread across space. As a result, musicians struggle to find the time to write new songs, maintain their online storefront, apply for grants, book shows, and promote their products. Several respondents complained about the creative conundrum in which they struggle to allocate their time and energy to creative and non-creative tasks and end up with mediocre results on both fronts. This section highlights the ways in which some musicians are reconfiguring their organizational approaches.

According to Scott (2006), the competitive pressures of capitalism force firms to continually revitalize their core competencies in the search for production and marketing advantages. To do this, firms observe and appropriate knowledge and strategies from other co-located firms and create their own internal solutions through a "learn-by-doing" process. As entrepreneurs, independent musicians also have the freedom to evaluate and reconfigure ineffective organizational models. To overcome the main limitations of the DIY model, some musicians are developing new ways to refocus on being creative while still completing all of their other tasks. In so doing, they are changing the way they practice networking and organizing their operations.

The existing literature on the networking practices of individuals in the creative industries suggests that social networking—cultivating weak ties through face-to-face interaction—is the best way to access local buzz, find sources of paid work, and mediate risk (Christopherson 2002; Grabher and Ibert 2006). In his study of Wicker Park, Chicago in the 1990s Lloyd (2006) describes artists as spending long hours working and "hanging out" in coffee shops waiting for the lightning bolts of inspiration or a meaningful collaborative opportunity to organically materialize. Although my interviews confirm that coffee shops and third spaces remain popular sites of interaction for musicians in Toronto, several respondents explained the need to become more efficient with their time by strategically scheduling interactions and agendas. As this musician put it: "We are so busy that we actually book meetings just to see each other. We might meet at places like this coffee shop, where there is Internet access, to work on our websites or promotion."

In creative industries such as new media, advertising, and publishing, social networking is vital to securing short-term contracts and projects. But there is a lack of paid work for musicians in Toronto, and they have realized that every minute spent fruitlessly networking is time not spent on other tasks. As a result, the value (and practice) of social networking is declining. As one musician argues: "It is difficult to balance everything and although networking is important . . . if I don't take time to practice and be good at what I do . . . then nobody is going to hire me anyway . . . These are economic decisions and everybody does informal cost-benefit calculations."

These calculations have also resulted in a strategic solution to the inefficiency of the DIY model. Rather than hanging out with musicians who have redundant skills, and are often viewed as competitors, some musicians in Toronto are shifting to what Grabher and Ibert (2006) call "connectivity" networking. This entails "getting help" with the range of creative and non-creative tasks from collaborators with complementary skill-sets including publicists, fashion designers, artists, and managers (Hracs 2015). For example, to complete important tasks, which required skills she lacked, this musician contacted a web designer and a photographer: "I definitely have been involved with some collaborations, for my website, and photographs for the website and press kit" Or as this musician explains:

> I have recently paid a manager for specific services. I have my own little time and money equation in my head, so it made sense for me to hire somebody to do some work for me. He does specific things like book shows or business planning. He is more experienced and efficient with these things than I am. Plus it looks more professional to have somebody call on your behalf.

Connectivity networking also implies a shift to "just-in-time" interactions through virtual channels instead of face-to-face encounters in coffee shops, bars, and other third spaces. As this music industry insider argues: "You don't have to necessarily be in physical proximity . . . There is the virtual component of message boards, blogs and file sharing." Musicians use these virtual spaces, and increasingly social media, to promote their shows, interact with fans/consumers, recruit new collaborators, learn about music-related tasks, buy and sell equipment, and to distribute their music-related products. Virtual channels of communication also allow musicians to connect asynchronously and work when gaps in their hectic schedules appear. As this musician explained:

> Networking has changed so much. It happens on the Internet. Everyone has got a Facebook page and who knows what else and you work a lot in that forum. That's where the hanging out happens . . . It is much more strategic . . . An enormous piece of my schedule is coming home from gigs at 12 or 2 in the morning and spending an hour on the computer answering emails because that is when I have the time. Now I've got an iPhone and I can do it on a break during the gig.

Although virtual spaces allow musicians to network and collaborate with individuals located anywhere in the world, there is still a strong preference and propensity for locally rooted relationships. As one musician argued:

> You can easily make a record with somebody in Australia without actually seeing each other these days, and that kind of thing happens. But most collaborations are project-specific and local. It's not just chatting with people all over the world for the sake of it.

Far from becoming "flat," the specificity of the "local" remains crucial because musicians can only borrow equipment from people within physical proximity or learn about government grants from people who understand the local institutional landscape. In this way interactions in virtual spaces are not replacing face-to-face interaction but rather facilitating and extending the shift toward connectivity networking. Indeed, as this musician asserted: "There is a generous overlap between the local physical community and the local electronic community."

Changing networking practices underpin the shift toward re-specialization and the re-configuration of the DIY model (Hracs 2015). In exactly the same way that firms identify their core strengths and outsource functions that others can do cheaper, faster and better, some musicians are getting help from a range of skilled specialists and free laborers. Interestingly, these helpers can be compensated in different ways depending on career stage and financial resources. Indeed, "helpers" can be equal partners, scene members who exchange services through bartering, or contractors who are simply hired to perform tasks for a fee (Hauge and Hracs 2010). Given their limited economic resources, musicians also make extensive use of free labor from family members, fans, and pseudo creatives/hipsters who volunteer on creative projects to earn social and cultural capital (Bourdieu 1984).

As the size of the team and organizational complexity of the enterprise grows, musicians run the risk of allocating too much of their time and energy to project management. Interestingly, I found that musicians who reach this conundrum apply the same logic and simply outsource management tasks, which are becoming more available in affordable a la cart packages. Services, including business planning and project coordination, are being provided by pioneering managers who work freelance in Toronto's creative sector after losing their industry jobs during the "MP3 Crisis" (Hracs 2015). But beyond choosing where and how to work, the biggest challenge facing indie musicians is making enough money to support their creative vision and avoid taking on additional jobs.

EMBRACING ENTERPRISE: THE COMMERCIAL STRATEGIES OF INDEPENDENT MUSICIANS

> "The best thing about technology is that now anyone can make music but the worst thing is that now anyone can make music"
>
> —Interview

Digital technologies, global integration, and broader restructuring have altered the way music-related goods, services, and experiences are produced, curated, promoted, distributed, valued, and consumed. In the early 2000s illegal downloading and the "MP3 Crisis" reduced the value of recorded music. As one key informant put it: "Now we have an entire generation that is used to not paying for music." At the same time, declining entry barriers and the rise of digitally-driven DIY created fierce competition and market saturation. Consider, for example, that Apple's iTunes music store offers over 37 million songs. Together, the "dilemma of democratization" curtails the ability of independent musicians to market and monetize their creative content (Hracs et al. 2013). Moreover, whereas music once enjoyed a privileged position atop the entertainment pyramid, consumers can now choose to spend their time, money, and attention on a greater range of alternatives such as video games, social media, cell phones, and the Internet itself (Hracs 2012). Thus, beyond the struggle to produce music and complete tasks, independent musicians struggle to stand out in the crowded marketplace, and more specifically, to generate distinction, value, and loyalty (Hracs et al. 2013). This section will outline some of the strategies musicians are using to enhance their live shows, sell recorded music, and interact with fans/consumers.

Whereas live shows used to promote the sale of recorded music, MP3s and CDs are now often given away to promote shows which have become the dominant revenue stream for independent musicians (Young and Collins 2010). In Toronto, however, the market for live music has become saturated due to a steady inflow of musicians and a static number of venues (Hracs et al. 2011). As musicians (and venue owners) realize that the originality of individual songs and quality of musicianship is no longer sufficient to attract paying fans/consumers, some musicians are trying to stand out by crafting unique visual styles that work in tandem with their sonic styles. As one musician put it: "[Musicians] are not playing behind a wall. They are on stage and people are looking at them. Every little thing, it is so visual . . . People need an image, you can sell an image." And this musician added: "We wear different outfits for every show and we want people to keep coming back to see what we're wearing this time."

Although the DIY model requires musicians to develop visual campaigns and clothing on their own, many musicians lack the creative and technical expertise. Thus, strategic musicians use connectivity networking to get help from artists, photographers, and, above all, fashion designers. As this musician explained: "Fashion is an area that I am constantly involved in because it is important. I teamed up with this designer and she made clothes for me for a while . . . I found her through social media."

Interestingly, although the fashion designers may be friends, scene members, or simply contracted, their "help" is almost always described as a favor. As this musician explained: "Audiences are becoming more skeptical and are able to smell bullshit from a mile away. So [on stage] I would say 'do you like my outfit? It's by my friend so-and-so.' Or 'look at what my friend made,' or 'this is a test outfit what do you think?' . . . So I'll just try to be genuine." This example demonstrates how musicians shrewdly invoke the same bohemian ethic that they have abandoned to guard against accusations of "selling out." Indeed, independent musicians and fashion designers need to brand and collaborate to compete, but they also need to disguise these strategies to make it appear unplanned, organic, and authentic because "trying too hard" is not cool.

To enhance the value of their goods musicians use the constructed concept of exclusivity (Hracs et al. 2013). As Simmel observed in *The Philosophy of Money* ([1900] 1978), consumers desire objects that are not merely given but attained by the conquest of distance, obstacles, and difficulties. While global producers use technology to make consuming easier than ever, some musicians are strategically restricting supply and access in order to turn their inability to afford larger production runs and mass distribution into a source of symbolic value. For example, musicians produce handcrafted albums that feature hand-painted artwork, photographs of the band, poetry, individual numbering, and handwritten thank-you cards. These albums are marketed as unique products that contain layers of value that are not offered by digital downloads or mass-produced CDs. As one respondent explained:

> It ends up being a package that you wouldn't normally see. It is not a mass-produced package and with all of the handcrafted detail we only issue about 300 units. We take it on the road and sell it for [CAD] $25

> instead of $15 so we are selling them for a premium . . . People start saying 'I was one of the few to snag this new cool album.'

Just as the literature suggests, musicians have realized that consumers will pay more for products that they perceive to be exclusive and unique because finding and obtaining such products requires high levels of cultural, social, and economic capital which puts consumers in select company (Bourdieu 1984; Hracs et al. 2013; Shipman 2004).

Despite finding ways to enhance the symbolic value of their live shows and recorded music, strategic musicians understand, like many firms, that building and maintaining a positive and trusting relationship with their fan/consumer base is vital. Yet, in the contemporary era where infinite consumer choice, inauthentic marketing, and ephemeral interactions pervade, capturing the attention of consumers and their loyalty is difficult, especially with limited economic resources.

To overcome this challenge some musicians are adding "members only" portals to their websites to attract, reward, and stay connected with fans/consumers. In Toronto, musicians offer members the experience of previewing new material (songs, videos, live shows, photos, contests) before it is officially released to the public and provide access to exclusive "members only" content (rare demos, behind the scenes footage and photos, private performances). According to Choi and Burnes (2013), fans/consumers value participating in these online communities because they enhance their sense of identity. Beyond exclusive content, however, fans/consumers seek interaction with musicians. As one respondent explained: "Fans want that experience. I think people are craving the human touch and that's what they can't get in a digital download. They want that human interaction. They want a piece of the artist as well."

To accommodate this demand, some musicians are developing on-going relationships that generate value through personalization, trust, loyalty, and repeat business. Musicians were early adopters of social media. By 2007, for example, 80 percent of all musicians maintained a MySpace page (Antin and Earp 2010). Yet, with modern social media applications, such as Facebook and Twitter, musicians can engage directly with fans/consumers on increasingly personal levels and the relationship between these groups is becoming blurred. Many of the musicians in my sample have established online blogs and forums through which they invite selected fans/consumers to experience and participate in their creative endeavors, businesses, and private lives. Although developing online personas, constantly updating creative and personal content, and answering on-going correspondences with fans/consumers is demanding, my research suggests that "creating conversations" and making "meaningful emotional connections" is crucial to building a stable client base and surviving the volatile marketplace (Hracs and Leslie 2014).

CONCLUSION

As the contemporary marketplace for music continues to evolve, this chapter contributes to our understanding of digitally-driven independent music production. At a time of ongoing industrial crisis, global competition, market volatility, the corrosion of creativity, and pessimism about the precarious working lives of musicians, and "creatives" more broadly, this chapter highlighted how some independent musicians in Toronto are re-writing the rules of the game. Overall, it argued that as entrepreneurs, musicians are professionalizing (working harder) and becoming more strategic (working smarter). Crucially, this has meant abandoning bohemian lifestyles and embracing enterprise. More specifically, the chapter demonstrated that musicians are exercising their newfound spatial freedom and relocating from Toronto's downtown core to spaces in the inner and outer suburbs that are more affordable and conducive to the creative process. Organizationally, musicians are forgoing traditional social networking in favor of "just-in-time connectivity networking." This shift facilitates the re-configuration of the DIY model by allowing musicians to re-specialize on making music while "getting help" from a diverse range of collaborators. The chapter also explored some of the innovative commercial strategies that independent musicians are using to market and monetize their products in the increasingly competitive and global marketplace. Specific examples included the strategic fusion of sonic and visual styles to enhance their live performances and harnessing the construct of exclusivity to generate value, distinction, and loyalty.

Before concluding, it is important to raise two caveats. First, despite their promise there is a danger of romanticizing the transformative potential of these strategies. For although they can improve the working lives of those who develop and adopt them, independent musicians still face a battery of risks and challenges including self-exploitation, temporal and spatial fragmentation, and extremely uncertain and low incomes. Moreover, the strategies themselves can bring new hardships. For example, whereas websites and social media enable independent musicians to establish relationships with fans/consumers, build brand loyalty, crowd source creative ideas, and secure funding for new projects (using sites such as "Kickstarter"), these activities are time-consuming and require investments of aesthetic labor which create new risks and barriers to creativity (Hracs and Leslie 2014). Therefore, although working harder and working smarter may help independent musicians realize their creative freedom and become economically self-sufficient, the majority are destined to fail (Banks 2007).

Second, it is important to acknowledge the role that local conditions in Toronto have played in driving the development of these strategies and to refrain from speculating about other markets without empirical evidence (Vinodrai 2013). Indeed, whereas intense competition within Toronto forces its musicians to develop innovative strategies and the city's creative field possesses the right mix of spaces, collaborators, and market dynamics to underpin them, this is not the case in other Canadian music scenes such as Halifax and most likely those in other countries around the world (Hracs et al. 2011). Therefore, future research should examine the evolution and diffusion of these strategies across space and the extent to which they are effective in helping independent musicians to reach their career goals over time.

REFERENCES

Antin, Judd, and Matthew Earp. "With a Little Help from My Friends: Self-interested and Prosocial Behavior on MySpace Music." *Journal of the American Society for Information Science and Technology* 61, no. 5 (2010): 952–963.

Bain, Alison L. "Constructing Contemporary Artistic Identities in Toronto Neighbourhoods." *The Canadian Geographer* 47, no. 3 (2003): 303–317.

Banks, Mark. *The Politics of Cultural Work*. Basingstoke: Palgrave, 2007.

Berman, Stuart. *This Book Is Broken: A Broken Social Scene Story*. Toronto: House of Anansi Press, 2009.

Bourdieu, Pierre. *Distinction: A Social Critique of the Judgment of Taste*. Cambridge: Harvard University Press, 1984.

Canadian Independent Recording Artists' Association (CRIAA). "FAQ." Accessed January 10, 2010. http://www.thenewindie.com/faq.php

Choi, Hwancho, and Bernard Burnes. "The internet and value co-creation: the case of the popular music industry." *Prometheus: Critical Studies in Innovation*, 31 no. 1 (2013): 35–53.

Christopherson, Susan. "Project Work in Context: Regulatory Change and the New Geography of Media." *Environment and Planning A* 34 (2002): 2003–2015.

Connell, John, and Chris Gibson. *Sound Tracks: Popular Music, Identity, and Place*. London: Routledge, 2003.

Cummins-Russell, Thomas, and Norma Rantisi. "Networks and Place in Montreal's Independent Music Industry." *The Canadian Geographer* 56, no. 1 (2011): 80–97.

Fox, Mark A. "Market Power in Music Retailing: The Case of Wal-Mart." *Popular Music and Society* 28, no. 4 (2005): 501–519.

Grabher, Gernot, and Oliver Ibert. "Bad Company? The Ambiguity of Personal Knowledge Networks." *Journal of Economic Geography* 5, no. 6 (2006): 251–271.

Hauge, Atle, and Brian J. Hracs. "See the Sound, Hear the Style: Collaborative Linkages Between Indie Musicians and Fashion Designers in Local Scenes." *Industry and Innovation* 17, no. 1 (2010): 113–129.

Hracs, Brian J. "Beyond Bohemia: Geographies of Everyday Creativity for Musicians in Toronto." In *Spaces of Vernacular Creativity: Rethinking the Cultural Economy*, edited by Edensor, T., D. Leslie, S. Millington, and N. Rantisi, 75–88. London: Routledge, 2009.

Hracs, Brian J. "A Creative Industry in Transition: The Rise of Digitally Driven Independent Music Production." *Growth and Change* 43, no. 3 (2012): 442–461.

Hracs, Brian J. "Cultural Intermediaries in the Digital Age: The Case of Independent Musicians and Managers in Toronto." *Regional Studies* 49, no. 3 (2015): 461–475.

Hracs, Brian J., Jill L. Grant, Jeffry Haggett, and Jesse Morton. "A Tale of Two Scenes: Civic Capital and Retaining Musical Talent in Toronto and Halifax." *The Canadian Geographer* 55, no. 3 (2011): 365–382.

Hracs, Brian J., Doreen Jakob, and Atle Hauge. "Standing Out in the Crowd: The Rise of Exclusivity-based Strategies to Compete in the Contemporary Marketplace for Music and Fashion." *Environment and Planning A* 45 (2013): 1144–1161.

Hracs, Brian J., and Deborah Leslie. "Aesthetic Labour in Creative Industries: The Case of Independent Musicians in Toronto." *Area* 46, no. 1 (2014): 66–73.

Leyshon, Andrew. *Reformatted: Code, Networks, and the Transformation of the Music Industry*. Oxford: Oxford University Press, 2014.

Lloyd, Richard. *Neo-Bohemia: Art and Commerce in the Post-Industrial City*. New York: Routledge, 2006.

McRobbie, Angela. "Clubs to Companies: Notes on the Decline of Political Culture in Speeded Up Creative Worlds." *Cultural Studies* 16, no. 1 (2002): 516–531.

Power, Dominic, and Daniel Hallencreutz. "Competitiveness, Local Productions Systems and Global Commodity Chains in the Music Industry: Entering the US Market." *Regional Studies* 41, no. 3 (2007): 377–389.

Scott, Allen J. "Entrepreneurship, Innovation and Industrial Development: Geography and the Creative Field Revisited." *Small Business Economics* 26, no. 1 (2006): 1–24.

Shipman, Alan. "Lauding the Leisure Class: Symbolic Content and Conspicuous Consumption." *Review of Social Economy* 62 (2004): 277–289.

Simmel, Georg. *The Philosophy of Money.* Routledge and Kegan Paul, London, 1978; first published 1900.

Spencer, Amy. *DIY: The Rise of lo-fi Culture.* New York: Marion Boyars, 2008.

Vinodrai, Tara. "Design in a Downturn? Creative Work, Labour Market Dynamics and Institutions in Comparative Perspective." *Cambridge Journal of Regions, Economy and Society* 6 (2013): 159–176.

Watson, Allan. *Cultural Production in and Beyond the Recording Studio.* New York: Routledge, 2014.

Young, Sherman, and Steve Collins. "A View from the Trenches of Music 2.0." *Popular Music and Society* 33, no. 3 (2010): 339–355.

5 From Artist to Entrepreneur

The Working Lives of London-Based Rappers

Laura Speers

In the changing musical marketplace where regular live performances, sense of community, and CD sales are being replaced by digital purchases, piracy, and a shift to merchandise, rappers are having to make sense of their changing role as artists. To be a professional rapper requires that you promote yourself, that you are resourceful, and that you network—all aspects of entrepreneurship. With little mainstream or commercial interest and backing, independent hip-hop rappers have to navigate the myriad opportunities and challenges facing them in the digital age in terms of production, promotion, distribution, and performance.

In contrast to dominant perceptions of hip-hop rappers as either gangsters with a penchant for bling and violence as portrayed in mainstream media (Perry 2004), or as a marginalized group battling oppression (Watkins 2005), my research suggests that there is an emerging community of rappers who are better understood as "cultural entrepreneurs." These cultural entrepreneurs have a strong DIY ethic and organize and exploit cultural, financial, social, and human capital to their advantage to generate revenue from their music (see also: Bürkner, this volume; Haijen, this volume; Hracs, this volume). Instead of only focusing on writing music, rappers now need to maintain their online presence, organize gig bookings, manage digital distribution, make music videos, and plan promotions—thus developing a portfolio of multiple roles. However, this creates a tension between their creative spirit and the need to make their living economically viable. As such, the wider structural implications of media and music industries, the Internet and social networking, and the fragmentation of underground hip-hop into microscenes (Harkness 2013), means they are "forced" cultural entrepreneurs and are required to meet increasingly challenging working conditions.

Although there is growing scholarship on hip-hop and its practitioners, there have been few attempts to study rappers as workers. My research on rappers in London indicates that their lives are underpinned by challenging tensions. These can be summarized as autonomy versus being forced to adapt, economic viability versus underground values, and creative practice versus entrepreneurial activity. By locating London-based rappers in the critical lexicon of studies of cultural entrepreneurship, this chapter aims to generate new ways of thinking about work identity, exploitation, and motivation in relation to cultural labor.

The argument and data presented in this chapter is drawn from 14 months of ethnographic fieldwork exploring a hip-hop community in London. Within this time, I attended 65 gigs, open mic nights, and other events that rappers were speaking at to immerse myself in the scene. I conducted 21 in-depth interviews with hip-hop artists, of whom 20 were male and one female. The interview sample was purposive in order to get a range of artists across the professional spectrum from "veteran" rappers, to more amateur ones just starting out, to understand creative labor at different stages of a rapper's career. All interviewees have been granted confidentiality through the use of a pseudonym.

I begin this chapter by highlighting the contributory factors as to why the focus of rappers has shifted from music to business and entrepreneurialism. In an overview of the London hip-hop scene, I suggest how its underground infrastructure and processes of digitization and fragmentation have influenced scene dynamics and artist roles. The theory behind cultural entrepreneurship, focusing on "forced entrepreneurship," is then discussed and explained using empirical data. I conclude by discussing the implications of the study and where future research could lead.

THE CHANGING NATURE OF THE LONDON HIP-HOP SCENE

Underground Versus Mainstream

American hip-hop was exported to the UK in the late 1970s and early 1980s. Other media channels introduced hip-hop to England, including radio shows, mixtapes from New York, and imported 12-inch vinyl from independent record labels (Wood 2009). During the 1980s, mainstream media and record companies were slow to respond to the UK's burgeoning hip-hop scene but this allowed rap music to develop highly localized scenes in urban areas, sites of both creativity and consumption based largely on live shows and parties. The London scene bolstered support through the exchange of mixtapes, videos, live performance, fanzines, and pirate radio broadcasts, developing a strong DIY (do-it-yourself) mentality in the process (Wood 2009). Despite the underground nature of the scene, a few acts broke through to achieve mainstream success such as Derek B and the female duo Cookie Crew reaching the UK Top 40 Singles Chart in the late 1980s. Although UK hip-hop has never enjoyed the same commercial success as American hip-hop and has been a predominantly independent scene, there was a period when it seemed the London scene would "blow up," a hip-hop term for achieving stardom and making money in the music industry (Lee 2009).

In parallel to the pervasive discourse surrounding 1990s U.S.-based hip-hop, UK hip-hop also had a supposed "Golden Era." Although there is some discrepancy as to when exactly this golden era occurred, many hail the period of 1998–2003 as a prime time of UK hip-hop in terms of the vibrancy of the scene, the regular nights, the number of artists, the close-knit community, and the volume and quality of records being sold. Joey described in an interview that during this golden era, his crew "were earning good money" and were the first hip-hop group to tour Eastern Europe and Australia. They in fact became so popular and successful that EMI offered them a record deal. The group turned them down because "at the time we were doing so well, we thought we didn't need the help and it would be derogative of us to accept. The amount of money wasn't enough because we were seeing that much without them so we said 'no'." Maintaining their subcultural underground values, the group did not want to "sell out" to a major label. However, it was not long before the so-called "MP3 crisis" hit, when the introduction of MP3 files and file-sharing sites such as Napster spread the practice of illegally downloading copyrighted music files and induced a structural shock to the music industry (Hracs 2012). This had a significant impact on the working lives of artists and groups such as Joey's who were on the brink of enjoying commercial success. Joey commented, "It used to bother me because we were making money and then we stopped so I had to readjust myself." However, he understands the mentality of fans in relation to illegal downloading: "Why would they buy it if you can get it for free? I wouldn't neither."

Despite the changes undergone in the music industry, the lure of a record deal and "blowing up" still holds for many artists in the scene today. Jim confessed that securing major backing is a prime motivation for him to rap: "I do it for the tiniest chance that it could get me out of the mundane life I'm in and take me somewhere better. That's in the back of any MC's mind, always." Similarly, although with more awareness regarding the way major labels work, female rapper Deena said, "I used to dream about getting signed and becoming rich. But now, the record companies want you to already pretty much do everything. Like they want you to fucking have a fan base, to be selling your CDs already." The success of other rappers being "discovered" by industry scouts and having lucrative careers, such as Example (signed to Epic Records and Sony Music) and Plan B (on 679 owned by Warner Music), fuels these hopes. Signing to a major record label provides a degree of financial security and also means the artist can focus solely on music-making while the label takes care of the business side. However, it is important to note that these sentiments are not shared by all artists because of the pervasive desire to "keep it real" and to hip-hop's underground values. For instance, in an interview Sean emphasized, "I want success but money is not my priority." Sean, in this statement, indicates he would like a large fan base but wouldn't compromise his creative integrity by selling out to a major label.

For the vast number of artists unable or uninterested in getting signed, the DIY disposition of the scene, that started in the 1980s, continued throughout the 1990s and 2000s, means rappers have had to set up their own record labels in order to record and release their own material. Of the UK hip-hop community I studied, rappers were either unsigned or on independent record labels they had built themselves, indicating their entrepreneurial mindset. For instance, Jehst launched the self-financed YNR Productions in 1998 in his university halls of residence and more recently in 2010, rapper Fliptrix set up High Focus Records which is now home to a host of currently popular UK hip-hop acts. Having to set up one's own record label highlights that as well as the creative processes of song writing, recording, and performance, artists now need to self-promote, self-publish, and self-release (Hracs 2015). As the scene has mostly functioned at an underground level for several decades now, artists to some extent have always worked according to a DIY model. However, with the digital revolution affecting hip-hop print media, radio, and the shift from vinyl to MP3, rappers have had to significantly broaden the scope of their entrepreneurialism to successfully leverage digital technologies in order to remain competitive.

Digitization

The onset of the digital age has had profound repercussions on UK hip-hop. The Internet and in particular social networking sites have revolutionized how scene members communicate, inform, promote, and interact. Downloading and peer-to-peer file sharing, podcasts, YouTube, and social networking sites are producing new spaces of creativity and social collaboration while old hierarchies between professional and amateur musicians are destabilizing and the boundaries between producer and consumer are blurring (Deuze 2007). However, there are some scholars (Cammaerts et al. 2013) who challenge the rhetoric of "new" media as crude technological determinism by suggesting that there has been less of a rupture than we think.

Although few statistics are available for hip-hop consumption specifically in the UK, more general data on music downloads reveals the rapidly changing context within which rappers are required to work. The 2009 IFPI Digital Music Report found that 110 million tracks were downloaded in 2008, up 42 percent from 2007 and that seven out of ten music consumers download music illegally. Although it can be a struggle for artists to make money from their music in the MP3 era, digital resources afford more opportunities than existed before. Whereas recording facilities were previously costly and only available to professionals at studios, digital technology has opened access to the recording process for amateur and aspiring artists (Arditi, this volume; Hracs 2012; Watson, this volume). However, most of the creative labor in these DIY and underground music collectives is voluntary and unpaid. The shift towards downloading and sound-sharing websites like

SoundCloud and YouTube has resulted in non-monetized music production and distribution, as well as consumption. Artists are mostly unpaid for their creative output and day-to-day work, so being able to make a living from one's music is highly precarious. For rappers wanting to make money in the London scene, they are required to be ever more entrepreneurial in diversifying their "products" to include merchandise such as hoodies and caps, and selling instrumental beats alongside their albums.

Proliferation of Related Music Genres and Fragmentation of the Hip-Hop Scene

Technological advances fused with diasporic and local musical influences have spurred a proliferation of "bass" music genres and subgenres in the last 20–30 years. The UK has a strong musical heritage with various spin-off genres emanating from hip-hop and 1980s rave music including jungle, breakbeat, trip hop, garage, drum and bass, grime and dubstep. Grime, a distinctly British transformation of hip-hop that hails from East London and emerged during the 2000s, is comprised of an amalgamation of influences ranging from UK garage to dancehall and hip-hop, and features MCs rapping (Dedman 2011). However, grime has a bpm of 140 which is a much faster tempo than hip-hop's 90 bpm. The success of grime has often overshadowed the music of UK hip-hop artists, despite the two genres being connected. In 2009, grime crossed over into mainstream popular music in Britain with a string of top ten hits in the singles chart by artists such as Wiley, Wretch 32, Lethal B and Chip.

This diversifying of sound and range of musical offshoots means existing and potential hip-hop fans are instead opting for something novel and contemporary. Many rappers view this as diluting the scene, as well as creating more competition. As choice increases, reaching consumers and "standing out in the crowd" (Hracs 2015) becomes more of a challenge. However a positive by-product is London's status as a musical hub with an expansive and vibrant community of artists and culture of experimentation. Furthermore, rappers can exploit these particular conditions by crossing over into other styles of music and collaborating with different artists. But a danger can be leaving your fan base behind. Foreign Beggars, a rap group who made their name in underground UK hip-hop circles with two critically acclaimed albums, diversified their sound with grime and dubstep, but were harshly criticized by stalwart fans after becoming a successful commercial crossover group. This again highlights the multitude of opportunities and constraints rappers are required to navigate, as well as the need for an entrepreneurial spirit to be successful in the scene and beyond.

In comparison to U.S. hip-hop, the London scene is quite distinct because of its particular development largely outside of a commercial remit. Although global hip-hop is a rapidly growing area of scholarly research, most studies to date are based on identity and appropriation, or are linguistic and musicological analyses of rap. Little research has explored the working conditions and lives of rappers, nor investigated hip-hop from a creative labor perspective. As such, it is unclear whether the London scene can be generalized to other hip-hop scenes, say in other European cities that have also experienced prevalent shifts in migration, globalization, marketization, and digitization. Nevertheless, there is significant mounting research on independent musicians more generally (in a range of genres) in varying countries that highlight the extent to which artists are having to adapt to digital technologies, perform a wider variety of tasks, and develop entrepreneurial traits to stay competitive (Hracs 2012).

CULTURAL ENTREPRENEURSHIP

The ever-growing scholarship on labor in the cultural and creative industries emerging over the last two decades has offered various terms and phrases to frame the increasingly challenging nature of working in the creative sector. These range from "cultural worker" (Banks 2007), "precarious labor" (Gill and Pratt 2008), and "the independents" (Leadbeater and Oakley 1999) to "creative proletariat" (Arvidsson 2008) and "cultural entrepreneur" (Ellmeier 2003). Of these terms, I argue the most suitable for capturing the wide-ranging and dispersed labor of rappers in the London hip-hop scene is cultural entrepreneur.

Within the field of cultural entrepreneurship itself, differing definitions abound of what it is and what it entails. Wilson and Stokes (2005) argue that the ability to coordinate artistic and managerial resources can be seen as a defining characteristic of the cultural entrepreneur. Ellmeier (2003, 11) suggests it is "all-round artistic and commercial/business qualifications, long working hours and fierce competition from bigger companies," while Deuze (2007) views it as encompassing aspects of self-employment, freelancing, and portfolio working. A common thread unifying much of the cultural entrepreneurship literature is the acknowledgement that there is a disappearing separation between "creative" skills and "non-creative" skills. According to McRobbie (2002a), the processes of despecialization and multitasking, typical of the shift to modes of entrepreneurialism, result in the corrosion of creativity. As Ellmeier (2003) has argued, the image of artists or creators is changing profoundly as the much-favored separation between creator/artist on the one hand, and non-creators/artists on the other hand, no longer fits because of the changing structure of cultural production. As such, a defining characteristic of the cultural entrepreneur is the ability to manage both artistic and business capital.

Although some scholars have questioned the usefulness of the term "cultural entrepreneur" (Oakley 2014), I argue that applying the concept to rappers is a productive exercise for the following three reasons. Firstly, it recognizes the agency of rappers and highlights they are not an "oppressed" community but rather economic and political agents trying to make a living from their art form. Secondly, it legitimizes their often unpaid work as labor in the cultural and creative industries. Finally, it forces us to take into account the changing nature of the independent music scene and it being a forerunner of technological change that places favor on market-driven entrepreneurialism. Building on this third point and following Oakley (2014), "forced entrepreneurship" is an even more accurate term than cultural entrepreneur in describing the labor and working conditions of London-based hip-hop artists.

Forced Entrepreneurship

The term "forced entrepreneurship," coined by Oakley (2014) captures how working patterns of cultural work are often not under self-selected circumstances. Oakley suggests that the forced entrepreneurship label fits those who have never expressed any desire to be self-employed but have simply had to adapt in rapidly changing industries to worsening working conditions. Previously, successful hip-hop artists would have signed to a major label and let them take control of advertising, promotion, and selling the music but in the wake of the economic turndown and "MP3 crisis," major labels started signing fewer acts and focused on more established and commercially viable artists to reduce risk (Hracs 2012). Compounded with the expansion of digital technologies and abundance of rappers trying to "make it," there is now less chance of music providing a steady job than perhaps before, making the current hip-hop landscape more challenging and competitive. Although rappers may dislike the "forced" nature of entrepreneurialism, in many respects by pursuing a career path in music today, they are choosing to be an entrepreneur. For cultural producers such as hip-hop artists, there is an inability to fit their cultural practice into a paying job so they either have to diversify into other avenues such as merchandise or juggle multiple other forms of employment that allows them to produce and perform rap music in their spare time.

Forced entrepreneurship can result in dissonance between work roles and identity (Wilson and Stokes 2005). In the case of London rappers, this is felt most readily in the perceived division between "creativity" and "business." In order to be successful, rappers need to leverage resources by cooperating and collaborating with industry professionals, promoters, funders, and agents. Producing creative work whilst trying to hone business expertise can result in a sense of conflicting identity because of the differing management behaviors typical of the cultural entrepreneur. One rapper described this tension as feeling "schizophrenic." Most artists started their working life with a set of personal motivations based on creativity and autonomy, but then had to shift to be commercial in outlook, as well as mobilize resources through their networks, which resulted in a much more instrumental approach to making music. Focusing on being economically successful was considered to be at odds with artists' original subcultural values. This continues to be a key source of tension for rappers in the scene and something they struggle with in their working lives.

THE WORKING LIVES OF LONDON-BASED RAPPERS

My research suggests that the working life of London-based rappers is experienced as highly ambivalent where pleasure and obligation become blurred in an extremely challenging way (Hesmondhalgh and Baker 2009). Drawing on 14 months of ethnographic research, this section uses empirical data to position the work of rappers in London as forced cultural entrepreneurialism. It suggests that rappers' lives are often characterized by conflict and tension: between autonomy and being forced to adapt; between economic viability and underground values; and between creative practice and entrepreneurial activity. To understand the context of these challenges, the tension between creativity and business is discussed, as well as pay and working hours, the need to multitask, and a consideration of what motivates rappers to continue in these tough circumstances.

Creativity versus Business

A central feature of cultural entrepreneurship, which is arguably heightened in an underground scene, is the tension between utilizing one's creative talents whilst needing to be business oriented. Although in many ways this is a false dichotomy, this strain was articulated in various ways throughout the scene, sometimes explicitly and other times implicitly. In an interview, rapper Eduardo summed up most UK artists feelings regarding needing to be business savvy:

> Making music, that's the easy part and that's the fun part. That's why you do it. When you've got to put that release out, you've got to promote it and you don't have a team around you, doing stuff like that for you and you're doing it off your own back, and you're trying to do it in between everything else that you've got to do, then that's when it gets difficult, you know? That's the horrible side of independent music . . . You're fighting against thousands of other people going, "Watch my video. This is my tune. Download my latest."

This quote indicates the competitive nature of music performance and promotion where quite often, especially in the case of a relatively small scene, artists are competing against their colleagues and friends. Many artists did not consider the commercial aspects of making music when starting to rap, for instance Thom commented, "I never had a five-year plan or anything. I just had fun and it became something." This makes the transition to managerial and entrepreneurial thinking and acting even more challenging.

Eduardo highlights what Hracs (2009) terms "professionalization" whereby anti-market attitudes and behaviors are eschewed in favor of market-driven entrepreneurial subjectivities and the realization that one's creativity must be buttressed by business acumen to achieve success.

The desire and need to generate interest and fans, with the hope it translates into sales, is so ingrained that some open mic nights allow rappers to deliver a speech resembling a sales pitch after their performance. At London Lyricist Lounge, one of the most vibrant and popular hip-hop events in London, following performances the host asks artists where the audience can find out more about them. Rappers can utilize the thirty seconds to one minute offered to their advantage by listing their various online profiles or advertising the CDs with them for sale. Some clearly dislike the sales pitch so say nothing at all or something vague, such as "Find me on YouTube." At the culmination of the creative process—performing to an audience on stage—rappers still need to be thinking in terms of a business strategy. However, there are rappers who are uncomfortable with selling themselves in this way. At a hip-hop event in the East London area of Shoreditch, rapper Kashmere had a very different approach to selling his albums. Mid-performance, he stopped the record and donned an MF Doom-style mask.[1] Accompanying strange ethereal sci-fi music, and speaking in an altered voice, Kashmere held up a CD and announced, "This is when I have to sell shit." By almost becoming a different person through wearing a mask, Kashmere distanced himself as a musician from that of the salesman. This example highlights the "forced" nature of entrepreneurship where rappers experience a dissonance in their work roles and identity (Wilson and Stokes 2005).

Pay, Working Hours, and Day Jobs

Of the 21 rappers I interviewed, only four are able to make a living from their music. However, these are not comfortable salaries, but rather meager existences usually subsidized by benefits, merchandise, or other streams of cash. The idea of making a living for most artists is based on goals of economic self-sufficiency and is not about becoming rich, but making enough money from their music to drop their other jobs. For example, Josh stated, "If I could make as much money to be able to afford rent and go for a few beers on the weekend, that would be fine, that would be awesome. It's not about money." For the first time since beginning to rap, Tino is able to live off his music but only because he does not pay rent:

> Well I live in a squat at the moment, which means I don't pay rent, electricity, water, or anything like that. I don't have a day job anymore but I used to when I was renting. Now I'm at a stage where I can live pretty comfortably off it. I can't buy new clothes and gadgetry all the time but just eating and getting around and going out and doing things, I can do that.

This quote from Tino (who in many other rappers' eyes has "made it") indicates the standard of living level that these workers are at and why their careers are so precarious.

Making music in the changing underground London scene and earning money in the age of digitization is extremely challenging. Many rappers have to maintain day jobs to fund their music. Eduardo emphasized the precariousness and difficulty of fitting hip-hop into his everyday life, "it's a juggling act; work and family and then still trying to put my heart and soul into music as well, finding time to write and record." He captures the conflict of being a cultural entrepreneur and the continual negotiation of personal motivations with that of being an artist, family obligations, and economic demands. In contrast to Leadbeater and Oakley (1999), there is not a blurring of work and non-work, as many rappers experience the opposite in that they would prefer to wholeheartedly commit to music rather than maintain a division between their work identity and personal identity.

Smithy is one of the few rappers who has managed to establish hip-hop as a full-time career:

> As of last September, I've been 100 per cent self-employed off this rap shit. I've just been selling beats, trying to do singles obviously, selling merch. The thing is, a lot of people think we make a lot of money off the record itself but we don't. We make money off the gigs—the things we can sell to double up our money afterwards. That's how I make money at the moment. My wife's my manager and we've got the website, I just try and sell, sell, sell. It's hard but this is what I want to do and I'm happy.

Although trying to make a full-time living from hip-hop is challenging, especially when you have three children to support as in Smithy's case, he is "happy" enjoying strong integration between his personal and professional identity. Being a rapper offers the opportunity for self-actualization and autonomy, which outweighs the negative side of needing to "sell, sell, sell" or the precariousness of not knowing when the next gig or festival performance will be. Employing his wife as his manager adds to the sense that Smithy's whole life and sense of self is bound up with his cultural work (Blair 2001). Furthermore, as Smithy comments, he's had to diversify his creative labor to incorporate selling t-shirts and merchandise in order to make ends meet.

Dispersed Labor and Being Multi-Skilled

To attain any kind of success or exposure, rappers have to build a portfolio of skills beyond their creative talents that encompasses management, finances, leveraging resources, and legal knowledge. These hybrid work identities (Hracs 2012) are not taken up by choice but necessity for rappers who want to make music, gain listeners, earn money, and function as part of the scene. The requirement to be multi-skilled and the accompanying sense of frustration at the ongoing dispersion of labor is captured in a humorous tweet posted by a London-based rapper: "Unless you're willing to become a manager, booking agent, distributor, editor, graphic designer, PR executive and dogs body, don't become a rapper." The tweet highlights the reality of being a rapper in the current economic, cultural, and social landscape and the DIY ethos of independent artists.

The tension between creative practice and entrepreneurial activity is highly pronounced when rappers feel they have little time for their music-making and performing as their focus has to be on distribution and promotion. Rapper Sean complained, "I would love to perform more but it's hard when you're an independent artist." Before signing to a booking agent, he had to "do everything": "I had to source my own shows, I had to deal with all the logistics while dealing with booking studio time, while dealing with arranging artwork for a single, while dealing with updating my website, which I had to learn to build without any knowledge." Rappers need to be multi-skilled in publicity, design, social media, management, accounting, as well as creativity, musical ability, lyricism, and imagination, in addition to numerous other qualities associated with being an artist. As Hracs (2015) found with independent musicians in Toronto, the myriad demands imposed by a DIY model reduces artists' ability to produce high-quality creative content, which in turn reduces their ability to stand out in the crowded marketplace and make a living.

Although managing diverse work responsibilities can go against rappers' initial musical aspirations and intentions, there are benefits to learning the intricacies of music production and promotion. Josh stated:

> The thing is you can't just be a sick[2] MC and a good producer, you've gotta have business acumen to a degree. Everyone in UK hip-hop is really doing everything at an independent level so don't have the benefit of being on a major and have someone that handles press for you. But the more you do, the more you just have to learn the other aspects of putting music out. It's quite DIY and hopefully makes people quite savvy. If they ever do get approached by a label, they're going to be able to weigh up the things that get presented with a more educated viewpoint, which can only be a good thing.

The cultural labor of rappers, whilst demanding and pressurized, is highly auto-didactical in having to build industry and market awareness and keep abreast of the altering technology, trends, and market. This autonomy and knowledge gives artists agency in navigating the independent scene, but little power in being able to change the status quo. However, as critics such as Chapman (2013) have argued, the multitasking virtuoso is the idealized subject of neoliberalism whose multiple skill sets enable him or her to remain agents, rather than objects of volatile market conditions.

Why Continue If It Is So Hard?

The prevalence of exploitation, precarious working conditions, and "free work," raises the question of why rappers and other cultural workers continue working in these taxing and often unpaid circumstances. When I asked rappers this question in interviews, there were generally two types of response. The first was for "the love" of hip-hop, which harkens back to Romantic ideals of the artist and positive emotional qualities (Gill and Pratt 2008). The second type of reply articulated a sense of self-actualization and personal fulfillment (McRobbie 2002a). Jim describes the ongoing internal struggle he experiences regarding continuing when it is tough but comes to the conclusion it is about his personal happiness and fulfillment:

> I ask myself that all the time—what is driving me to do it? As an MC, when you've done a shit gig to like ten people and your stuff isn't selling like it should and you're putting in all this effort into videos and music, and people aren't responding like you want them to, you ask yourself "what is the point?" It just comes down to if you're happy doing what you're doing and you're getting something out of it.

Jim justifies his casualized and unacknowledged labor by holding on to a sense of self-realization through creative expression. A different artist, Sean, explained his rationale as follows: "I fucking love it. Well, I like making music but I love performing. I'm like unbelievably addicted to being on stage." Sean emphasizes he prefers the "creative" to the business side of being a rapper. He then goes on to say, "I always liken it to an abusive relationship in that I get sick of it and I've had enough of it and want nothing to do with it and then I go back—I love it!" Using the metaphor of an abusive relationship highlights the emotional toll and challenging nature of being a cultural entrepreneur, yet also the driving motivation for many artists: a profound passion for their art form. However, this masks the exploitation occurring as an attachment to "my work" provides "both a justification and disciplinary mechanism for staying, often unprofitably, with cultural work and not abandoning it altogether" (Oakley 2014, 151).

In contrast, Smithy espoused a discourse in accordance with the successful cultural entrepreneur, a positive understanding of his achievements based on combining his creative talent with business shrewdness, which he can take full credit for. He said: "What I love about hip-hop is that it's given me an opportunity to feed my kids, given me an opportunity to do something creative. The thing I love most is the fact I've just made something out of nothing." Smithy exudes pride at being able to exploit and utilize his creative talents and relishes being solely responsible for making and selling music with no resources or financial backing. The rapper's resourcefulness in making "something out of nothing," combined with his musical aptitude, indicates his entrepreneurial ethic has become an important source of self-actualization, even freedom and independence (McRobbie 2002a). As these feelings of deep attachment, affective bindings, and the idea of self-expression run throughout the hip-hop scene, Gill and Pratt (2008) suggest we might call this kind of labor "passionate work." However, as McRobbie (2002a) points out, a distinctive feature of this type of cultural work where people show enthusiasm and love for their job is that insecure and often exploitative markets are continually oversupplied with labor. Therefore, if rappers are not prepared to multitask, brand, and sell themselves, there is an abundance of others willing to do so.

CONCLUSION

This chapter has mapped out the structural, technological, and economic factors that have contributed to London-based rappers experiencing a shift from being a music artist to cultural entrepreneur. Although the scene to a certain extent has always included DIY and entrepreneurial components, the processes of globalization, marketization, and especially digitization has resulted in rappers having to widen their scope of entrepreneurialism to encompass digital technologies in order to operate in the scene and be competitive. As such, the current conditions are harsher and the engagement with business has intensified, resulting in more challenging working lives. The shift from artist to entrepreneur has been difficult because of being forced to adapt, which depletes the autonomy, choice, and satisfaction that motivated many rappers to be artists in the first place. Although the Internet offers useful tools and entrepreneurial opportunity, many artists are still adjusting and learning how to maximize and exploit the various resources at their disposal.

In contrast to Sköld and Rehn (2007, 52) who argue that "an entrepreneurial disposition seems to have become a highly coveted virtue" in hip-hop, I argue that this entrepreneurialism is because of necessity rather than choice, therefore not coveted but a result of "forced entrepreneurialism" (Oakley 2014). Indeed, in the case of UK hip-hop, the notion of entrepreneurialism is particularly undesired because of its perceived contradiction with the subcultural values of being underground and not selling out that are prevalent in the scene. This chapter also highlights that rappers are not marginalized or oppressed but often astute businessmen with up-to-the-moment knowledge on production, law, technology, and industry trends, and how to leverage and exploit that capital.

McRobbie's (2002b, 99) observation of the general valorization of creative labor, "where work comes to mean much more than just earning a living; it incorporates and takes over everyday life" resonates in the London hip-hop community where rappers' work is a labor of love yet is also exploitative. The working conditions raise several ethical issues around labor in the cultural industries and the need to address the affective experience of contemporary cultural work and conceptualization of labor in modern societies. For example, where pleasure and autonomy might in fact be conceived as tools of control, encouraging self-exploitation. Further research on cultural entrepreneurs that takes into account wider structural factors and their everyday lived experience is vital in improving the working lives of rappers and other cultural producers.

NOTES

1. MF Doom is an American hip-hop artist known for having several stage names and personas. He wears a mask similar to that of super-villain Doctor Doom in the Marvel Comics.
2. "Sick" is a slang word used to state something is good or great.

REFERENCES

Arvidsson, Adam. "The Ethical Economy of Customer Coproduction." *Journal of Macromarketing* 28, no. 4 (2008): 326–338.

Banks, Mark. *The Politics of Cultural Work*. Basingstoke: Palgrave Macmillan, 2007.

Blair, Helen. "'You're Only as Good as Your Last Job': The Labour Process and Labour Market in the British Film Industry." *Work, Employment and Society* 15, no. 1 (2001): 149–169.

Cammaerts, Bart, Robin Mansell, and Bingchun Meng. *Copyright and Creation: A Case for Promoting Inclusive Online Sharing*. London: LSE Media Policy Brief, 2013. Last Accessed December, 28, 2014. http://www.lse.ac.uk/media@lse/documents/MPP/LSE-MPP-Policy-Brief-9-Copyright-and-Creation.pdf

Chapman, Dale. "The 'one-man band' and Entrepreneurial Selfhood in Neoliberal Culture." *Popular Music* 32 (2013): 451–470.

Dedman, Todd. "Agency in UK Hip-Hop and Grime Youth Subcultures—Peripherals and Purists." *Journal of Youth Studies* 14, no. 5 (2011): 507–522.

Deuze, Mark. *Media Work*. Cambridge: Polity Press, 2007.

Ellmeier, Andrea. "Cultural Entrepreneurialism: On the Changing Relationship Between the Arts, Culture and Employment." *International Journal of Cultural Policy* 9, no. 1 (2003): 3–16.

Gill, Rosalind, and Andy Pratt. "In the Social Factory? Immaterial labor, Precariousness and Cultural Work." *Theory, Culture and Society* 25, no. 7–8 (2008): 1–30.

Harkness, Geoff. "Gangs and Gangsta Rap in Chicago: A Microscenes Perspective." *Poetics* 41, (2013): 151–176.

Hesmondhalgh, David, and Sarah Baker. "'A Very Complicated Version of Freedom': Conditions and Experiences of Creative Labor in Three Cultural Industries." *Poetics* 38 (2009): 4–20.

Hracs, Brian J. "Beyond Bohemia: Geographies of Everyday Creativity for Musicians in Toronto." In *Spaces of Vernacular Creativity: Rethinking the Cultural Economy*, edited by Edensor, Tim, Deborah Leslie, Steve Millington, and Norma Rantisi, 75–88. London: Routledge, 2009.

Hracs, Brian J. "A Creative Industry in Transition: The Rise of Digitally Driven Independent Music Production." *Growth and Change* 43, no. 3 (2012): 442–461.

Hracs, Brian J. "Cultural Intermediaries in the Digital Age: The Case of Independent Musicians and Managers in Toronto." *Regional Studies* 49, no. 3 (2015): 461–475.

Leadbeater, Charles, and Kate Oakley. *The Independents*. London: Demos, 1999.

Lee, Jooyoung. "Open Mic: Professionalizing the Rap Career." *Ethnography* 10, no. 4 (2009): 475–495.

McRobbie, Angela. "Clubs to Companies: Notes on the Decline of Political Culture in Speeded Up Creative Worlds." *Cultural Studies* 16, no. 4 (2002a): 516–531.

McRobbie, Angela. "From Holloway to Hollywood: Happiness at Work in the New Cultural Economy." In *Cultural Economy*, edited by du Gay, Paul, and Michael Pryke, 97–114. London: Sage, 2002b.

Oakley, Kate. "Good work? Rethinking Cultural Entrepreneurship." In *Handbook of Management and Creativity*, edited by Bilton, Chris, and Stephen Cummings, 145–160. Cheltenham: Edward Elgar Publishing, 2014.

Perry, Imani. *Prophets of the Hood: Politics and Poetics in Hip-Hop*. USA: Duke University Press, 2004.

Sköld, David, and Alf Rehn. "Makin' It, by Keeping It Real: Street Talk, Rap Music, and the Forgotten Entrepreneurship from 'the 'Hood'." *Group and Organization Management* 32, no. 1 (2007): 50–78.

Watkins, Craig. *Hip-Hop Matters: Politics, Pop Culture, and the Struggle for the Soul of a Movement*. Boston: Beacon Press, 2005.

Wilson, Nick, and David Stokes. "Managing Creativity and Innovation: The Challenge for Cultural Entrepreneurs." *Journal of Small Business and Enterprise Development* 12, no. 13 (2005): 366–378.

Wood, Andy. " 'Original London Style': London Posse and the Birth of British Hip-Hop." *Atlantic Studies* 6, no. 2 (2009): 175–190.

6 Hip-Hop Tunity

Challenges and Opportunities for Indie Hip-Hop Artists in the Dutch Music Industry

Joni R. Haijen

In October of 2014 the Dutch rapper Mr. Probz reached the number one position in the Dutch music sales chart, the "Mega Top 50," with his song "Nothing Really Matters." Simultaneously, he was asked to perform at one of the biggest international dance festivals in the world, the Amsterdam Dance Event. Although the recent hit of Mr. Probz is not a typical rap song, it offers an example of how the Dutch music market for hip-hop is expanding. Rappers like Mr. Probz are independent—that is to say they are not signed by a record label. In addition, these rappers are not dedicated to making "pure hip-hop." The broadening appeal of this new wave of rappers became clear in the summer of 2013, when *Great Minds*—a collaboration between three well-known Dutch hip-hop artists—reached second place on the Dutch album sales chart. This is very unique since this is the highest listing of a Dutch hip-hop album ever. Dutch hip-hop—also known as "Nederhop"—is increasing in popularity in recent years, reaching a mainstream audience that appreciates the creative use of Dutch language in songs. However, it should be noted that next to using only Dutch lyrics, there is a growing group of Dutch rappers like Mr. Probz that produce songs both in Dutch and English. Nederhop is currently considered to be one of the most successful genres in the Dutch music industry (Cabenda 2013). This popularity is not only remarkable because hip-hop used to be a subgenre serving a niche market in the Netherlands, but also because, as this volume illustrates, the digital revolution has drastically transformed the landscape of the music industry. Digital technologies have altered the way music is produced, promoted, distributed, and consumed and has generated alternative business models with different opportunity structures (Hracs 2015). Due to the changes in the music industry, artists are no longer dependent on "major label" recording companies and skilled specialists. Rather they need to "do it themselves" (DIY). This new landscape of DIY has changed the nature of artists' labor, requiring them to diversify their skill sets and negotiate a range of challenges that are still relatively under-examined (Hracs and Leslie 2014).

The main focus of this chapter is to find out how indie artists negotiate opportunities in the Dutch hip-hop scene while paying particular attention to the changes digital technologies have brought about in the nature of their work, resources, and embeddedness within this artistic field (Granovetter 1985, 1990). It draws on an ethnographic study (2009–13), which included participant observation and 26 in-depth interviews. The sample included 18 indie musicians and 8 key informants who worked as managers, producers, and journalists in the Dutch music industry. In order to identify indie musicians who actively participate in the Dutch hip-hop scene—not always easy given the propensity of musicians to hold multiple jobs—a snowball sampling method was used. Verbatim quotes are used to demonstrate how respondents expressed meanings and experiences in their own words.

HIP-HOP IN THE NETHERLANDS

In the early 1980s hip-hop crossed the Atlantic Ocean and arrived in the Netherlands. Initially, the Dutch tried to imitate rappers from the United States but gradually developed their own style and created a new variant of hip-hop that would strongly characterize the Dutch hip-hop scene from the late 1980s onwards—Nederhop (Van Stapele 2002, 66). Critiquing commercial music derived from U.S. acts like Public Enemy and Run DMC, a group of Nederhop artists succeeded in creating an innovative and unique sound. On the one hand, this opened the eyes of many rappers in the Netherlands and suggested that it was possible to produce "cool" music by rapping in Dutch. On the other hand, as in the United States, hip-hop was still perceived as being part of a niche market, heavily influencing its contexts of production and distribution (Wermuth 1994). Since the Dutch music market as a whole is quite small, the reach of hip-hop music is even smaller. However, this simultaneously strengthened the process of the formation of a subculture—the Dutch hip-hop scene consisting of a group of "homeboys" and "flygirls" that regularly gathered together in the Randstad,[1] forming a close inward-oriented community.

In 1995 things started to change when journalist Kees de Koning founded his own hip-hop label, Top Notch. It was the first label that aimed to reach a broad audience with hip-hop music. In doing so, de Koning became and remains a key figure in the Dutch hip-hop scene. His strategy bore fruit as artists signed at Top Notch entered the Dutch national charts. From that time forward, Nederhop has been in an upward direction. As one key informant explained:

> Ten years ago, the Dutch hip-hop scene was relatively small. Everyone knew one another. Today, it is still small but the scene has developed: it reaches a much broader audience.

Interestingly, Nederhop has tapped into digital channels and blossomed beyond traditional media and the major label system. Indeed, Dutch rappers release their albums online and through small independent labels (Van Gijssel 2009).

THE CURRENT FIELD

In the contemporary digital era, respondents have emphasized the importance of networking and developing new business models. As one respondent explained:

> I need to connect! Expand my networks before I drop my album . . . The Dutch hip-hop scene is such a small world, you really need to have the right connections and produce commercially interesting tracks. I started to study *Interactive Media*, as it helps me to discover the new business structures in the music industry. [On] the positive side the industry has to find new business models and this will bring creativity back in the center of these new models. I have got big plans for the future, so I need to have professional people at my side before I release my album.

This particular respondent is a twenty-three-year-old indie artist, son of a Pakistani father and a Dutch mother, raised in a small village in the south of the Netherlands. He moved to Amsterdam in order to get better access to the "right connections" in the music industry. He also started his own record label—Millennium Music—because he wants to be his "own boss" and does not want to be dependent on other people. The name Millennium Music was chosen carefully and reflects his aim to promote himself as a socially involved "millennium goals rapper." He believes that this distinctive reputation will help him attract attention from the media and provide him with performance opportunities at particular occasions, like benefit concerts. At the same time, he feels the need for new connections and even seeks a professional manager as he hopes this will help him into the next phase of his career. Being an upcoming artist focused upon his reputation and developing his networks, his case is illustrative of the current developments many aspiring artists in the Dutch hip-hop scene confront. The rise of the Internet has had a massive impact on the ecology of the music industry and the ways of doing business. Like this respondent, many indie hip-hop artists want to start their own record label and learn how to promote themselves as an artist.

Opportunity Structure

Supply and demand remain important in the music industry despite recent and ongoing restructuring. On the supply side there is the stock of aspiring artists with their unique life stories and particular sets of resources at their disposal subjected to the will of the demand side. This will is driven by gatekeepers like journalists, managers, and consumers who "decide" which artists become superstars, while others are marginalized, possibly never going further than making music in their bedrooms (Brandellero and Kloosterman 2010). It is precisely this interplay between the demand and supply side in the music market that defines the "opportunity structure," or the kismet of the indie artist.

The concept of opportunity structure was introduced by Waldinger et al. (1990). It considers the set of openings, the market conditions at a certain time and place to make a living from economic activities. The opportunity structure of the cultural industry and the music industry in particular, is characterized by flexible forms of socio-economic organization, requiring creative skills, but not always formalized training, as innovation is considered a competitive advantage.

Becker (1982) offers that creative activities take place in complex networks of cooperation that he terms, "art worlds." Becker considers artistic production as collective action in which artists form the core, but all activities related to the process of creating a creative product has to be done within a wider field of collaborations (Hracs 2015). Therefore, economic actions and outcomes, especially in the creative sector, are affected by individual actors and their mutual relationships—their embeddedness—within the field of economic action. Becker emphasizes that "wherever an art world exists" boundaries of acceptable art are defined, assimilating those who create "acceptable" art, while excluding those who do not (Becker 1982, 35). These gatekeepers who identify and select emerging talent—playing a vital role in the creative industry as tastemakers by doing so—are called "cultural intermediaries" by the French sociologist Pierre Bourdieu (Hracs 2015). Moreover, following Bourdieu, each field of economic action, like the Dutch hip-hop scene, forms a particular domain of social life which has its own rules of organization generating a particular set of practices and positions of the actors active in it (Calhoun et al. 2008, 263).

As a distinct genre, indie artists in the hip-hop scene are not only confronted with the general gatekeepers of the music industry, but also with some specific gatekeepers, like hip-hop experts, special labels for hip-hop music, and a particular fan base (see also Speers, this volume). Being a rapper, you are part of the hip-hop subculture. The scene, therefore, forms a particular field within the music industry with a specific fan base that is strongly connected to the scene and its artists. In order to access this scene, you need to be able to rap but also need to know the particular "tricks of the trade," the rules of organization, and the general values and manners. According to Bourdieu (1984), the possession of different types of resources "provides the basic structure for the organization of fields, and thus the generation of forms of habitus and the practices associated with them" (Bourdieu 1984; Calhoun et al. 2008, 263). Thus, despite the fact that hip-hop is characterized by low entry thresholds—it is relatively easy to become a rapper; one does not need to have formal diplomas or be able to play an instrument—the respondents need to possess some specific resources in order to be able to access this particular art world (Kloosterman 2010). Therefore, it is important to examine the "rules" of this particular field and to consider what kind of resources the indie artists make use of to become embedded in order to expose their opportunities and challenges in the Dutch hip-hop scene.

RESOURCES

Each artist has his or her own specific package of resources, depending on their individual life stories. But what kind of resource packages do the respondents possess and which resources really matter if you want to have opportunities in the field of Dutch hip-hop? This section is an overview of the main characteristics of the resources artists have at their disposal—an examination of their human and financial capital as well as their social, cultural, and ethnic resources. Human and financial resources are important indicators for one's socio-economic position, while social, cultural, and ethnic resources also influence the opportunities one has as an indie hip-hop artist.

Financial resources are very important to the indie hip-hop artist. Due to digital technologies, an increased number of people have access to recording tools. According to the respondents, it is increasingly important to produce things of high quality to distinguish themselves from the crowd. In order to be able to produce videos and songs of high quality, the respondents indicate that they need to have large amounts of money at their disposal for purchasing high quality recording tools and to hire specialized producers. As one respondent stated:

> I only want to release music of high quality, but I lack the money to record in a studio and to hire a producer, but where can I find sources of money if the major record labels with money are disappearing?

So although digital technologies might have made it easier to enter the music business, it also has a paradoxical effect: it increased the need for the indie hip-hop artists to have more money at their disposal. Out of twelve respondents, six state that they do not earn enough money from their music (yet). Only two frequently complained about suffering from a lack of financial resources. Except for those respondents who are currently in school and receiving student grants, the other artists do not receive subsidies from the government. They argue that in the Netherlands you can get state support in the form of unemployment benefits or that some special projects are able to receive subsidies but none of them is eager to obtain money from the state. They prefer to eschew government support and make their own money. Moreover, they even frequently complain that hip-hop projects have been "over-subsidized" during the last ten years which has resulted in a lot of "fake hip-hop projects which do no good to the reputation of hip-hop."

Only two respondents are sometimes subsidized by being involved in social projects at community centers and cooperating with a NGO. Nonetheless, the respondents generally share the opinion illustrated by one of the key informants:

> If you are creative enough, you can make a living from hip-hop. However, most artists combine their musical career with another job. Those who are able to make a living from hip-hop music are the ones with brains—they have been able to develop strategic business plans.

The importance of having a business plan, even as an independent musician, is becoming more crucial. Training programs related to artist management and workshops about becoming a rapper are offered with increasing frequency. After visiting one of these courses at the Pop Academy in Rotterdam, one of the respondents explained:

> This is a course to become a professional artist, it provides you with tools to handle and act in the industry. Some have the naive idea that this study provides you with a plan that explains step by step what you need to do to become a professional artist. Many guys are straight from the streets and lack a business mentality. However, it is this business mentality that gives you the chance to distinguish yourself and to become a successful rapper.

Moreover, beyond acquiring skills and knowledge, respondents regard courses and training as a vital way to develop networks with other musicians and professionals (see Hracs, this volume):

> This school is a whole web of networks: you become friends with people who have their contacts in the industry and these, in turn, become also part of your network which helps you in developing your professional career.

Contrary to the assumption that hip-hop has low barriers to entry and that education is not necessary, most contemporary hip-hop artists have at least a few years of advanced education. Moreover, most respondents have taken a program related to their needs as an artist because they felt they needed to know the "tricks of the trade" in the music industry. Two respondents have established their own record label, not only because they are interested in the business side of their music career but also—and more importantly—because they do not want to be dependent on a record label, they want to pull the strings on their own. As one respondent explained:

> I have always been interested in the business side of music. How do you manage to earn enough money with your music? In order to find

> answers to these questions, I started to produce, release, and distribute an album myself. After that, I decided to start my own record label. It gives me freedom, while simultaneously I acquire insights in the music business.

In addition, they emphasize that, thanks to the fact that hip-hop forms a niche and, therefore, serves a relatively particular audience, there is some space for them to have their own record label. As one respondent put it:

> Because it is a specific subculture, the *real* fans prefer to keep the authenticity of hip-hop alive by buying their music from these small labels established by members of the scene itself instead of the big money makers.

Nevertheless, some respondents would like to have a contract with a record label, because that is the "lubricated machine" which would arrange the business part of their careers in order to provide them with more time to fully focus on their music.

These findings suggest that the "business side" of being an artist is more recognized, important, and formalized through targeted training. In addition—except for two respondents who have established their own record label—the respondents prefer to have a deal with a professional who is able to manage their businesses. This reinforces the work of Hauge and Hracs (2010, 114) which states, "the new demands of independent production and global competition are forcing individuals to become more professionalized and entrepreneurial." However, this is when certain limitations of the contemporary DIY model of music production and the recent shift to re-specialization become more evident. In his study of independent musicians in Toronto, Hracs (2015) argues that as musicians seek to break out of the DIY model, freelance managers are re-emerging as key intermediaries who can help musicians develop effective business plans. Furthermore, the digital era has introduced a range of new tasks in the working life of artists today. Hracs (2015, 466) offers that, "contemporary DIY entails individual responsibility for a traditional and modern range of creative and non-creative tasks . . . such as maintaining websites, digital distribution and promotion using social media." This is also what the respondents of this study indicate. Nevertheless, while some complain they "need to do everything themselves," they consider this range of creative and non-creative tasks inherent to the DIY model.

Much like Cummins-Russell and Rantisi (2012) observed in their study on the role of networks and place in Montreal's independent music industry, artists advance their careers by having access to a wide network of contacts, while creativity is encouraged by frequent face-to-face exchange. Additionally, the artists mitigate the risks of low-paying and unstable employment by functionally diversifying their contacts both vertically and horizontally within the scene (see Bürkner, this volume). Regarding their social resources, the respondents confirm the great importance of developing and maintaining their networks. The respondents who are already nationally known have well-developed networks within the scene. However, only one of them also has well-developed networks abroad, connecting with other rappers and producers in the United States. The other respondents mainly focus on their networks within the Netherlands because they predominantly make Nederhop, which they feel has little currency abroad. Furthermore, the Dutch scene forms a close community. From conversations with contacts within the scene, it is apparent that the Dutch hip-hop scene is characterized by mutual friendships, which also might explain why the respondents are not very active in developing contacts abroad. Moreover, as Cummins-Russell and Rantisi (2012) emphasize, despite recent technological advances, face-to-face contact between artists remains important. The same is true for indie hip-hop artists in Amsterdam. As one key informant stated, "Artists in the Dutch hip-hop scene are often close friends, they visit each other a lot, and maintain mutual relations. Many even share apartments." For this reason, local ties and connections remain important even in the digital age.

The artists interviewed indicate that social media platforms like Twitter, Facebook, and Whatsapp are increasingly important to the scene. Thanks to these digital tools, the respondents are able to interact and share information with their collaborators, extend personal networks, connect with audience members, and stay informed on the latest developments in the music industry. One respondent explains:

> Thanks to new digital tools, artists are able to keep each other and their audiences informed. It not only increased but also improved the mutual relations among the artists and their audience. New collaborations even appeared thanks to these new forms of communication.

Most of these networks have remained local, but more recently scene members have also discovered the ease of developing international relations by using the Internet.

Contrary to other studies (see: Gill and Pratt 2008; Hauge and Hracs 2010), the use of social media has not caused a rise of (net)working hours as the Dutch hip-hop scene consists of a close-knit group in which boundaries between work and social activities have always been blurred. As one respondent stated, "Many songs in the Dutch hip-hop scene are born by chilling together on the couch." However, not everyone appears to think this way as two respondents emphasized that being active on social media is very different from hanging out with others from the scene. For example, one respondent pointed out that he regrets the fact that he cannot "solemnly use Facebook for fun," but also has to use the digital tool "for promotional activities." Nonetheless, other respondents view social media platforms as welcome tools making it easier to promote their music.

The scene appears to be characterized by what Putnam (2000) has called "bonding capital" or the social contacts termed "strong ties" by Granovetter (1973, 2005). This has positive as well as negative sides—once you succeed in establishing the right friendships, you are "in the clover," but because it forms a relatively closed community, it is not always easy to have close friendships and occupy a place within the scene. The respondents who are still struggling to acquire a place within the scene repeatedly expressed complaints about the scene being "a very small and closed world." Spending various afternoons together with two of the respondents, this sentence frequently rang true:

> The Dutch hip-hop scene is such a small world, consisting of a group of friends which makes it closed to outsiders. If you are different, you are not able to enter the scene.

Others, talking about the "scene," emphasize the "positive vibe" within it among the artists and other key actors because most of them are friends with each other. In many cases, important gatekeepers within the scene—like journalists and radio hosts—are also friends with the respondents. One informant described it in this way:

> Being friends, many artists still meet face-to-face to chill with each other, but also regarding business with other actors active in the scene it is important to meet face-to-face. However, other forms of communication also have come to play an important role in maintaining contacts.

The number and content of the messages artists mutually send to each other confirm that the scene is characterized by friendships. One key informant stated:

> Of course, I am their business partner in the first place. But, if some of the guys call me to chill on a Friday night, I would not reject. They are also my friends.

Thus, the social resource base of the respondents is characterized by a lot of strong ties and bonding capital. The digital era has made it easier to get and stay in touch with each other, the gatekeepers, and their audience. Additionally, because hip-hop is a subculture and the scene consists of relatively spatial and concentrated close mutual relationships, the core of the fan base is also actively part of it. This became especially clear when visiting concerts and parties, but also on blogs, forum discussions, and other online applications. Fans regularly address artists to discuss issues and to voice opinions about their music. The respondents agree that it is important to have these contacts with their fans; they appreciate the small scale of the Dutch hip-hop scene, as it makes it very accessible for the fans.

From this analysis it also becomes clear that the Dutch hip-hop scene forms an island of its own because it is a particular subculture. As a consequence, the social resource base of the respondents is characterized by a relatively high number of social contacts within the scene itself—strong social ties or bonding capital—while lacking weak ties or bridging social capital like personal contacts with actors in the mainstream market. As a result, all respondents—including the key informants—would like to have more contacts outside the scene and express frustrations about hip-hop not being accepted by the mainstream media and "having a second-rate position in the music industry." Those respondents who do manage to reach out have established connections beyond the scene via key informants acting as mediators between the hip-hop scene and the mainstream. Social media and other digital tools have also been helpful in developing contacts beyond the scene.

Since hip-hop forms a subculture within the cultural industry, cultural resources are of great importance. This particular market demands unique, symbolic products be dedicated to hip-hop. The artists use these products to express their social status, represent hip-hop culture, and advertise a particular way of living through specific clothes, language, and manners. One of the most important aspects of hip-hop culture that every indie artist emphasizes is the cultural resource of "being real." This implies that you stay true to your background by representing hip-hop culture. While not specifically detailed by the respondents, "being real" and representing hip-hop culture included a shared love of the genre accompanied by specific manners, tastes, practices, and values. This ethos was observed during fieldwork through contact with the respondents. One example of a specific manner that is also a form of tacit knowledge in the scene is that you do not focus on money, instead you need to stay "real" by "doing your thing." Moreover, it implies that as artists in the hip-hop scene, you need to keep your authenticity, remain true to yourself, don't belie your background and your artistic integrity by choosing the "big money." Even from a business point of view, it is very important to stay true to your cultural authenticity in the Dutch hip-hop scene. If you want to achieve commercial success, you always need to keep in mind that you keep your authenticity, your artistic integrity. Otherwise, if you are perceived as too commercially-minded according to scene members, you will no longer be considered part of the scene, which has consequences for the future of your career. This causes tensions for the respondents as those artists experiencing this were no longer embedded within the scene, which heavily decreased the chance of scoring another hit and even made it hard to stay active as a hip-hop artist. Two respondents able to make a living from their music evaded blame for "not being real" by having a business strategy in which there is enough room for authenticity and to express a shared love for hip-hop culture. For example, they organize specific events dedicated to hip-hop and are continuously emphasizing their street credibility. Moreover, as Hauge and Hracs (2010) show in their study on musicians and fashion designers in Toronto, people active in the creative industry consider authenticity a very important part of the lifestyle and personal narrative; therefore, there is a need to find a balance between economic returns.

No remarkable differences have been found between artists of different ethnic backgrounds. However, ethnicity serves as a source of inspiration for the respondents. As such, ethnic resources can be viewed as "extra capital" to the respondents but do not play a dominant role. However, ethnic resources support the cultural resource base of the respondents in the sense that having a background as an ethnic minority contributes to one of the most important characteristics artists need to have in order to enter the scene—"being real." Having an ethnic minority background gives artists "street credibility" as they are perceived as being familiar with the "hard life of the streets" as an immigrant, amplifying their status of "being real."

OPPORTUNITIES AND CHALLENGES

The digital revolution has dismantled established (power) structures in the music industry, democratizing its business ecology. Major record labels have not disappeared and remain important. For example, they are reaching out to indie artists and assisting them with the distribution of their music. However, as technology has reduced entry barriers and provides new platforms to help promote and distribute music, especially subgenres like hip-hop, the supply of aspiring rappers continues to increase. As a result, the respondents indicate that they need to be more professional and creative in order to distinguish themselves from the mass of other indie artists. In particular, it is very important to have a professional business plan as an artist today. This also implies that you need to develop a public relations or "PR" strategy. As one respondent asserted:

> Nowadays, you need to have a story to tell in order to get attention from the media when you release a new album. For example, the cover of my album caused a lot of commotion. This provided me the opportunity to be in the spotlights with my album for more than one year, getting attention from the media, which would otherwise never have paid attention to a rapper like me.

Key informants confirm this by stating the scene is characterized by a self-filtering mechanism which automatically removes those artists who do not fulfill the admittance requirements set by the actors in the scene. If you want to become a successful rapper, it is important that your music brings something creative and innovative—be it textual, visual, or aural. Indeed, the artists among the respondents who are considered to be successful by scoring hits in the national Dutch charts distinguish themselves from the other respondents by having a solid business strategy in which bringing innovative and creative products to the market is paramount. As one respondent put it: "As an artist you need to supply yourself in different packages, make use of different resources to sell yourself and enlarge your market." Most respondents find themselves at the intersection between the mainstream and the subcultural market of Dutch hip-hop. This is a difficult position because the economic potential of the subcultural market of Dutch hip-hop is very small. If you want to make a living from hip-hop music in the Netherlands, you need to break out of the subcultural market and enter the mainstream. However, then the dilemma of "keeping it real" appears as the artists enter a market in which they are able to earn more money.

CONCLUSIONS

The contemporary digital era is one of low barriers to entry and increasing competition. The findings of this study demonstrate that the Dutch hip-hop scene consists of a very close community, which forms an "art world" of its own. Opportunities appear to those indie artists embedded within the scene, have access to the right social networks, and are able to develop a professional business strategy that also leaves room for ties to traditional aspects of hip-hop culture. Challenges appear to those who can't work within these parameters. The digital era can provide opportunities to those who are able to use constantly evolving digital tools in a strategic way, while also posing challenges to those indie artists who are not digitally savvy. The current opportunity structure demands indie production and requires musicians to diversify their skill-sets. As an indie artist you need to understand how the music industry functions, develop networks with important gatekeepers, and place high quality products on the market.

Although hip-hop in the Netherlands is blooming, it is still hard to earn enough money to make a living from it since this growth largely takes place outside the traditional mainstream channels. Despite this challenge, there are examples like Mr. Probz illustrating that the Dutch hip-hop scene operates as an art world, facilitating opportunity when you know the "tricks of the trade," offering a "hip-hop tunity" for the entrepreneurial-minded indie artist.

NOTE

1. *De Randstad* is a conurbation consisting of the four largest Dutch cities Amsterdam, Rotterdam, The Hague, and Utrecht.

REFERENCES

Becker, Howard. *Art Worlds*. Berkeley, Los Angeles, and London: University of California Press, 1982.

Bourdieu, Pierre. *Distinction: A Social Critique of the Judgement of Taste*. Trans. by Richard Nice. London, Melbourne, and Henley: Routledge and Kegan Paul, 1984.

Bourdieu, Pierre. *The Field of Cultural Production. Essays on Art and Literature*. New York: Columbia University Press, 1993.

Brandellero, Amanda, and Robert C. Kloosterman. "Keeping the Market at Bay: Exploring the Loci of Innovation in the Cultural Industries." *Creative Industries Journal* 3 (2010): 61–77.

Cabenda, Pablo. "Hiphop uit je smoel." *De Volkskrant*, 2013.

Calhoun, Craig, Joseph Gerties, James Moody, Steven Pfaff, and Indermohan Virk. *Contemporary Sociological Theory*. Hoboken and New York: John Wiley and Sons, 2007.

Cummins-Russell, Thomas A., and Norma M. Rantisi. "Networks and Place in Montreal's Independent Music Industry." *The Canadian Geographer/Le Géographe Canadien* 56 (2012): 80–97.

Gijssel, Robbert van. "De gescheiden werelden van neder- en hip-hop." *De Volkskrant*, October 9, 2009.

Gill, Rosalind, and Andy Pratt. "In the Social Factory? Immaterial Labor, Precariousness and Cultural Work." *Theory, Culture and Society* 25 (2008): 1–30.

Graham, Gary, Bernard Burnes, Gerard J. Lewis, and Janet Langer. "The Transformation of the Music Industry Supply Chain." *International Journal of Operations and Production Management* 24 (2004): 1087–1103.

Granovetter, Mark. "The Strength of Weak Ties." *The American Journal of Sociology* 78 (1973): 1360–1380.

Granovetter, Mark. "The Old and the New Economic Sociology: A History and Agenda." In *Beyond the Marketplace: Rethinking Economy and Society*, edited by Friedland, Roger, 89–112. New York: Aldine de Gruyter, 1990.

Granovetter, Mark. "The Impact of Social Structure on Economic Outcomes." *Journal of Economic Perspectives* 19 (2005): 33–50.

Granovetter, Mark. "Economic Embeddedness." In *Contemporary Sociological Theory*, edited by Calhoun, Craig, 162–170. Malden and Oxford, Carlton: Blackwell Publishing, 2007.

Hauge, Atle, and Brian J. Hracs. "See the Sound, Hear the Style: Collaborative Linkages Between Indie Musicians and Fashion Designers in Local Scenes." *Industry and Innovation* 17 (2010): 113–129.

Hracs, Brian J. "Cultural Intermediaries in the Digital Age: The Case of Independent Musicians and Managers in Toronto." *Regional Studies* 49 (2015): 461–475.

Hracs, Brian J., and Deborah Leslie. "Living Under the Lights: The Intensification and Extensification of Aesthetic Labour for Independent Musicians in Toronto." *Royal Geographical Society* 46 (2014): 66–73.

Jeffcutt, Paul, and Andy Pratt. "Managing Creativity in the Cultural Industries." *Creativity and Innovation Management* 11 (2002): 225–233.

Kloosterman, Robert C. "Matching Opportunities with Resources: A Framework for Analysing (Migrant) Entrepreneurship from a Mixed Embeddedness Perspective." *Entrepreneurship and Regional Development* 22 (2010): 25–45.

Putnam, Robert. *Bowling Alone*. New York: Simon and Schuster, 2000.

Waldinger, Roger, Howard Aldrich, and Robin Ward. *Ethnic Entrepreneurs*. London: Sage, 1990.

Wermuth, Mir. "Rap from the Lowlands (1982–1994). Global Dichotomies on a National Scale" (Paper presented at the conference Popular Music Studies in a New Dutch Perspective, Amsterdam, 1994).

7 "Working at the Candy Factory"

The Limits of Nonmonetary Rewards in Record Industry Careers

Alexandre Frenette

Careers in the music industry are highly uncertain—and often quite short—due to several factors including the advent of technological innovations, frequent restructuring of operations and business models, and the industry's overarching inability to predict the success of recorded music releases (Caves 2000; Hracs 2012; Leyshon 2014; Peterson and Anand 2002). Research on a variety of music-related workers confirms that such unpredictability translates to chaotic and precarious careers for musicians (Haijen, this volume; Hracs, this volume; Speers, this volume), songwriters (de Laat 2015), film score composers (Faulkner 1983), as well as record producers and engineers (Watson, this volume). Conversely, the emphasis on "psychic" or nonmonetary rewards among artistic workers such as these complicates typical understandings of what marks professional success/failure and good/bad jobs (Menger 1999; Oakley 2009).

Much like workers in the artistic roles above, record industry personnel forgo money in exchange for nonmonetary rewards such as autonomy and self-expression (Hesmondhalgh and Baker 2011). Record industry workers produce and disseminate recorded music, which, either in the context of (large) major record companies or (smaller) indie labels, involves producing, promoting, marketing, distributing, selling, etc. Caves (2000) refers to these non-artistic roles as "humdrum" (or ordinary), but according to record industry workers their positions are far from humdrum. Hesmondhalgh and Baker (2010) refer to work in the creative industries as "a very complicated version of freedom" because, on one hand, the record industry workers they interviewed describe deriving powerful nonmonetary rewards, but, on the other hand, they report long work hours, low pay, and considerable job insecurity. Similarly, McRobbie (2004) describes creative work as characterized by the *pleasure-pain axis*; I briefly expand on this concept below, first by contextualizing the challenging state of the record industry, then by building on what is meant by the "pleasure" of nonmonetary rewards.

During the first decade of the twenty-first century, global revenues for the sale of recorded music fell from $36.9 billion to $15.9 billion (Smirke 2011). In the United States, the sales figure went from almost $15 billion to $8.5 billion annually (Friedlander 2010). In 1999, major record companies employed approximately 25,000 people and by 2010 that figure fell below 10,000 (Friedlander 2010). Consequently, the remaining jobs are extremely competitive and demanding. Moreover, the status, excitement, and prestige of music industry work are generally offset by relatively low incomes, particularly early in one's career. A report by Berklee College of Music's Career Development Center (2012) establishes starting salaries in the record industry (excluding music attorneys) as ranging between $24,000 and $28,000 per year. Not only are starting salaries low, job security in the music industry is scarce (Hesmondhalgh and Baker 2011). The oversupply of potential workers—including in the form of unpaid interns willing to work for free—makes it extremely challenging (and often expensive) to start and sustain a career in the music industry (Frenette 2013).

Nonetheless, music industry personnel describe a strong passion and attachment for music, which inform their choice of occupation and thus constitute their occupational identity (Frenette 2014). Wright (2005, 115) similarly shows how bookstore employees accentuate passion for books as a precondition for employment and there is "an evangelism at work in their orientations to the [books] they sold." These employees construct their special status as connoisseurs and elevate their low-paid work as creative, moral work motivated by nonmonetary rewards. According to this perspective, which Watson (2013, 334) aptly summarizes in his work on record producers and engineers: "It is frequently suggested that cultural work is invariably more than a job; rather it is a labor of love." Therefore, recent studies on the subjective experiences of workers in creative fields shed much light on how nonmonetary rewards—and the strong potential for self-exploitation (Banks 2010)—explain why so many people want to work in a sector like music despite challenging employment conditions (Hesmondhalgh and Baker 2011; Watson 2013). However, little research analyzes how workers make sense of the limits of nonmonetary rewards, particularly over time.

Although McRobbie (2004) helpfully describes the pleasure-pain axis as the normative expectation of pain among creative workers, balanced by various forms of nonmonetary rewards such as pleasure and passion, the evidence presented in this chapter suggests that such equilibrium is tenuous, especially in the digital age. Building on the work of Tavory and Winchester (2012, 369) on experiential careers, I propose that record industry personnel undergo "changes in their ways of experiencing a 'cared about' object of their career." These shifts in experience can be summarized as an early period of strong excitement followed by routinized behavior ("becoming jaded") on the part of music personnel and, often, disenchantment that leads to exiting the music industry. Therefore, based on participant observation and data from semi-structured interviews with music industry interns, paid employees, and ex-employees, this chapter focuses on how record industry workers make sense of the limits of nonmonetary rewards and asks: What factors challenge the sustained commitment of workers towards their record industry careers?

Following a brief overview of research methods, I highlight how workers describe their work as a "passion job." Next, I consider how disenchantment (or the inability to deal with a loss or routinization of passion) is identified as a key reason for quitting or getting let go. Specifically, I show how the disenchantment of workers occurs due to three main factors: precariousness, a changing relationship to music, and aging out. In the process, I provide a snapshot of record industry work conditions—in the words of current or recent workers—and show how the digital era has exacerbated these three pressures to exit the industry early. I conclude with implications for future research.

DATA AND METHODS

This chapter is based on evidence from participant observation and semi-structured interviews with music industry interns and employees in New York City. Gaining entry as an intern, I was an overt participant observer at two companies: I spent two days per week for four months at the sales and marketing department of a major record label I call "Major Records USA" and at least one day per week for six months at the digital sales department of "Indie Distribution," an indie-oriented music distribution company. Assuming the position of intern provided a privileged access point to situate the meanings and cultures of music industry work. I assumed a highly participatory (although low status) role, which occasionally brought me beyond the context of the office; much like creative workers need to be mobile and extend their work beyond the confines of the office (Gregg 2013; Hracs and Leslie 2014), research brought me to music venues, bars, coffee shops, and birthday parties. I wrote field notes daily, frequently re-reading these to help me locate gaps and themes later clarified in interviews. To protect the confidentiality of respondents, all individual and company names were changed to pseudonyms.

Also, I completed semi-structured interviews with 60 music industry workers: 33 men and 27 women, ranging from 18 to 54 years old (average age = 29.1). I conducted at least one formal follow-up interview with 16 of the participants to expand and revisit findings. All but five of the interviews were digitally recorded, transcribed, and coded using ATLAS.ti software. Interviews, which on average lasted over 90 minutes, were conducted to test, expand, and counterbalance data from participant observation. Questions elicited participants' biographical and occupational backgrounds, their perceptions regarding recent music industry struggles, and workplace culture.

Variation and Limitations

The participants in this study generally tend to be (1) young, (2) live in New York City, and (3) work or intern at major record labels or well-established indie music companies. As I describe below, these characteristics simultaneously constitute the sample's strengths and its limitations.

In order to capture varying experiences within the trajectory of music industry careers, from those of neophytes to veteran employees, interviewees ranged from recent or current unpaid interns (N = 12) who had not yet secured their first jobs to "old timers" (N = 5) who had already ended their music industry careers. Interview data suggests that workers might become disenchanted and exit the industry at any age, but in this chapter I draw especially from the insights of entry- to mid-level employees.

Moreover, by focusing on workers at well-established companies in New York City, the present study succeeds at analyzing the experiences of personnel in a traditional music production market (akin to Los Angeles or London). However, some of the career challenges this chapter describes might not emerge as saliently for entrepreneurial members of smaller, more independent-driven, "non-traditional" music scenes (which grew significantly in recent decades) such as Omaha, Nebraska, and Seattle, Washington (Seman 2010). Notably, high rents in cities like New York exacerbate the precariousness of workers as compared to cities like Indianapolis, Indiana. Similarly, enchantment at work might (or might not) be easier to sustain at a smaller company or in a more DIY/indie music context. Therefore, this chapter tells part of a larger story on music industry work in the digital age.

THE PASSION JOB: MEANING AND/OR MONEY IN THE DIGITAL AGE

Before discussing potential reasons for disenchantment, it is important to expand slightly on the professional context in which record industry personnel operate, which is rich in opportunities for nonmonetary rewards. Record companies generally have a no-collar office culture where self-expression in and outside of the office is encouraged and, at least superficially, well received. Workplaces in the creative industries are understood as ideal sites for worker self-realization and the blurring of work and fun (Florida 2002). No-collar workplaces such as record companies appear to present "an environment where personal identity could be deeply felt and shaped" (Ross 2003, 51). For record industry personnel, the crafting of one's identity at work occurs in a professional context that stresses the salience of nonmonetary rewards.

Employees commonly emphasize the nonmonetary rewards of their work more so than whatever money they receive; they describe music industry work as a "passion job," a "lifestyle job," or not a job at all (i.e., an extension of their affinity for music). "It's definitely a passion job," Kevin tells me after spending five years promoting indie records to college radio stations. He goes on, "It's all about the music." When discussing how the job is different than what he originally conceived, however, Kevin describes a familiar tension: "There's the beauty of working with music which is my one true love, but it's not a lot of money to start off with especially with all the hours and stress that's put into it." Despite the challenges of music industry work, Kevin concludes, "At the end of the day it's definitely worth it." Kevin deploys a "love for" metaphor, which carries a sense of moral worth and accentuates psychic rewards according to a narrative of passion and engagement (Benzecry 2011). Workers are expected to convey strong passion not just for music, but for their vocation as well (Frenette 2014).

However, to recognize or imbue work in the music industry as special does not occur automatically and often wanes over time. To illustrate this point, I will consider Grace (22 years old) and Susan (38 years old) as exemplars; the former represents the early stage of enchantment at work whereas the latter is approaching the end of her music career.

Grace is relatively new to the industry. She is a "jill-of-all trades" at a well-respected indie record company, working as a receptionist, office assistant, and internship coordinator. During an interview, she describes her various job responsibilities to me, from managing guest lists for shows to hiring interns to office upkeep. Grace does not sound very attached to the hodgepodge of tasks she routinely takes on, but depicts her current work environment enthusiastically.

Posters of bands from the record company's roster are pinned or taped to the walls in the small lobby where Grace works. She recalls her early impressions upon visiting the record company's office: "It feels very loose and not too stressful, and interesting. You walk in and there are all sorts of people just sitting around, wearing jeans and some graphic t-shirt, playing tons of music." After seven months at her job, she still describes the music industry as "sexy and exciting." Grace also tells me she still likes getting into shows for free, a common perk in the business. Not every office is equally fun, nor are all departments within a company equally alluring. In Grace's case, the excitement she describes comes from factors beyond her immediate work responsibilities. Her everyday tasks do not appear to be sexy and exciting, but she describes her work environment, the informal office culture, her co-workers, and the music they work with affectionately.

For the various rewards of working in the music industry, employees like Grace take on work they describe as unfulfilling. Similarly, although with 15 years of music industry experience, Susan speaks unenthusiastically of her everyday tasks. During an interview, Susan described her accounting-related position at a major record company with marked ambivalence: "My job is the kind of job I could do for almost any business and I wouldn't want to do it for any [other] business. If I'm not working here I don't want to do Excel spreadsheets for Procter & Gamble." I asked Susan how her day would be different doing this job at a place like Procter & Gamble. Again, like Grace, she accentuates nonmonetary rewards:

> I couldn't wear jeans and a t-shirt to work. I wouldn't have a TV in my office [*pointing to a TV*]. I wouldn't be able to listen to music. The CDs

> I get, the shows I go to, these are all . . . [*Speaking in a more animated manner*] We have a bin in our kitchenette that says, 'Do not throw CDs into this trash,' because we get so jaded, we get so many CDs we just throw them away. This is a kind of 'working at the candy factory.' This is the place that puts out the stuff that excites you and it's such a dream for so many people.

While employed in the music industry, Susan claimed that she knew her job was a special one—implying a certain prestige and status—yet she also made a comment about the sign on the trash bin (a sign that I saw above or on many other trash bins in that building). Susan noted that people become jaded. To be jaded means to become tired or bored with something, typically from too much contact with it. In the case of music industry personnel, to become jaded is not necessarily negative. Socialization into a music industry workplace involves a healthy level of jadedness to achieve the proper fan/professional balance of industry cool (Frenette 2014). However, jadedness can become disenchantment.

Less than six months later Susan told me she was bored and burnt out with the music industry and was moving on to attend graduate school. Although working in the music industry—in whatever capacity—is a dream for so many people, several respondents described a shift in experience where the nonmonetary rewards no longer produce sufficient levels of commitment to continue working in the "candy factory." The sections below consider some potential reasons for disenchantment in music industry work, particularly in the digital era.

BECOMING DISENCHANTED

Faulkner (1974, 157) calls the early career a period of "illusionment" when young adults attempt to establish footholds and success seems possible; depending on what the worker achieves, dreams are replaced by "new mobility outlooks and motivations." After working for an indie record label for two years, Shane has already seen employees lose their sense of excitement and decrease their level of commitment. This process of disenchantment, he adds, exists in every industry:

> There are people who worked at *Indie Label X* and over the course of time you just sense they're not really committed, they're not really *into* it, and you get the vibe that they're not really happy because they know that they're not making that much money, they're working long hours, you could just sense either you're excited about your job or you're not. It happens in every industry I'm sure.

People become disenchanted in other industries, yet music industry employment is often characterized by precarious work conditions and low pay.

Therefore, when perks count as payment and workers portray their source of livelihood as a passion job, disenchantment (or the inability to deal with a loss or routinization of passion) is identified as a key reason for quitting or getting let go.

Below I will delineate some overlapping factors in music industry personnel's experience that challenge the continuation of their careers, namely: precariousness; a changing relationship to music; and aging out. In so doing, I provide a snapshot of record industry work conditions and show how the digital era has exacerbated these three pressures to exit.

Precariousness

Record industry employment in the digital era is exceptionally precarious. With the downturn in record sales and consistent restructuring of record companies, even full-time permanent employees have very little job security (Hesmondhalgh and Baker 2011). Increased precariousness in the digital age has also brought with it several interrelated effects on working conditions: workers must assume more responsibilities (many of them mundane); they experience considerable stress regarding their job security day-to-day; and face an uncertain future.

Despite its potential for glamour and excitement, everyday tasks carried out by the music industry workers are neither necessarily glamorous nor glamorized by others. The arrival of the digital age has not eliminated mundane tasks; in fact, with so many positions eliminated at increasingly lean record companies, there are less people to handle unexciting work. While tasks like burning or delivering promotional compact discs have largely been eliminated, new tedious digitally driven work has emerged. At a music distribution firm, Nate manages YouTube content for record companies, i.e., ensures official record company content is on the website (and incorrect, inappropriate, or illegal videos are not). It is slightly technical and low profile work that needs to get done, but an afterthought for most people: "No one gives a fuck what I do on YouTube, really. But [record companies] need that. . . . Is your average fan going to thank me? No. They don't give you a second thought." Workers at all levels can draw from the music industry's nonmonetary rewards, yet this may be more challenging for certain workers within the industry's hierarchy. While working in the music industry is described as high status, and newcomers or outsiders may expect exciting work, employees also realize that their actual day-to-day tasks might tend towards the mundane and thankless.

In the digital age music industry employment is becoming even more insecure and unstable. As one record industry veteran told me, compared to previous (more successful) decades, "It's not a constant party anymore." He continues, noting changes compared to the 1990s and before:

> It wasn't that long ago, records sold themselves: press a bunch of vinyl records, you send them out to stores, and people came to stores and

> bought them. There was a lot of money going around, a lot of drugs going around; it's not really that way anymore. Profits are shrinking. Labels are closing [or merging].

What was previously considered a fun industry is becoming a difficult context in which to build a career. While visiting a respondent at a major record company for a follow-up interview, he told me about a large round of layoffs that took place a few weeks before. The layoff rumors, he said, were the worst part of this process; after weeks of job uncertainty, he tells me the stress had left him too nervous to eat. While some cultural workers are inherently "risk-seekers" and entrepreneurial, for many the stress caused by insecurity takes its toll.

Even the committed and the relatively successful workers have uncertain futures—or feel as such. An A&R employee at a major record company tells me in an interview about his impressive accomplishments and rapid ascent through the company's ranks. He was involved in signing and putting together several hit albums in the last year. The head of the company's A&R department even introduced him to me as a rising star at the company. Yet, as the interview progressed, this 26 year-old A&R employee reflected soberly about what might be ahead: "I wonder . . . where I'm going to be in two years. Am I still going to be in the industry?" Workers are aware of their precariousness and mention it occasionally. The precariousness of music industry work provides potential sources of disenchantment for workers, which may translate to tenuous levels of commitment.

A Changing Relationship to Music

Workers identified numerous day-to-day challenges and long-term career concerns; while issues related to precariousness were most prevalent, some of the other (overlapping) reasons identified for disenchantment have to do with the workers' fluid relationship with music. As described below, music industry personnel likely need to work with some music they do not like, struggle with the art/commerce tension, and often lose interest in "keeping up."

Although the music industry lends itself to psychic rewards from being involved with artists and their oeuvres, workers also report the need to develop professionalism that allows distance when such a connection is absent (or, worse yet, they abhor the music with which they are involved). Several respondents brought up the necessity—although not always a pleasant one—to work with music they did not like. One respondent joked about a friend who left the music business because all he could find was work in the adult contemporary genre. As an intern, Danielle describes learning to work with music she does not love as an early challenge: "I think that was something I learned, that you can respect something without necessarily being a *fan*, having all the paraphernalia and what not." Music personnel rarely like all of the releases they work with, although they may not freely admit it. Moreover, with the frequent restructuring of companies and the difficulties workers face to find stable employment, record industry personnel in the digital age are especially unlikely to control the genre, let alone the artists, with which they work.

Related to the fan/professional tension above, by virtue of their position, at least some of the time music industry workers must treat music as a "product," albums as "units," fans as "customers." These are practical examples of workers managing the art/commerce tension day-to-day—their professionalism (mixed with occasional cynicism) allows them to maintain aesthetic integrity while bringing to market music they may not like, but fulfills their employers' commercial imperatives (Wei 2012). Simultaneously, these examples portray the struggle between sustaining passion and routinely doing work that seems to challenge the worker's reverence for music in a passion job.

Working in the candy factory, it is a challenge not to take things for granted and get used to the activity of music making. At the same time, workers describe it as a challenge to consistently become excited by new music. Despite their professed passion and seemingly strong identity, music industry personnel change their relationship to their work and to music. I ask Bela, a 29 year-old employee, if her relationship to music has changed through working in the music industry. She quickly retorts: "God, now I'm so much more fucking jaded, and I don't go to as many rock shows, and I don't really care about being a sponge and learning about every new band and reading *Billboard* and *Magnet*." Later on during our conversation, she diagnoses part of the problem: "I'm not *that* excited by new music. I listen to a band; very rarely do I like the new band." She expands on why she has gotten bored with most new music: "You listen to a lot of the same stuff, you just get a little bit bored and you want to hear something new or maybe you want to hear something familiar. You realize what you really like. You know?" Bela describes having identified her preferences—in contrast to a few years ago when everything sounded so fresh and exciting. A few months after the interview, Bela applied for graduate school and left the music industry.

The changing relationship to music, as Bela's case shows, overlaps with the process of aging out. While difficulties in maintaining the desire to stay abreast of new music is nothing new, the coming of the digital age has vastly increased the quantity of new music available and accelerated the "lifespan" of a new song. Therefore, in addition to the longstanding challenges of managing the fan/professional and art/commerce tensions inherent in their jobs, it is an especially difficult time for record industry workers to remain abreast of new music.

Aging Out

Although staying abreast of trends in music might never cease to interest some individuals, employees such as Bela above suggest how laborious such a process might become. Some respondents de-emphasize the importance of age among workers in the music industry, insisting that age matters less than enthusiasm. Nonetheless, because music industry employees tend to be young, it is difficult to extract age as a factor affecting disenchantment and career decisions. The contemporary structure of the record industry seems to accelerate the aging out process. According to current and ex-employees, age matters in that it is difficult to continually come off as credible regarding new cultural and technological developments, and these are evolving at startling speeds—i.e., workers have a perceived "shelf life." Paired with the precariousness and low pay of music work, as well as changing life priorities over time, age becomes a key factor that challenges the enchantment (and, therefore, the continuation) of record industry careers.

Uncertainty and self-awareness regarding one's status as an older worker can essentially begin at the beginning of a music career. Eddie, a 54 year-old music industry ex-employee, recalls his start at a major record company when he was in his 20s:

> I was this new kid on the block that just walked in the door and before you could blink I was starting to badmouth these guys who are 40 . . . I'm saying, 'These guys, man, they don't know what's going on, they're old, they need to get out of here!' And sure enough, when I had started getting close to that age, there were a bunch of guys coming in and saying, 'This guy, he doesn't know what's going on. He needs to get out of here.' So I understood from early on that you probably have a shelf life.

Eddie equates aging out with becoming too old to retain credibility in an artistically inclined role. He adds that, for example, a sales employee might be able to "hold on" later, but an employee in an artist-facing role will rarely last beyond the age of 40. Of course, there are numerous notable exceptions—people who retain their creative roles well into their 60s or older, but of significance is the predominant idea that workers have a shelf life.

As a youth-oriented industry, it is crucial for music personnel, to varying extents, to remain abreast of cultural and technological developments. One method record companies use to address this need is to regularly host unpaid interns and, when convenient, to treat these (usually) college-age workers as a de facto focus group (Frenette 2013). Yet, especially in the face of a constant influx of youth, employees sometimes become sensitive about their elder status. After telling me that an intern first informed him of Facebook many years ago, Karl (32 years old) responds defensively when I ask whether interns help him stay abreast of new music: "I'm not *that* out of touch where I need someone a little younger than me to tell me, you know, what the kids are listening to. I feel like I still have a pretty good grasp on that" (Frenette 2013, 382). He later turns the age-related tension into a joke: "But maybe I don't [have a good grasp]. My Dad probably says the same thing . . . So I don't know!" As Karl confirms, workers feel pressure to remain abreast of new music and the proliferation of technologies, virtual spaces, etc. The constantly evolving realities of the industry favor younger workers and new practices.

Aging out overlaps with precarious work conditions as a factor leading to disenchantment. Some workers, like Oliver, are not ushered out, but report ending their music career because they feel old and broke—and they feel old and broke, at least in part, due to the precariousness that has been exacerbated in the digital age. A few years removed from working at an esteemed indie record company in New York, Oliver recalls his decision to leave the music industry: "I was starting to get old for it. . . . Being like 31–32, I'd never done anything but alternative music, you know? I've never made *that* much money! This city is getting really expensive." Oliver had hit a plateau and could not land a senior position. His middling job led to boredom and, paired with age, motivated him to make a change: "I was getting bored there with what I was doing. And I was just like, 'Oh my god, I'm 31.' And, you know, I love music so much [but] maybe it doesn't *have* to be what I do for my job." He started considering work in other fields: "I was like, 'anything would be more exciting and lucrative than this!'" Oliver went back to school and transitioned to the graphic design field. Significantly, he recalls that his age, paired with challenging work conditions, led to his disenchantment; shifting life priorities, notably the perceived need to make more money, no longer made music industry work viable.

Finally, although aging in a youth-oriented industry affects both men and women, it should be noted that the latter tended to frame the topic as more problematic. Several women questioned how they could continue to attend shows and remain active members of the industry when they would also become mothers. One female A&R employee admitted that she frequently lies about her age, fearing that she will come off as irrelevant. Abby more generally tells me: "There's this idea that as you get older you get farther and farther from this idea of cool. You might be trying to capture it or reclaim it." She also points out that the idea of attending a show in her 30s (she is currently 26) scares her, but she considers it easier for her male colleagues to "hold on" longer. After all, she concludes, older employees in the music industry tend to hold senior positions, and senior management at record companies is primarily male.

CONCLUSION

Record industry work involves a peculiar combination of precariousness and passion—or, as McRobbie (2004) put it, the pleasure-pain axis. Based on interview and participant observation data, this chapter considers how balancing both extremes can prove tenuous over time. While nonmonetary rewards count as payment, disenchantment (or the inability to deal with a loss or routinization of passion) is identified by music personnel as a key reason for quitting or getting let go, and occurs for three main reasons: precariousness; changing relationship to music; and aging out. I thereby provided a snapshot of record industry work conditions and showed how the digital era has exacerbated these pressures to exit the industry.

Attempts to generalize these findings should consider differences in demographic, geographical, subcultural, and company size. Since workers in the record industry (and creative industries in general) must consistently rely on informal networking practices and show temporal as well as geographical flexibility (Eikhof and Warhurst 2013), further research particularly needs to consider how the sources of disenchantment are experienced differently based on class, race, and gender. Considering the high cost of living and notably challenging arts-related employment conditions in New York City (de Peuter 2014), more research should consider the paradoxically increasingly important role of place for music industry work in the digital era (Wynn and Dominguez-Villegas, this volume).

Finally, further research should address the role of firms in cultivating the enchantment and reacting to the disenchantment of workers. How is the lure of work in glamorous fields utilized by employers in the music industry? How do employers help instill passion and commitment, and how do workers make sense of these practices? The micro-level processes related to worker subjectivity in the record industry described above should be further linked to theories of employability and "enterprising subjects" (Vallas 2012) in order to articulate more broadly the challenges of sustaining careers at large, in and outside of the music industry.

REFERENCES

Banks, Mark. "Autonomy Guaranteed? Cultural Work and the 'Art–commerce Relation'." *Journal for Cultural Research* 14, no. 3 (2010): 251–269.

Benzecry, Claudio E. *The Opera Fanatic: Ethnography of an Obsession*. Chicago: University of Chicago Press, 2011.

Berklee College of Music, Career Development Center. "Music Careers in Dollars and Cents, 2012 Edition." www.berklee.edu/pdf/pdf/studentlife/Music_Salary_Guide.pdf

Caves, Richard E. *Creative Industries: Contracts Between Art and Commerce*. Cambridge, MA: Harvard University Press, 2000.

de Laat, Kim. "'Write a Word, Get a Third': Managing Conflict and Rewards in Professional Songwriting Teams." *Work and Occupations* 42, no. 2 (2015): 225–256.

de Peuter, Greig. "Confronting Precarity in the Warhol Economy: Notes from New York City." *Journal of Cultural Economy* 7, no. 1 (2014): 31–47.

Eikhof, Doris Ruth, and Chris Warhurst. "The Promised Land? Why Social Inequalities Are Systemic in the Creative Industries." *Employee Relations* 35, no. 5 (2013): 495–508.

Faulkner, Robert R. "Coming of Age in Organizations a Comparative Study of Career Contingencies and Adult Socialization." *Work and Occupations* 1, no. 2 (1974): 131–173.

Faulkner, Robert R. *Music on Demand.* New Brunswick, NJ: Transaction Publishers, 1983.

Florida, Richard L. *The Rise of the Creative Class: And How It's Transforming Work, Leisure, Community and Everyday Life.* New York: Basic Books, 2002.

Frenette, Alexandre. "Making the Intern Economy: Role and Career Challenges of the Music Industry Intern." *Work and Occupations* 40, no. 4 (2013): 364–397.

Frenette, Alexandre. "Consuming Labor: Charisma and Identity in Music Industry Work." *Presentation at the Annual Meeting of the American Sociological Association*, San Francisco, CA, August 16–19, 2014.

Friedlander, Joshua P. "Nobody Stole the Pie." *Music Notes Blog.* March 3, 2010. http://www.riaa.com/blog.php?content_selector=riaa-news-blog&blog_selector=Nobody_Stole_Pie&news_month_filter=3&news_year_filter=2010&searchterms=friedlander&terminclude=&termexact

Gregg, Melissa. "Presence Bleed: Performing Professionalism Online." In *Theorizing Cultural Work: Labour, Continuity and Change in the Cultural and Creative Industries,* edited by Banks, Mark, Rosalind Gill, and Stephanie Taylor, 122–134. New York: Routledge, 2013.

Hesmondhalgh, David, and Sarah Baker. "'A Very Complicated Version of Freedom': Conditions and Experiences of Creative Labour in Three Cultural Industries." *Poetics* 38, no. 1 (2010): 4–20.

Hesmondhalgh, David, and Sarah Baker. *Creative Labour: Media Work in Three Cultural Industries.* New York: Routledge, 2011.

Hracs, Brian. J. "A Creative Industry in Transition: The Rise of Digitally Driven Independent Music Production." *Growth and Change* 43, no. 3 (2012): 442–461.

Hracs, Brian J., and Deborah Leslie. "Aesthetic Labour in Creative Industries: The Case of Independent Musicians in Toronto." *Area* 46, no. 1 (2014): 66–73.

Leyshon, Andrew. *Reformatted: Code, Networks and the Transformation of the Music Industry.* Oxford: Oxford University Press, 2014.

McRobbie, Angela. *Creative London-Creative Berlin: Notes on Making a Living in the New Cultural Economy.* Kunstverein München, 2004.

Menger, Pierre-Michel. "Artistic Labor Markets and Careers." *Annual Review of Sociology* 25 (1999): 541–574.

Oakley, Kate. "From Bohemia to Britart–Art Students over 50 Years." *Cultural Trends* 18, no. 4 (2009): 281–294.

Peterson, Richard A., and Narasimhan Anand. "How Chaotic Careers Create Orderly Fields." In *Career Creativity: Explorations in the Remaking of Work,* edited by Peiperl, Maury A., Michael B. Arthur, and Narasimhan Anand, 257–279. New York: Oxford University Press, 2002.

Ross, Andrew. *No Collar: The Humane Workplace and Its Hidden Costs.* New York: Basic, 2003.

Seman, Michael. "How a Music Scene Functioned as a Tool for Urban Redevelopment: A Case Study of Omaha's Slowdown Project." *City, Culture and Society* 1, no. 4 (2010): 207–215.

Smirke, Richard. "IFPI 2011 Report: Global Recorded Music Sales Fall 8.4%; Eminem, Lady Gaga Top Int'l Sellers," *Billboard Magazine*, March 30, 2011. http://www.billboard.com/biz/articles/news/global/1178545/ifpi-2011-report-global-recorded-music-sales-fall-84-eminem-lady

Tavory, Iddo, and Daniel Winchester. "Experiential Careers: The Routinization and De-routinization of Religious Life." *Theory and Society* 41, no. 4 (2012): 351–373.

Vallas, Steven. *Work: A Critique*. Malden, MA: Polity Press, 2012.

Watson, Allan. " 'Running a Studio's a Silly Business': Work and Employment in the Contemporary Recording Studio Sector." *Area* 45, no. 3 (2013): 330–336.

Wei, Junhow. "Dealing with Reality: Market Demands, Artistic Integrity, and Identity Work in Reality Television Production." *Poetics* 40, no. 5 (2012): 444–466.

Wright, David. "Mediating Production and Consumption: Cultural Capital and 'Cultural Workers'." *The British Journal of Sociology* 56, no. 1 (2005): 105–121.

Part IV

Playing

8 The Resilience of a Local Music Scene in Dalston, London

Tarek E. Virani

The digital revolution has had a profound impact on local music scenes. Local music scenes are understood here as the locally interconnected spaces and places of musical production, performance, and consumption where cultural meaning is created and shared through face-to-face interaction (Bennett and Peterson 2004; Cohen 1991; Finnegan 1989; Shank 1994). These scenes are often geographically located in neighborhood districts within cities (Currid 2007a; Florida and Jackson 2010) and usually have trans-local links (Hodkinson 2002; Kruse 2010, 2012). The term "trans-local" is used to identify the parallel links (usually cultural and/or subcultural) that exist between the local and the regional, the national and the global, in music production, consumption, and distribution (Kruse 1993). These links are enhanced by the use of information and communications technology (ICT) and the global media (see: Gosling 2004; Hodkinson 2004; Schilt 2004). Spatially, local music scenes are typically demarcated by a cluster of performance venues, record shops, recording studios, and record labels (Connell and Gibson 2003; Currid 2007a, 2007b; Gallan 2012; Florida and Jackson 2010; Johansson et al., this volume; Lena 2012; Watson 2008, this volume).

It has been argued that the allure of local music scenes has been diminished in the digital age (Connell and Gibson 2003; Florida et al. 2010; Frith 2007; Hodgkinson 2004; Kruse 2010, 2012; Sheffield 2010; Williams 2006). The argument states that through the increased use of ICT and the global media's influence, the local and/or the notion of locality, is being uncoupled from our traditional understanding of what local music scenes are. The literature outlines three developments that elucidate this: first, a shift away from physical subcultural participation (Williams 2006) which has given rise to virtual scenes (Bennett and Peterson 2004; Hodgkinson 2004). Second, a decline in a sense of local identity and local history coupled with the rise of trans-local identities (Connell and Gibson 2003; Hodkinson 2002; Kruse 2010, 2012; Sheffield 2010). Third, the demise of local sounds affiliated with local music scenes (Connell and Gibson 2003).

Another body of literature argues that when it comes to music, localities remain highly relevant. This is because they are: First, the places where musical and other artistic activities still cluster creating important social and economic benefits for those involved (Caves 2000; DiMaggio 1987; Florida and Jackson 2010; Florida et al. 2010; Gill and Pratt 2008; Seman 2010). Second, localities affirm the legitimacy and value of a cultural product such as music, giving the local scene a level of credibility (Currid 2007b; Molotch 2002). Third, live performance in local venues is still viewed as necessary (Frith 2007; Gray 2006) and as a marker of "authenticity"—depending on genre (Auslander 2008). Fourth, music scenes in general rely on local infrastructure, such as performance venues and recording studios, to support them (Currid 2007b; Gallan 2012; Gray 2006). Many of these businesses tend to cluster and co-locate at the local level (Florida and Jackson 2010).

This chapter argues that although the digital revolution has contributed significantly to a renegotiation of what locality means, the local, nevertheless, has not been diminished. This argument can be understood as a middle road between the two aforementioned sets of literature. Through the use of interview data and by focusing on one significant performance venue in the Dalston area of Hackney in London, this chapter argues that in exceptional circumstances, localities and the infrastructure that exists within them can become elevated, thereby causing a realignment of what the local means. In this particular case, Dalston's music scene has become elevated as well as established through the activities of one particular venue, leading to the development of a resilient music scene. I argue that this resilience is a result of a number of innovative activities that the venue has undertaken in order to establish itself as an important cultural node in London.

This chapter will briefly examine the literature on the digital revolution and how it has affected local music scenes. It will then explore the literature on why localities remain important to musical activity followed by a brief discussion of the site and methods used for this research. The subsequent sections will present the research findings and discuss the resiliency of the scene, followed by a conclusion.

THE DIGITAL REVOLUTION AND LOCAL MUSIC SCENES

Although a strong link exists between music and place (Connell and Gibson 2003; Hudson 2006), and between music and the local (Finnegan 1989; Gallan 2012), the digital revolution has altered the way this link is perceived and subsequently maintained. Williams (2006) found that, within a straightedge hardcore music scene, an internet forum was not only used as a supplement to face-to-face participation but as a primary or sole source of subcultural participation. Furthermore, Williams (2006) identified a subcultural divide within the scene between physical scene participants and members that only participated online. Both claimed to be authentic scene participants except that some members chose not to attend shows, which caused friction and disagreements within the scene. This suggests that traditional local subcultural participation, such as attending shows and physically participating in the scene as it is manifest in localities, must now contend and negotiate with newer types of subcultural participation that are entirely mediated digitally.

Bennett and Peterson (2004) use the term "virtual scene" to describe scenes that only or partially occur online—such as the one examined by Williams (2006). Virtual scenes are different to, but not dislocated from, local scenes in that they rely on detached communication processes that exist online, as opposed to face-to-face interaction prevalent at the local level. This detachment means that the scene is primarily built on virtual displays of knowledge. For instance, Atton (2010) found that in online fanzines it is the art of writing that is used as a marker of subcultural capital, thus displays of knowledge are often articulated in this manner. Hodgkinson (2004), in his study of a post-rock online fanzine, found that levels of knowledge about the scene were expertly articulated by virtual scene participants as they negotiated the aesthetic dimensions of that scene. These displays take place online as virtual scene participants try to express their levels of competence, as well as their levels of subcultural capital, through their overall knowledge about their respective genre and/or scene. This is done in order to build networks and allegiances within the scene (Baym 2007; Bennett and Peterson 2004).

The physical constraints of participating in a local music scene are thus removed, which allows for forms of musical communication and interaction unhindered by age, sexual orientation, ethnicity, gender, geography, money, or the need for face-to-face social interaction.

This is further articulated by Connell and Gibson (2003) who have stated that the Internet has been able to lessen the importance of the local since it enables a sense of offline "imagined community" that is crucial to music scenes but not tied to geography. As an extension of this, Kruse (2010) discusses local indie rock scenes and suggests that as Internet options for the discussion and sharing of indie music increase, the local spaces devoted to interaction around music are changing and sometimes disappearing. An article in *The Guardian* acknowledges the loss of local places such as performance venues and the rise of online blogs and forums which, they argue, have resulted in a new reality for musicians—a reality that does not necessarily involve needing to be a part of any local scene (Sheffield 2010). Artists can now find success before ever playing a show, bypassing the "local" entirely (Ibid). As participation based on ICT increases, physical participation becomes optional—meaning that individuals can potentially be lured away from local music scenes.

This being said, virtual scenes are usually connected to a respective local or trans-local one. In her study of the Champaign-Urbana indie music scene in Illinois, Kruse (2010) suggests that traditionally (meaning pre-Internet) this particular local scene was not autonomous but part of a larger network of local scenes. Today, this process has been accelerated due to the digital revolution which has made looking at local scenes in total isolation redundant (Ibid). This has further strengthened the argument that local scenes may be giving way to trans-local tendencies which in turn may have adverse effects on the feeling of a sense of identity that comes from participating in local music scenes. Connell and Gibson (2003) confirm this trans-local perspective where they claim that the Internet has "de-linked" the notion of "scene" from locality. Their claim goes further by stating that the notion of local sounds are in effect being cancelled out by the influencing power and speed of technological change and globalization in the music industries.

THE IMPORTANCE OF LOCALITIES

Florida and Jackson (2010) view music scenes as geographically bordered markets rooted in location. This is because most artistic activities tend to create colonies marked by clusters of people engaged in the production and consumption of cultural products such as music (Caves 2000). Clustering, in the creative and cultural industries, happens because cultural goods are intangible and demand for them is difficult to determine or predict (Ibid). Thus, cultural workers, like those involved in music, benefit substantially by being co-located (Gill and Pratt 2008). Florida et al. (2010) found that while musicians have every reason to disperse and not be consolidated in clusters they do not, instead they tend to continuously cluster and aggregate. Co-location and/or clustering of musicians, and other music-related scene participants, not only provides a sense of security in a precarious line of work, but also allows for engagement with other aspects of music such as the generation of taste and genre (DiMaggio 1987), which are the building blocks of music scenes (Kruse 1993).

Currid (2007b) suggests that scenes arise as subcultures focusing on particular niches—and these scenes are very much rooted in the localities that they inhabit. She also offers that localities, in turn, affirm the legitimacy and value of a cultural good, giving the local scene a level of credibility. Molotch (2002) calls this "place in product," where the value of producing something in a particular location is fundamental to its successful consumption.

Another element that demonstrates the importance of the local is live performance (Johansson et al., this volume). Performing live in venues, local or otherwise, is still viewed as a marker of authenticity (Auslander 2008; Frith 2007). This, of course, depends on the type of music being discussed; however, live performance is usually tied to discussions of authenticity in many genres of popular music ranging from hip-hop to indie rock to free jazz (Anderton et al. 2013; Frith 2007). Live performance is crucial because it is here that audiences can: judge performances (Frith 2007), see the amount of work that goes into a performance (Moore 2002), and watch an artist develop (Auslander 2008). "Liveness" legitimizes musicians and performers in many genres of music, thus proximity to audiences, as well as gatekeepers and taste-makers, is crucial. Location itself is an important component of this infrastructure (Florida and Jackson 2010).

Music scenes are also marked by the industries and infrastructure that surround them. Currid (2007b) states that venues, clubs, recording studios, and performance spaces act as physical conduits for economic and social relationships. Local music scenes depend on this local infrastructure in order to enact themselves. The history of music scenes is littered with the names of infamous venues and record shops that catalyze local scenes. Venues such as The Haçienda in Manchester, CBGB in New York City, and Crocodile Café in Seattle were central to their respective local music scenes. This being said, the ways in which music venues remain successful in music scenes—especially in the wake of the digital revolution—have yet to be the subject of sustained academic inquiry (Gallan 2012).

SITE AND METHODS

The research for this chapter focuses on the experimental music scene in Dalston. The scene is physically active in many parts of London, but has a strong focus in the Dalston area. It is particularly active at two performance venues located close to each other. The focus of this chapter is on one of these venues—the venue will remain unnamed for anonymity purposes. It opened in 2008 and since then has become an institution for experimental music in London. It hosts concerts, lectures, workshops, roundtables, festivals, and visual art performances. It curates a number of large projects in collaboration with important cultural institutions in London and is a pillar of the experimental music scene within the cultural fabric of London.

The data used in this chapter came from fieldwork that was conducted between June 2011 and January 2012 in the Dalston area. A total of 32 in-depth interviews were conducted with scene participants that were connected to the venue in some way and lasted from one to two hours in duration. Interviews were conducted with a range of scene participants including venue owners, promoters, musicians, music journalists, audience members, and venue staff. All interviews were open-ended in nature with a few probing questions and were recorded and then transcribed. The transcripts were then analyzed using coding which entailed looking for relevant themes. The codes were then assigned to the themes.

The main reason behind choosing this particular scene as a field site is my interest in experimental music, especially because I also perform and create music. My knowledge of experimental artists and music aided my acceptance as a researcher; in essence my knowledge of the music and its influences helped me to gain access. It would have been very difficult for me to converse with people in the scene if I did not have a working knowledge of free improvisation and other types of experimental music.

THE CONCERT CALENDAR

The venue is renowned for its eclectic concert schedule and books local, out-of-town, and international acts from the world of experimental music. However, experimental music is an umbrella term that encompasses a number of genres and sub-genres (Bailey 1992). At the core of the venue's programming are musicians who view themselves as free improvisers. Free improvisation is a sub-genre of experimental music where musicians improvise with each other in a live setting (Bailey 1992; Watson 2004).

> I don't think [the owners] are dogmatic in the sense that they believe that there's one sort of God-endorsed way to look at all this. I mean free improvisation is obviously a core but they also book avant-rock and folk
>
> (Interview with music journalist, 2012).

Many of the local musicians that are part of this scene are free improvisers. This allows them to be relatively flexible when it comes to who they perform with. The music is expressionistic, which means that composition and preparation are not usually necessary (see Bailey 1992 and Watson 2004 for more on free improvisation). This means that when curating the concerts, it allows local musicians to improvise/perform with international and out-of-town musicians or acts.

For instance, in May 2014, Thurston Moore (of famed rock bands Sonic Youth and Chelsea Light Moving) had a two-day residency at the venue where he improvised with two local musicians who are well-known in the free improvisation scene. "Residencies" are, usually, when an international or out-of-town act performs there for a number of consecutive evenings. The local musicians act as support acts for many international and out-of-town performers, which adds to the originality of the concert programming. Most importantly, however, it maintains a local element in the curation of these concerts, therefore, elevating local musicians as they play with renowned international musicians within the global experimental music scene. At the same time, the venue creates trans-local networks that are reciprocal and equally important.

> I think Otomo Yoshihide is okay, [the owners] really like what he does and sometimes they contact musicians directly to invite them to come and play. People like Mika Mika, they really like the guy and they invited him. For some reason he's quite popular in France. He was invited to play in France, and [the owners] got to know about it and then they asked him to come and play, with, I think it was [respected local artist] over here
>
> (Interview with venue staff member, 2012).

The quote above was another example of an internationally renowned artist who was brought over from abroad, in this case Japan, to play with a local musician who is equally renowned but happens to be part of the local free improvisation scene in Dalston. These types of musical collaborations allow for the building of networks within the global, as well as the local, experimental music scene. As international acts are booked to play at the venue, musicians from the local scene get to play overseas or cross-nationally. This reciprocity allows for the extension of the local scene but also benefits it as more and more musicians build these types of networks. As a result of this type of reciprocal curation, the venue creates and maintains important local and trans-local links that enable the owners to book the acts that they would like to see perform there.

In order to manage the programming of the concerts, the owners created a not-for-profit organization housed within the venue. This looks after the venue's calendar, deals with local and international promoters, and manages other performance projects that take place in collaboration with other venues. The venue's calendar boasts an event (usually a concert) on most evenings of the week. Tickets can be bought through the venue's website or collected at the door in some cases—rather than going through a mainstream ticket agency. The majority of performances are either collaborations between local acts and international or out-of-town ones, or purely local acts.

The calibre of the programming has, rather remarkably, created a local scene that revolves around local and trans-local (especially global) connections. These connections are part of the scene's local identity thanks to the venue's programming and the continued support of local acts. It also actively engages with other venues in the borough and beyond, strengthening its position as a cultural institution in London.

VENUE-BASED RECORD LABEL AND ARCHIVING PROJECT

Due to the originality and uniqueness of the concert programming, many of the concerts that take place are inimitable, meaning there is a very good chance they will not happen again. The owners, and others within the scene, were aware of this and wanted to have a record of the shows that took place at the venue. Through this they slowly built an archive of unique material, including video and sound experiments, and then decided that it would be beneficial to share it. This thought process led to the archiving project slowly being transformed into a record label that was launched in 2012. The label now boasts a large catalog where releases, in multiple formats including vinyl, are available through the website or in the venue only. This is a unique model of working because it quite figuratively brings the local experimental music scene into the venue, giving it a home and developing a genre, a way of working, and an aesthetic based around the venue.

Significantly, many of the recordings that are now part of the catalogue feature collaborations between local and international acts. There are multiple instances of the same local musicians reappearing on different recordings because they were booked repeatedly. This goes a long way in supporting the local acts that contribute to the recordings, but also builds reciprocity with the local scene to the point where it ends up being a virtuous circle.

As an extension of the archiving project, the venue strives to expand the potential audience for what they are producing, as well as their global networks in the field of archiving experimental music. One very important example is through a connection with an American-based archive where the venue acts as a curator and contributor. This particular collaboration also acts as a platform for the venue itself. The venue's contribution includes a diverse array of artists that have all been recorded live.

As another extension of the label, the venue does a regular broadcast on one of London's premier art radio stations. It usually features a mix of guests, concert recordings, interviews, and the occasional live broadcast transmitted directly from the venue. The collaboration with the radio station strengthens the local scene because it unites the people that are actively interested in experimental music in London. It does this while, at the same time, elevating the status of the venue by advertising upcoming performances.

PUBLIC FUNDING AND NETWORK BUILDING

The owners are incisive when it comes to examining the arts funding landscape in London. The United Kingdom has a sophisticated and robust arts funding infrastructure. It includes many organizations and many types of funding, ranging from arts performance to community revitalization projects to regeneration. This means that small arts-based businesses, such as performance venues, can potentially plug themselves into a number of funding networks. Recently, the venue was awarded a large grant in recognition of its contribution to experimental music in London as well as its contribution to the local area. The owners, quite astutely, directed this funding into an arts program designed to assist emerging musical artists in the development of ideas, networks, collaborations, and platforms to present new works. Additionally, this connects the venue to higher education institutions that focus on experimental music in London.

The venue has also forged a partnership with an organization that is funded by Arts Council England. The organization focuses on new music where it aims to raise the profile of this particular cultural sector. It provides composer and artist support and development, partnerships with a range of organizations, live events and audience development, touring advice and information, network building, and education. By partnering with this organization, the venue has been able to embark on a number of projects, curating concerts and installations with more international acts and at a range of much larger venues.

> [The organisation] does a wide range of stuff, like big gigs. One thing that [the venue] can't do is put on big gigs. For example Chris Watson's 40 channel installation of wildlife sound, which happened at Kew Gardens. That would equally be at home in the aesthetic of [the venue]
> (Interview with musician and sound artist, 2012).

The venue owners very cleverly use this type of partnership to not only elevate their status locally, but to increase their global network.

> In 2011 [the organisation in partnership with the venue] asked for event proposals to be submitted to feature acts from outside of the UK who had not previously played here. Four acts won awards of £2,000 each, out of a possible 200 entries from across the globe. This resulted in four nights of music granted to four events organisers
> (Interview with music journalist, 2012).

This is a testament to the international profile of experimental music that has been steadily growing, but also to how the owners of this venue are positioning themselves locally and internationally.

> But the funny thing is people, like Japanese pop artists, they actually contact us. People outside the country actually contact us to play shows here. I mean they talk to their friends, you know I played in London or whatever and a lot of people who haven't been here know about this place
> (Interview with member of venue staff, 2012).

Using partnerships with arts funding organizations and through the acquiring of public funds, the venue owners are able to elevate the status of this venue to one that is pivotal to experimental music in London. Thus, the venue has expanded the local scene's boundaries and plugged it into the arts funding network within the UK.

A RESILIENT MUSIC SCENE IN DALSTON

The owners of this venue were always interested in making it more than just a performance venue. The venue is now a home for a community of local musicians—it is where they meet, collaborate, talk, listen, and perform. It is also a place where fans of experimental music, and others that are part of the scene, congregate and contribute in multiple ways. In reality, the venue has elevated itself to a cultural hub entrenched in the cultural fabric of the experimental music scene in Dalston. At the same time, this venue has embedded the scene into the cultural landscape of London, making it resilient to changes that might negatively affect it.

This local music scene can be characterized as resilient due to three areas of activity: first, a sophisticated network of local and trans-local (including global) acts that all perform at the venue. This elevates the status of the venue, the scene, and the area of Dalston. Through shared and reciprocal networks it attracts the world of experimental music to Dalston, while also presenting this local scene to the world. Second, it provides an erudite and innovative way of delivering the music to its audience locally and beyond through the use of the record label and the archiving project. Essentially, this has afforded the scene its own market. Due to the level and vibrancy of the musical collaborations that take place at the venue, and their uniqueness, they are able to capture these live performances and release them to the public in a number of formats. They are also able to market these recordings in a unique way, since most of these concerts are one-off performances unlikely to take place again. This allows the label to occupy a unique place in a market, mainly created and sustained by the scene. It also, importantly, entrenches local musicians within the larger marketing apparatus which affords them ample opportunities for exposure. Finally, the venue is plugged into funding networks that pay for performances and also help developing musicians. This funding enables collaborations with larger cultural institutions, resulting in a highly sophisticated way of engaging their local audience, as well as potentially expanding their global audience. Most importantly, they initiate ways of working with these larger, established cultural institutions that enable network sharing and more opportunities for experimental musicians—locally and globally. All of this ensures the sustainability and success of the local music scene, and is an example of how local music scenes can emerge as highly sophisticated and influential cultural bodies and/or nodes. Thus, the local experimental music scene in Dalston is established within this backdrop of cultural institutions, allowing them to secure a very important place within both the arts community and the arts funding landscape in London.

CONCLUSION

This chapter argues that although the digital revolution has contributed significantly to a renegotiation of what locality means, the local, nevertheless, has not been diminished. The allure of local music scenes in the wake of the digital revolution is shaped by two forces. On one hand, there is a renegotiation of what locality means. This is exemplified by a shift away from physical, subcultural participation and the rise of virtual scenes, the decline in a sense of local identity, and the demise of local sounds affiliated with local music scenes. While on the other hand, there is the reality that localities remain crucial to musical activity and music scenes. This is exemplified by the appeal of co-location/clustering for local musical activity, the credibility of being associated with the local, the importance of live performance, and the existence of local infrastructure.

Through studying this particular venue in Dalston, it is clear that there exists a middle ground between these two points of view. Localities—and the infrastructure that exists within them—can be elevated through a renegotiation of what the local means. In this case, the local benefits from trans-local networks. These trans-local connections can sustain the scene. Thus, the local benefits in three ways: First, the venue sustains local performers through reciprocal concert curation and programming. This provides them with a platform to create trans-local and local networks within and beyond the scene. Second, the venue ensures that local musicians are promoted through the record label as well as through any subsequent collaboration with organizations such as radio stations and archiving projects. Finally, the venue uses public funding to create larger trans-local networks through the curation of larger projects and performances, all the while helping local emerging artists in a number of important ways.

In this particular case the local has become reinvigorated as shared local and trans-local networks extend outward nationally and globally and return to coalesce at the local level in Dalston. This provides the scene with the potential for sustaining itself since the venue, and the scene, is now established within the cultural fabric of Dalston and more importantly, London. Essentially, this venue has created and used its local and trans-local networks to re-establish the identity of the local scene, and in doing so, has made it resilient, thereby ensuring the local scene continues to have the place and space to coalesce.

REFERENCES

Anderton, Chris, Andrew Dubber, and Martin James. *Understanding the Music Industries*. London, UK: Sage, 2013.

Atton, Chris. "Popular Music Fanzines: Genre, Aesthetics, and the 'Democratic Conversation'." *Popular Music and Society* 33, no. 4 (2010): 517–531.

Auslander, Philip. *Liveness: Performance in a Mediatized Culture*. London and New York: Routledge, 2008.

Bailey, Derek. *Improvisation: Its Nature and Practice in Music*. Boston, MA: Da Capo Press, 1992.

Baym, Nancy K. "The New Shape of Online Community: The Example of Swedish Independent Music Fandom." *First Monday* 12, no. 8 (2007).

Bennett, Andy, and Richard A. Peterson. *Music Scenes: Local, Translocal and Virtual*. Nashville, TN: Vanderbilt University Press, 2004.

Caves, Richard E. *Creative Industries: Contracts Between Art and Commerce No. 20*. Cambridge, MA: Harvard University Press, 2000.

Cohen, Sara. *Rock Culture in Liverpool: Popular Music in the Making*. Oxford: Oxford University Press on Demand, 1991.

Connell, John, and Chris Gibson. *Sound Tracks: Popular Music Identity and Place.* London and New York: Routledge, 2003.

Currid, Elizabeth. "How Art and Culture Happen in New York: Implications for Urban Economic Development." *Journal of the American Planning Association* 73, no. 4 (2007a): 454–467.

Currid, Elizabeth. *The Warhol Economy: How Fashion, Art, and Music Drive New York City*. Princeton, NJ: Princeton University Press, 2007b.

DiMaggio, Paul. "Classification in Art." *American Sociological Review* 52 (1987): 440–455.

Finnegan, Ruth. *The Hidden Musicians: Music-Making in an English Town*. Middleton, CT: Wesleyan University Press, 1989.

Florida, Richard, and Scott Jackson. "Sonic City: The Evolving Economic Geography of the Music Industry." *Journal of Planning Education and Research* 29, no. 3 (2010): 310–321.

Florida, Richard, Charlotta Mellander, and Kevin Stolarick. "Music Scenes to Music Clusters: The Economic Geography of Music in the US, 1970–2000." *Environment and planning A* 42, no. 4 (2010): 785–804.

Frith, Simon. "Live Music Matters." *Scottish Music Review* 1, no. 1 (2007): 1–17.

Gallan, Ben. "Gatekeeping Night Spaces: The Role of Booking Agents in Creating 'Local' Live Music Venues and Scenes." *Australian Geographer* 43, no. 1 (2012): 35–50.

Gill, Rosalind, and Andy Pratt. "In the Social Factory? Immaterial Labour, Precariousness and Cultural Work." *Theory, Culture and Society* 25, no. 7–8 (2008): 1–30.

Gosling, Tim. "'Not for Sale': The Underground Network of Anarcho–Punk." In *Music Scenes: Local, Translocal, and Virtual*, edited by Bennett, Andy, and Richard A. Peterson, 168–185. Nashville, TN: Vanderbilt University Press, 2004.

Gray, Oliver. *Access One Step: The Official History of the Joiners Arms*. Winchester: Sarsen Press, 2006.

Hodgkinson, James A. "The Fanzine Discourse over Post Rock." In *Music Scenes: Local, Translocal, and Virtual*, edited by Bennett, Andy, and Richard A. Peterson, 221–237. Nashville, TN: Vanderbilt University Press, 2004.

Hodkinson, Paul. *Goth. Identity, Style and Subculture.* Oxford, UK: Berg Publishers, 2002.

Hodkinson, Paul. "Translocal Connections in the Goth Scene." In *Music scenes: Local, Translocal, and Virtual*, edited by Bennett, Andy, and Richard A. Peterson, 131–148. Nashville, TN: Vanderbilt University Press, 2004.

Hudson, Ray. "Regions and Place: Music, Identity and Place." *Progress in Human Geography* 30, no. 5 (2006): 626–634.

Kruse, Holly. "Subcultural Identity in Alternative Music Culture." *Popular Music* 12, no. 1 (1993): 33–41.

Kruse, Holly. "Local Identity and Independent Music Scenes, Online and Off." *Popular Music and Society* 33, no. 5 (2010): 625–639.

Kruse, Holly. "Local Independent Music Scenes and the Implications of the Internet." In *Sound, Society and the Geography of Popular Music*, edited by Bell, Thomas L., and Ola Johansson, 11–31. Farnham, Surrey, UK: Ashgate Publishing, Ltd., 2012.

Lena, Jennifer C. *Banding Together: How Communities Create Genres in Popular Music*. Princeton, NJ: Princeton University Press, 2012.

Molotch, Harvey. "Place in Product." *International Journal of Urban and Regional Research* 26, no. 4 (2002): 665–688.

Moore, Allan. "Authenticity as Authentication." *Popular Music* 21, no. 2 (2002): 209–223

Schilt, Kristin. "'Riot Grrrl is . . .': Contestation over Meaning in a Music Scene." In *Music Scenes: Local, Translocal, and Virtual*, edited by Bennett, Andy, and Richard A. Peterson, 115–130. Nashville, TN: Vanderbilt University Press, 2004.

Seman, Michael. "How a Music Scene Functioned as a Tool For Urban Redevelopment: A Case Study of Omaha's Slowdown Project." *City, Culture and Society* 1, no. 4 (2010): 207–215.

Shank, Barry. *Dissonant identities: The Rock'n'Roll Scene in Austin, Texas*. Middleton, CT: Wesleyan University Press, 1994.

Sheffield, Hazel. "Has the Internet Killed Local Music Scenes?" *Guardian. co. uk* 10 (2010).

Watson, Allan. "Global Music City: Knowledge and Geographical Proximity in London's Recorded Music Industry." *Area* 40, no. 1 (2008): 12–23.

Watson, Ben. Derek Bailey and the Story of Free Improvisation. London: Verso, 2004.

Williams, J. Patrick. "Authentic Identities Straightedge Subculture, Music, and the Internet." *Journal of Contemporary Ethnography* 35, no. 2 (2006): 173–200.

9 Landscapes of Performance and Technological Change

Music Venues in Pittsburgh, Pennsylvania and Nashville, Tennessee

Ola Johansson, Margaret M. Gripshover and Thomas L. Bell

Local music scenes consist of a multitude of different elements—artists, record labels, studios, music media, and ancillary music industry infrastructure (Johansson and Bell 2009; Virani, this volume). An important aspect of local scenes is live music and the venues where performances take place. As venues have thus far received only modest attention in scholarly research, this chapter will investigate the landscape of performance venues and how the Internet and social media have impacted these places of performance. While many segments of the music industry are less profitable in an era of rapidly changing technology, live music entertainment remains robust and an important source of income for artists (Wynn and Dominguez-Villegas, this volume; Virani, this volume). As live performances involve face-to-face contact between the artists and the audience, they are, paradoxically, both more immune to, and enhanced by, technological changes taking place elsewhere in the music industry.

The scant academic literature on venues contextualizes their role in cultural, economic, and urban development. However, the implications of the digital age on live music, and specifically the operation of venues, has so far only been addressed in music industry publications (e.g., *Billboard* magazine). The drawback of this literature is that the spatial elements of the live music industry are often given short shrift. We, therefore, combined an examination of the industry literature with that of venues in two cities—Pittsburgh, Pennsylvania, and Nashville, Tennessee—to explore the spatial configuration of live musical landscapes and how they have been affected by the Internet and social media. Both cities have similarly sized music scenes and number of venues, and yet their urban morphologies differ. Pittsburgh is a post-industrial city with a built environment that still reflects its industrial history. The city is also filled with urban neighborhoods with their own unique cultural characteristics and small business districts. Nashville, on the other hand, manifests rapid Sunbelt sprawl. Beyond the immediate downtown and surrounding mixed land-use district, the city is characterized by low density single-family housing. The live music scenes may, therefore, be organized differently in each city and may be affected by the digital age in different ways.

EXISTING RESEARCH ON VENUES

The limited academic literature on music venues—which has virtually nothing to say on the impact of the Internet—suggests three perspectives on their importance. From a cultural perspective, they are important elements of local music scenes (Virani, this volume). Economically, they are integral parts of an increasingly important live music industry and potential catalysts for local and regional economic development (Virani, this volume). Finally, venues shape, and are shaped by, other urban land uses.

According to Grenier and Lussier (2011), venues are important for local scenes, as this is where audience and performers meet; they can be crucial as sites where musical synergy may result in a particular "sound"; and they are also "training grounds" for artists where scene and sound coalesce. Some venues are more "scene forming" than others. Scene formers include the famous CBGBs in punk-era New York City (Kozak 1988), the Cavern Club in Beatles-era Liverpool (Leonard and Strachan 2010), as well as more obscure venues in less heralded places, such as town pubs in Australia (Gallan and Gibson 2013). In fact, Australian scholars, more so than others, have explored the importance of venues. Oldham (2013), for example, points out how particular styles of music develop hand-in-hand with the type of venue that was popular at the time, e.g., Australian pub rock of the 1970s where the rowdy and irreverent music performed was fueled by excessive alcohol consumption and a predominantly male, working class audience. Thus, the social and musical space of venues has a profound impact on shaping music.

From a broader perspective, a prominent venue can also be symbolic of the musical identity of a city, such as the iconic Apollo in Glasgow, Scotland, which was reputed to have the "best" audience in the world (Forbes 2012). The closure of Glasgow's Apollo also symbolized a post-industrial reshaping of the urban landscape. A new, clean performance space in Glasgow has replaced the old, grungy Apollo as the city's main music venue. In fact, *Music Week* (2005, 2007a) suggests that an older and wealthier generation of concertgoers is seeking out the more comfortable live experiences in newer venues.

There has been a sea change in the manner in which people receive, play, and share music in this digital age. Record sales have declined in this era of file sharing, downloading, and music streaming (Connolly and Krueger 2005; Hracs, this volume; Leyshon et al., this volume). But, live music has become increasingly important for the music industry (Wynn and Dominguez-Villegas, this volume; Jansson and Nilsson, this volume): the revenue from live performances in the United States more than doubled from 1997–2005, while record sales declined during the same period and have continued to do so since (Black et al. 2007).

Compared to recorded music, live music is centered on the experience of attending a unique event. In economic terminology, it is a "non-substitutable" good for which audiences are willing to pay an increasingly high price (Frith

2007). Live music is, therefore, one of the few growth segments of the music industry in the Internet era. Not surprisingly, then, the live music industry (e.g., venue management, promotion, and ticketing) has consolidated into a handful of large transnational corporations, such as Live Nation and AEG. Larger venues in cities like Nashville and Pittsburgh often exist within this globalized music business, while smaller venues are more likely to be owned locally and conduct business with local and regional promoters, booking agents, and artist managers. The typical live club often faces financial struggles (Alexander 2008), but recent higher revenues have reportedly also resulted in more investment in facilities (*Music Week* 2004).

The exact location and physical character of music venues matter. The existence of venues may enhance the symbolic value of the area where they are located. Playing live is part of the perceived authenticity of rock music. Venues with a less-than-polished appearance suggest strong ties to a place and its history, roots in the local music community, and less corporate and commercial emphases. Smaller to mid-sized rock clubs with these characteristics tend to be especially important within a local scene (Forbes 2012). The dynamics of urban socio-economic processes may, however, prove problematic. Cutting-edge venues located in urban spaces that are perceived as creative and cool are often a precursor to gentrification in that neighborhood. As gentrification progresses real estate prices increase and, without public subsidy, the financial viability of such venues may be in jeopardy–ironically, a victim of their own success (Homan 2008).

METHOD AND DATA

To explore the role of the Internet and social media on live music, we examine venue performance spaces used by touring musicians in both Nashville and Pittsburgh. Despite its slightly smaller size (1.7 million vs. Pittsburgh's 2.3 million people), Nashville's metropolitan area is a tour destination on par with Pittsburgh (Johansson and Bell 2014) and probably has more live music because of the abundance of local musicians who play in venues that cater primarily to tourists who visit "Music City USA" (Johansson 2010).

The questions we seek to answer are the following: How is the live music scene organized spatially in each city? And, have web-based technologies impacted the operation of venues? To answer these questions, we created a sample of venues by analyzing tour schedules for artists who played in both Nashville and Pittsburgh. The artists were those on the top 20 playlists of college radio stations, as published in the *College Music Journal*. Using data that we previously collected for a 2004–06 study period, 161 artists had tour dates in both cities as recorded in an industry source called *Celebrity Access* (Johansson and Bell 2014). The artists played in 50 different venues in Pittsburgh and Nashville—25 in each city. The same types of data were gathered from January 2013 to January 2014 to yield a more current set of performances. Venues were again recorded from *Celebrity Access*—13 additional venues were identified (five in Pittsburgh and eight in Nashville). The venues were then categorized, mapped, and their spatial patterns analyzed. We determined which venues were operational in 2014 and which had subsequently closed their doors since the time of our earlier inquiry that used 2004–06 data.

We then developed a set of questions for local venue owners/managers and promoters to address in order to explore how their venues were operated. The questionnaires primarily addressed whether or not the Internet and social media had changed the venue's operation and what the spatial implications of such changes were. Eight individuals agreed to participate and had the option of answering our brief questionnaire either by telephone or email. To contextualize the relatively limited survey data, we also accessed publications that are primarily targeted to the music industry using the database *International Index to Music Periodicals*. The keyword combination "venue" and "Internet" yielded more than 1,000 hits, of which approximately 30 articles were deemed relevant to address our research questions.

DIFFERENCES AND SIMILARITIES IN PITTSBURGH AND NASHVILLE VENUE COMPOSITION

In Pittsburgh, there were 30 different venues frequented by the touring acts and in Nashville there were 33. We have not systematically visited the interior spaces of all the venues, although we have attended performances in many of them, have explored the immediate location surrounding most venues, and collected online information about them.

The geographic location of venues from downtown, to urban neighborhoods, to the suburbs, is also similar in the two cities, although downtown Nashville is more attractive as a music venue location. Downtown Pittsburgh has recently experienced growth, but largely in the form of restaurants and non music-based entertainment (e.g., theatrical performances) rather than music venues.

We categorized the music venues in each of the metropolitan areas and identified a size-based hierarchy. The largest performance spaces were huge outdoor amphitheaters and indoor arenas that host major artists (Table 9.1). Next in size were iconic venues that were often formerly vaudeville houses and movie palaces. Some of these medium-sized iconic venues were even former churches such as Ryman Auditorium in Nashville and Mr. Small's in Pittsburgh. At the lowest level of the venue hierarchy are the small clubs that tend to cluster near the downtown, universities, gritty former wholesale/industrial/commercial districts, or trendy gentrifying neighborhoods. The musical scenes in both metropolitan areas are dominated numerically by

Table 9.1 Venues in Pittsburgh and Nashville

Category	Pittsburgh	Nashville
Clubs	7	10
Arenas	4	2
Auditoriums	2	4
Seated Theatres	2	3
Amphitheatres	2	1
Multipurpose Art Spaces	3	0
Outdoor Festivals	1	2
Cafés and Coffee Houses	1	1
Closed/Demolished (of any category)	5	9
Other	3	1
Venue Location*		
Urban Neighborhood	19	18
Downtown/CBD	5	9
Suburban/Exurban	4	4
Suburban Downtowns	2	2

* Including closed/demolished venues

such small clubs. Certain genres of music are also sporadically performed in non-traditional spaces. Some "arty" musicians, for example, play to small audiences in art galleries and studios.

Generally, the mix of venues in the two cities mirrors each other. The small club is the most numerous category in both cities, although more dominant within the Nashville scene. Small arts venues that also occasionally double as music performance spaces have found a home in Pittsburgh, but less so in Nashville. Venues that have been discontinued since they appeared in the earlier 2004–06 database are more numerous in Nashville. This shakeout is related to the more rapid pace of urban change in Nashville. A fast-growing city puts redevelopment pressure on older buildings and the venues that are housed therein. Of the 14 closed/demolished venues, six are categorized as clubs, but venue "death" is distributed among most of our venue categories.

MUSIC VENUE LANDSCAPES IN NASHVILLE

Music venues in Nashville cluster in the central part of the city, perhaps more so than those in Pittsburgh (Figure 9.1). Most of the venues are

Figure 9.1 Venues in Nashville (adapted by the authors from OpenStreetMap [© OpenStreetMap contributors, http://www.openstreetmap.org/copyright])

contained within two loops of the interstate highway system, one defining the downtown area and a mixed land use area immediately south of the CBD, and the other covering the predominantly commercial area of Nashville's West End.

Downtown Nashville is a major part of the city's musical landscape. There are several large venues located there including the iconic Ryman Auditorium, original home of the Grand Ole Opry. Today the Ryman is equipped with modern amenities as a premier music venue for all musical genres. Due to the redevelopment pressures associated with a rapidly growing city, there are currently no rock clubs in the immediate downtown area. Just outside that area, there are clubs—most notably the Mercy Lounge and the Cannery Ballroom in the Gulch, an aging warehouse complex—but they are slowing meeting similar fates. There are also venues west of downtown located in commercial buildings that were previously retail stores or wholesale establishments. The location of Vanderbilt University and Music Row, where the music industry is situated, also makes this area of Nashville a popular venue place.

Three relatively new music venues are located in the newly gentrifying neighborhood of East Nashville. One of these, the Limelight, is located is an "urban development area" near the city's professional football stadium. East Nashville is what Lloyd (2011) calls a form of "hip urbanism" that consists of youthful, creative class individuals and new urbanist planning that emphasizes higher densities. One may expect a growth of venues in this part of the city, but currently there is no strong rock music venue presence in either East Nashville or the largely African American Northside. Nashville's venue locations have, then, a strong southwestward directional character.

MUSIC VENUE LANDSCAPES IN PITTSBURGH

A significant number of Pittsburgh's venues are located in older buildings formerly used for non-entertainment purposes. This is not surprising as Pittsburgh has seen significant economic and population decline for many decades. Such buildings tend to be located in relatively densely settled urban neighborhoods throughout Pittsburgh, although not necessarily in the CBD or near a university as is more the case in Nashville (Figure 9.2). These older Pittsburgh neighborhoods are typically of mixed land use including both commercial spaces in transition and industrial buildings in proximity to working-class neighborhoods. Not only is the moderate rent attractive, but smaller club venues thrive in an economically marginalized urban environment because they signal that an area is "hip." Nineteen out of 30 venues in the Pittsburgh area are located in areas we classified as "urban neighborhood." More specifically, concentrations of venues are found in four areas of central Pittsburgh—the Southside, Station Square, the Strip District, and the Penn Avenue area.

The Southside is a mixed-use area dominated by its commercial spine—Carson Street—which once served the needs of the surrounding residential neighborhood, but now acts as an entertainment district for the entire city. Four venues are located here with perhaps the best known being the Rex Theater, a former vaudeville theater opened in 1905. On the same side of the Monongahela River, but closer to the CBD, is Station Square—a former railroad complex turned into a restaurant, hotel, and entertainment center that attracts tourists. As a space for music venues, however, Station Square appears problematic as all venues in the data set have closed.

The third concentration is the Strip District—a warehouse area adjacent to the downtown. It retains some of its warehouse character while

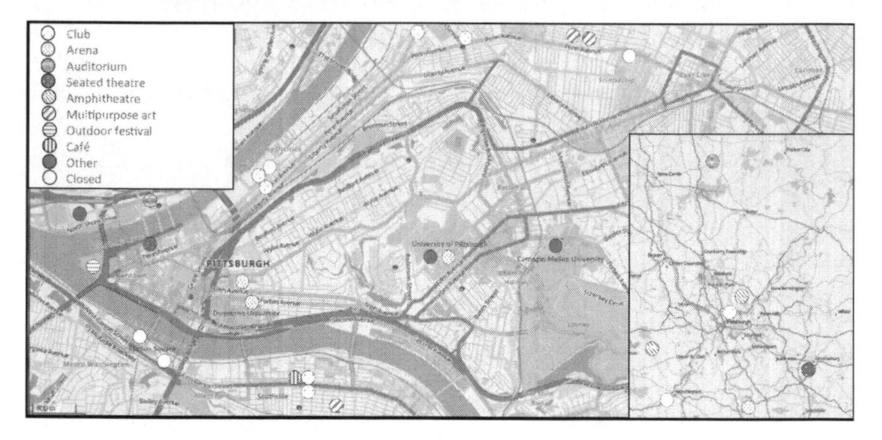

Figure 9.2 Venues in Pittsburgh (adapted by the authors from OpenStreetMap [© OpenStreetMap contributors, http://www.openstreetmap.org/copyright])

entertainment, food, and retail establishments currently flourish. Further out from the Strip District, a cluster of venues along Penn Avenue run in a northeasterly direction for several miles. The Penn Avenue area has relatively inexpensive real estate and is comprised of somewhat derelict working-class row houses. Five small venues were found in this area.

Farther away from the city center is Mr. Small's, one of the most unique adaptive reuse venues. It is located in a former Catholic church in the Millvale neighborhood. The conversion of churches to other uses is common in the Pittsburgh area because of the dual forces of population decline and the wide variety of central and eastern European settlers who built an abundance of ethnically based churches in the city, which also make good clubs. One musician who frequents Mr. Small's said that the shared buzz of the intimate atmosphere gave the audience a "contact high" (O'Toole 2004).

Perhaps surprisingly, few venues are close to the main universities in Pittsburgh. The only such venues are university-owned auditoriums and arenas. Except for the corporately managed arena at the University of Pittsburgh, music performances are only intermittent in these venues. No clubs are near any of the campuses. The established entertainment districts in other locations in the city appear to have outcompeted and prevented near-campus clusters of venues from emerging.

VENUES IN THE DIGITAL AGE

We identify five ways in which the live music industry and venues have been transformed in the digital age: 1) flow of information about concerts has increased; 2) ticketing has been streamlined; 3) the music industry has been restructured; 4) cyber concerts have emerged; and 5) performance characteristics have undergone changes. These insights and their spatial manifestations are drawn from the questionnaire responses and a close reading of music industry literature.

First, the Internet has facilitated the flow of information about performance events. The capacity of promoters to identify potential concertgoers is greater than ever through online-derived databases and social media (Peters 2012). The most important factors determining whether someone chooses to attend a performance are price considerations and the level of awareness that a show is happening (Waddell 2013). Even in the digital age, "getting the word out" about performances matters. Thanks to the Internet and social media, more people are aware of shows locally, according to many of the venue owners and operators we interviewed. Web-based advertising is considered an efficient way to reach the market compared to traditional forms of advertising, and it is available at a lower cost. But as recently as 2012, however, 80 percent of advertising spending for concerts was still allocated to traditional media outlets (e.g., radio, television, print ads, billboards) and only 20 percent online (Peters 2012). Our questionnaire respondents consistently mentioned the increasing importance of online marketing, although the operating manager at the Palace Theater outside Pittsburgh suggested online marketing is still used as a supplement, rather than "taking over" traditional advertising outlets (Baughman 2014).

Knowledge about shows varies among potential audiences depending on their location. The geographic range to which a venue markets, and from which it draws its audience, is now more extensive. A Pittsburgh venue manager said that "the Internet provides a conduit to reach a wider geographic area than the old print ads and radio spots. Typically you would have a fixed budget to spend on . . . advertising which meant you would have to forgo advertising in the outlying areas as it would start having diminishing returns. Thus the audience now comes from a wider demographic and geographic footprint" (Michaels 2014). This sentiment was echoed by several other questionnaire respondents. At the same time, traditional factors such as interstate access to attract audiences and airport access to attract artists are locational variables that still matter greatly (Baughman 2014).

Internet-based concert marketing takes many forms. Websites and apps are used to ask fans for information about music preferences and location, which can then be followed up by e-mail "blasts." This enables advertisers better to target potential concertgoers than, for example, radio advertising, which is a scattershot approach over a more territorially limited range. "Narrow-casting" to a targeted audience includes social media notifications, cell phone messages, interest-specific online advertising, and marketing from venue or ticketing companies' databases. Online marketing tools allow one to identify Facebook "friends" of individuals who have recently purchased tickets, and those friends will subsequently receive notifications of an impending show. Other advertisers and marketers use "geotargeting" to identify individuals carrying GPS-enabled cell phones in their vicinity. If a potential fan is within a certain distance from a venue based on cell phone location, the promoter will message the fan (Waddell 2013). One Pittsburgh venue owner observed that digital marketing technology allows him to target fans of individual artists. A "like" on Facebook can be tracked in order to target concert ads on their website to a likely attendee (Drusky 2014). These online marketing techniques enable venues and promoters to reach a more geographically dispersed, yet specific, audience.

Developing sophisticated concert marketing systems involves technical skills and effort. The marketing prowess of promoters varies, which influences the geographic reach of different venues. Heretofore, corporate promoters with larger financial resources have had an advantage in the digital era. Today, affordable web-based marketing services are also available to smaller venues and promoters. The capacity to use these digital technologies has filtered down to smaller locally owned and operated venues, although cost and technology are constantly in flux. Nashville venue manager Andrew Mischke (2014) noted that it has only been since 2014 that social networks adjusted pricing (upward) of their services to small businesses in order to better reflect their actual costs and the venues' potential revenues. The Pittsburgh manager of Stage AE, stated "our marketing has to stay more elastic in the ability to adapt and embrace the changes of social media, Internet, apps, etc." (Herrman 2014). The use of social media is especially expected to grow in the future in terms of marketing (Peters 2012).

In a real sense, venues are not only marketing concerts but also themselves. Social media platforms have been a boon for iconic venues such as the Ryman Auditorium. Its following is "large, vocal and loyal and is not just composed of Nashvillians" (Dupont 2014). Such web exposure allows venues to expand their reputation. As a result, clubs like San Francisco's Fillmore are developing nationwide franchises (Alexander 2008). While the Ryman has not done that, successful venues are often becoming part of a branded economy.

Digital technology also enables artists to disseminate information and connect with their audience on websites and social media (Arriagada, this volume; Ault 2002; Hracs, this volume). Fans develop taste preferences over the web and have virtually unlimited ability to try out new music. Jared Hoffman of the Knitting Factory, an expanding set of franchised venues across the United States, said "I think the live music industry has grown and is thriving thanks to the Internet, with audiences further and further afield from the major cities getting instant exposure to what's next and what's new" (as quoted in Alexander 2008, 51). A Pittsburgh venue manager says "the Internet has been a good thing for venues as it has created a proliferation of music, and provides a means for fans to know exactly where their favorite artists will be playing on any given night" (Herrman 2014). Information translates into greater interest in concerts; thus, the Internet encourages a thriving live scene. Nashville venue manager Andrew Mischke (2014) agrees, but also adds that it is difficult for industry people to identify the impact of social media on increases in show attendance. Others have noted that even if it seems counterintuitive, the Internet increases "musical awareness and creating a yearn for a 'real' experience away from the computer screen" (*Music Week* 2004, 7). This, accompanied by a good physical location, may be why the manager of Stage AE in Pittsburgh says "we are more desirable, because we have easy access for 'digital' impulse attendance" (Herrman 2014).

Working with the artists, booking agents and concert promoters use online databases with past concert information—including *Pollstar*, *Celebrity Access*, and *Billboard*—to schedule tours and seek out the best match between performer and venue (Krueger 2005). For example, the Palace Theater in Greensburg, Pennsylvania uses *Celebrity Access*, which helps with revenue planning and pricing of artists (Baughman 2014). Other Pittsburgh promoters and venue owners said that the Internet is of use to know where artists are playing and if they are "doing solid numbers" in other venues, which other promoters are booking them, and to receive audience feedback to help them improve operations. All of this makes the live music industry more efficient and lowers the transaction costs of concert booking. An alternative opinion is offered by Scott Michaels at the Peterson Events Center in Pittsburgh for whom booking "is still driven by relationships with promoters and agents" (Michaels 2014).

A second area where venues have been transformed is ticketing. The most important revenue stream in live music is the purchasing of tickets; therefore, "ticketing, once an industry stepchild, is the linchpin of the industry" (Waddell 2011). The trend in ticketing is towards online purchases. As early as 2004, the industry leader Ticketmaster reported that 50 percent of tickets were sold online (Ault 2004). Today, online sales not only dominate, but a significant portion of transactions, 14 percent, come from mobile devices (Waddell 2013). Online ticketing is more expedient for buyers and for venues compared to box office purchases or over-the-phone purchasing. Venues believe the ease of purchase has translated to more tickets being sold (Ault 2003). Tickets can be acquired with the same ease no matter where someone is located, which means the catchment area of a venue increases as well.

Internet ticket purchases allow the ticketing company to build a database of fans based on music preferences; they can then promote upcoming performances in the area, as well as promote other ancillary products and services. In 2000, the benefits of such new technology accrued to big promoters with national or international shows (Waddell 2000). More recently, smaller venues have developed comparable capacities. In 2003, analysts predicted that only venues with a capacity over 6,000 seats would use barcoded ticketing as scale economics were needed to make investment in the technology worthwhile (Ault 2003). Now, most small venues also use the barcode technology.

The ticketing industry is increasingly competitive. A number of ticket operators have emerged to challenge the industry leader, Ticketmaster (Waddell 2011). As technology has diffused, processing prices have declined, which means venues have more options available to them. Eventbrite, Ticketfly, ShowClix, DIY Tix, and StubHub are some alternative ticket vendors that venues use. These developments in ticketing are examples of digital technology becoming cheaper and filtering down the venue hierarchy.

Venues are also able to by-pass the ticket companies and establish their own websites where tickets are sold, although the functionality of these sites is often "powered" by an outside tech provider with which the venue partners. If venues have their own ticketing websites, they can also keep ticket transaction surcharges that would otherwise go to the ticket companies. If the venue previously maintained its own "analog" ticketing, labor-intensive box offices and call centers can be phased out, which is highlighted as an advantage in the digital era by the questionnaire respondent at the Palace Theatre in Greensburg, Pennsylvania (Baughman 2014). Venues also scan tickets and identification cards of the patrons, which may yield georeferenced data such as residential ZIP codes. Georeferencing, therefore, allows the venue to build a database of customer information which is useful for marketing purposes (Ault 2004). Specific venue databases are especially valuable because they are market-specific and geographically precise.

A third impact of the digital era is that the boundaries between the main actors in the live music industry—agents, promoters, and venues—are increasingly blurred. Today, agents are negotiating with the venues, promoters route tours, ticketing companies are promoting and marketing, promoters tap into concessions and parking revenue, and venues are promoting and putting tours together (Waddell 2004). "With the impact of the Web on our business, which makes it so easy and inexpensive to reach fans and to conduct commerce with them, I think you're seeing barriers coming down and new opportunities coming up" says a national promoter from Clear Channel Entertainment (Waddell 2004, 68).

One example of new technology triggering industry restructuring is that tour promoters may prefer to book concerts at a venue with an in-house marketing department because it is more likely to have effective online and local media capacities (Waddell 2005b). This is especially true for national promoters who book shows in places where they do not have a local presence. As venues take on these new roles, smaller venues may not have staffing or resources to be as successful as their larger, often corporate, counterparts.

Sharing concessions and parking revenues with promoters has been reported in the industry literature on industry restructuring, although parking revenue is traditionally the purview of the venue. Based on questionnaire responses, parking appears to be a key consideration for venues. The potential revenue stream from parking depends on where the venue is located in the city. Venues in central locations and repurposed buildings typically do not have access to dedicated parking. But venues are unlikely to relocate to suburbs. Three Pittsburgh venue managers say that a central location is important as they draw on a metropolitan-wide audience, while one respondent from suburban Greensburg pointed out that operating costs are lower and thus pricing is lower for them, which attracts audiences. New corporate-owned clubs have emerged in urban redevelopment areas where parking, by design, is more accessible and sometimes owned by the venue itself. Our examples include Limelight in Nashville and Stage AE in Pittsburgh. Both are in locations adjacent to the CBD and in proximity to the cities' sports stadiums.

A fourth area with which the industry has been experimenting is merging live concerts with the Internet to reach larger audiences. Performances can be made available on the Internet as live cybercasts or broadcast after the fact (Waddell 2005a). The Internet also has been used to supplement a "festival experience" where live songs can be downloaded afterwards (Koranteng 2003). Large venue owners such as Live Nation have developed the ability to record and redistribute live concerts on the web. Advanced recording technology at the venue is necessary (Weiss 2009), but the expense of equipping a venue with the technology to record video and audio of concerts is decreasing. Some venues outsource the recording, but stream the content on their own websites.

Cyber concerts are a way to further monetize live music as the selling of advertising space on websites provides an additional revenue stream for artists, venues, and ancillary website owners (Bruno 2007; Bruno and Waddell 2006). Concert streaming does not appear to "cannibalize" the live music experience and draw people away from the actual performance. One reason is that audiences are searching for both the immediate experience of a concert and a recorded "post-experience" (Weiss 2009). Live streaming has, however, had very limited success thus far (Daley 2014). None of our respondents in Pittsburgh or Nashville mentioned live streaming as something they were doing.

A fifth and final way live music may be affected by Internet technology is the style of performance. It is suggested artists are more conscious about the recorded sound, as heard on YouTube videos or other Internet outlets, than with their immediate connection with the live audience (Weiss 2009). On the other hand, artists with exciting live performances have more potential for success than even before as concerts provide the most reliable revenue stream (Alexander 2008). Even carefully packaged pop artists—e.g., the proverbial boy bands—have to perform well on stage (*Music Week* 2004). One respondent had an opposing viewpoint: "bands get popular, tour and make money without 'learning how to'," although he also acknowledged that "artists can be more 'genuine' . . . and market themselves without traditional label and radio support" (Herrman 2014).

CONCLUSION

The live music scenes in Nashville and Pittsburgh are approximately the same size with an almost equal number of venues. In both cities there is an identifiable hierarchy of musical venues, from large arenas and outdoor stage venues to similar types of mid-sized venues and smaller clubs. At the same time, there are some distinct spatial variations between Nashville and Pittsburgh based on their unique cultural geographies. More concerts were held in downtown Nashville than in Pittsburgh and non-downtown venues in Nashville are found along commercial roads and mixed land use districts, especially in areas dense with restaurants and small retailers catering to youthful consumers. Pittsburgh's music scene is, rather, more dispersed among the city's neighborhoods. While venues come and go, the overall provision of live music during the digital era has been robust in these markets.

Overall, "the Internet has been a boon" for live music in general (Ault 2002, 1). The industry considers live music "a great natural ally of the internet" and fans are seeking out live music in venues of all sizes (*Music Week* 2005, 13). Practically all of the music venues we surveyed had a web page and made use of social media and other digital technologies. They have been affected by at least three of the transformations that we identified in this chapter: increased flow of concert information, ticketing, and industry restructuring. The use of technology has made the industry operate more efficiently. Advanced and targeted marketing has extended the spatial reach of venues, which has had the intended effect of attracting an audience from farther away. At the same time, "creeping corporatization" characterizes the contemporary live music sector, and more economically robust venue ownership may be better able to adapt to urban and technological changes (*Music Week* 2007b). Larger venues had an advantage in the nascent digital era—the early 2000s—but the process has filtered down the venue hierarchy since then as the technology has become more ubiquitous and inexpensive. Still, it is the big corporations, such as Live Nation, that have the most extensive marketing tools and databases at their disposal. As the center of music industry has gravitated towards live music, further investment in corporate venues is likely. In the digital era there has been a proliferation of venues, but also more competition among them, according to a national promoter (Waddell 2004).

Examples of these trends are evident in our case study cities. For example, the manager of a competing venue in Pittsburgh points to Stage AE as a successful model in the new era of live music—a purpose-built modern facility, a good location with ample parking, and a mid-sized space that replicates the club "feel" but with large enough capacity to be profitable. Smaller, independent venues in more marginal locations—often venues that we mapped as clubs in urban neighborhoods—also benefit from the digital revolution, but the need for knowledge and skills in the live music industry has increased dramatically, which indicates that such venues must also "professionalize."

The viable venues of the future will be those that are run by managers who embrace digital technologies and anticipate the ongoing changes and challenges in providing customers with quality live music experiences. Smaller venues have to perform new functions in the ongoing restructuring of the live music industry while wrestling with the traditional internal challenge of operating at inherently low profit levels. The geographies of urban club space will likely remain similar compared to the recent past, but with the addition of corporate venues that seek out new revenue generating locations.

REFERENCES

Alexander, Jason Scott. "Clubs Go Beyond the Stage." *Mix* 32, no. 1 (2008): 44–51.

Ault, Susanne. "Web Is a Windfall for Touring Biz." *Billboard* 114, no. 51 (2002): 1, 72.

Ault, Susanne. "New Tickets to Ride." *Billboard* (Touring Quarterly insert) 115, no. 8 (2003): 1, 8–11.

Ault, Susanne. “Touring: Online Ticketing Wins More Fans.” *Billboard* 116, no. 2 (2004): 17–20.

Baughman, Teresa. Director of Operations, Programming and Marketing, the Palace Theatre. Personal communication, June 26, 2014.

Black, Grant, Mark Fox, and Paul Kochanowski. “Concert Tour Success in North America: An Examination of the Top 100 Tours from 1997 to 2005.” *Popular Music and Society* 30, no. 2 (2007): 149–172.

Bruno, Antony. “Concert 2.0: Monetizing Live Music Online and in Virtual Worlds.” *Billboard* 119, no. 22 (2007): 20.

Bruno, Antony, and Ray Waddell. “http://www.venues_get_wired.com/: everyone from tiny clubs to huge promoters is using the web to reach more fans—and new revenue streams—with concerts.” *Billboard* 118, no. 30 (2006): 21–23.

Connolly, Marie, and Alan Krueger. *Rockonomics: The Economics of Popular Music*. NBER Working Paper No. 11282, 2005.

Daley, Dan. “Streaming Concerts: Will This Time Be Different?” *Front of House* 12, no. 12 (2014): 56.

Drusky, Brian. General Manager, Drusky Entertainment. Personal communication, June 27, 2014.

Dupont, Lisann. Communications Manager, Ryman Auditorium, Personal communication. July 14, 2014.

Forbes, Kenny. “Glasgow as a Live-Music City: An Analysis of the ‘Legendary’ Apollo Venue and Its Audience.” *Social Semiotics* 22, no. 5 (2012): 605–621.

Frith, Simon. “Live Music Matters.” *Scottish Music Review* 1, no. 1 (2007): 1–17.

Gallan, Ben, and Chris Gibson. “Mild-Mannered Bistro by Day, Eclectic Freak-Land by Night: Memoirs of an Australian Music Venue.” *Journal of Australian Studies* 37, no. 2 (2013): 174–193.

Grenier, Line, and Martin Lussier. “Constructing Small Venues in Montreal: Theoretical Explorations in an Ongoing Project.” *MUSICultures* 38 (2011): 173–190.

Herrman, Doug. General Manager, Stage AE, Personal communication, July 2, 2014.

Homan, Shane. “A Portrait of the Politician as a Young Pub Rocker: Live Music Venue Reform in Australia.” *Popular Music* 27, no. 2 (2008): 243–256.

Johansson, Ola. “Form, Function, and the Development of Music-Themed Entertainment Districts in Nashville and Memphis.” *Material Culture* 42, no. 1 (2010): 47–69.

Johansson, Ola, and Thomas L. Bell. “Where Are the New US Music Scenes?” In *Sound, Society, and the Geography of Popular Music,* edited by Johansson, Ola, and Thomas L. Bell. Farnham, UK: Ashgate Publishing, 2009: 219–244.

Johansson, Ola, and Thomas L. Bell. “Touring Circuits and the Geography of Rock Music Performance.” *Popular Music and Society* 37, no. 4 (2014): 313–337.

Koranteng, Juliana. “Download Festival Offers ‘Legitimate’ Live Music.” *Billboard* 115, 20 (2003): 25.

Kozak, Roman. *This Ain’t No Disco: The Story of CBGB*. New York: Faber & Faber, 1988.

Krueger, Alan. “The Economics of Real Superstars: The Market for Rock Concerts in the Material World.” *Journal of Labor Economics* 23, no. 1 (2005): 1–30.

Leonard, Marion, and Rob Strachan. *The Beat Goes On: Liverpool, Popular Music and the Changing City.* Liverpool: University Press, 2010.

Lloyd, Richard. “East Nashville Skyline.” *Ethnography* 12, no. 1 (2011): 114–145.

Michaels, Scott. General Manager, Peterson Events Center, Personal communication, July 8, 2014.

Mischke, Andrew. General Manager, Mercy Lounge/The Cannery Ballroom/The High Watt/One. Personal communication, July 2, 2014.

Music Week. "Sold-out Sector Is Alive and Kicking." March 13, 2004, p. 7.

Music Week. "New Venues Take Live Music into a New Era." December 24, 2005, p. 13.

Music Week. "Live Music Takes a Step Towards the Middle Ages." September 29, 2007a, p. 8.

Music Week. "The Live Sector: Going Live." February 17, 2007b, p. 17.

Oldham, Paul. "Suck More Piss: How the Confluence of Key Melbourne-Based Audiences, Musicians, and Iconic Scene Spaces Informed the Oz Rock Identity." *Perfect Beat* 14, no. 2 (2013): 120–136.

O'Toole, Christine H. "Pittsburgh Rocks: The City that Made Steel Is Now Forging Some Serious Local Music." *Washington Post*. Last modified May 12, 2004. www.washingtonpost.com/wp-dyn/articles/A19203–2004May11.html

Peters, Mitchell. "The Social Network Hits the Road." *Billboard* 124, no. 16 (2012): 4–5.

Waddell, Ray. "Online Tickets Pay Off: Concert Promoters Exploit Ease of Web." *Billboard* 112, no. 42 (2000): 6–117.

Waddell, Ray. "New Deals Changing Tour Biz." *Billboard* 116, no. 7 (2004): 1–68.

Waddell, Ray. "On The Road—Sky's the Limit for Network Live Venture." *Billboard* 117, no. 31 (2005a): 22.

Waddell, Ray. "In-House Marketers Get the Gig." *Billboard* 117, no. 25 (2005b): 25–26.

Waddell, Ray. "The Truth About Ticketing." *Billboard* 123, no. 13 (2011): 18–24.

Waddell, Ray. "The Ticket Pushers." *Billboard* 125, no. 10 (2013): 32–36.

Weiss, David. "Beyond the Stage." *Mix* 33, no. 5 (2009): 40–42.

10 What's the "Newport Effect"?

Music Festivals, Touring, and Reputations in the Digital Age

Jonathan R. Wynn and Rodrigo Dominguez-Villegas

Music is a fruitful area of study for social scientists, with research examining on-stage interactions between musicians (Becker and Faulkner 2009), "in situ" exchanges between musicians and audiences (Becker 1951), and the effervescent experiences of performances themselves (Fonarow 2006).

The issue of music's emplacement has been an increasingly rich vein. Cultural geographers mapped the birthplaces of country (Carney 1979), blues (Strait 2010), and zydeco musicians (Kuhlken and Sexton 1991). Others examined the neighborhoods, venues, and scenes arising around music culture (Florida and Jackson 2010; Grazian 2004; Johansson et al., this volume; Seman 2010; Silver et al. 2010; Virani, this volume). Somewhat ironically, the importance of place has only increased in the digital age (see also Virani, this volume).

Despite the rising economic value of live performances for musicians, touring and festivals are still poorly understood. Live performances represent a considerable and growing concern for the industry at large, and a newfound importance for cities as they transition from centers of cultural production to entertainment machines (see also Virani, this volume). This chapter delves into these issues hoping to open a few new lines of inquiry to better understand how U.S. festivals affect the wider music map for touring musicians and disparate music scenes across the country.

First, we provide a brief review of music in the digital age to explain the rise of importance of live performances for the success of small- and independent-label contemporary musicians and how they link to efforts by urban placemakers.

Second, we describe the connectivity of musicians in general and under the umbrella genre called "folk" or "Americana" specifically through the lens of one of its major events: the Newport Folk Festival. This section highlights the value of collaboration and social ties among musicians of this ilk as an exemplary case of a social space that is crafted for artists to connect and exchange ideas by drawing upon interview data from the perspective of musicians, talent bookers, and the festival producer.

Expanding upon what the festival producer called the "Newport Effect," a third section opens a line of research on the relationship between bands, festivals, and the places they tour by matching the above qualitative data with quantitative data that maps the network that results from the connections between musicians and the cities where they perform. In so doing, this chapter points to a new way of thinking about the cultural geography of music—beyond the expected centers of cultural production (i.e., New York City, Los Angeles, Chicago, Nashville)—a "geography of genre." Bob Dylan once said that "being on tour is like being in limbo . . . It's like going from nowhere to nowhere" (Shelton 1986, 430). And yet, this somewhat sarcastic statement is assuredly not the case. This chapter provides an image of touring as an 'opportunity structure' for interactions and reputations different from more conventional approaches to cultural production because it shows not just the importance of cities as postindustrial cultural centers but how their music scenes interconnect for musicians.

METHODS AND FOCUS

As an extension of a larger qualitative study of three festivals—Austin, Texas's South by Southwest, Nashville, Tennessee's Country Music Association Music Fest, and Newport, Rhode Island's Newport Folk Festival—this chapter matches some of the insights gleaned from interviews and participant observation with social network analysis.

We focused on the Newport Folk Festival. The founding of this festival in 1959, along with its sister Newport Jazz Festival in 1954, serves as the start of the Festival Era in the United States. Although it has had several iterations, its present moment is very artist driven: an advisory board of five festival alumni selects musicians for the annual lineup. Although festival producer Jay Sweet is largely credited for its latest resurgence on the cultural landscape, he stated in an interview that for his board, "it's their festival too." Sweet believes that, unlike many festivals that book a diverse lineup to cater to as wide an audience as possible, Newport Folk has a strong allegiance to the genre of folk, or "Americana" music, and promotes the idea of a symbolic branding conferred upon festival performers that creates a larger "Newport Folk family" and a notable bump in prestige media professionals call the "Newport Effect." Perhaps most importantly, this group of musicians is largely associated with small- and independent-labels, which lack the logistical apparatus of large music labels especially regarding promotion, media impact, and tour support.

To learn more about the geography of this genre, we examined changes in connections among musicians defined through their common performance in a specific city. To measure this, we analyzed the social network of the 2013 Newport Folk Festival formed through the cities where bands performed three months before and after the festival—which correspondingly overlaps with the time of year most bands tour. We then compared this network with the network created by the same performers during exactly the same time period the year prior, when they were not performing at the festival. We gathered information from band websites and two popular online music resources (Songkick or Last.fm), creating a database with 42 bands and almost 400 tour locations.

Through the analysis of this two-mode network,[1] we saw how the festival affects musician ties and places concurrently. We obtained two networks: the performer-by-performer network, showing which performers performed at a common locale, and the city-by-city network, showing how cities are linked by the musicians that performed in them. We estimated the changes in network statistics, allowing us to see changes in the connectivity among folk musicians as well as changes in the centrality of cities in the U.S. folk music scene. All analyses were performed using the open-source statistical language R and the sna package (see Butts 2013).

LIVE PERFORMANCES AND ENTERTAINMENT CITIES IN THE DIGITAL AGE

Profound changes in the music business have impacted how music is received and enjoyed as this volume shows: from Edison's invention of the phonograph to the expansion and consolidation of record labels and changes in copyright laws, technology and market demands throughout the twentieth century, to more recent digital innovations of production and consumption (Madden and Rainie 2005; Peterson and Berger 1996).

More recently, economists who study the industry note that live concerts superseded album sales as the primary source of income for musicians (see also Johansson et al., this volume). According to a 2005 study on "rockonomics," the ratio of touring income to record sales income was 7.5 to 1 for the top thirty-five performers in 2002 (Connolly and Krueger 2005). A 2012 survey of over 5,371 musicians by the Future of Music Coalition found that respondents received only 6 percent of their income from recorded music over the last year, with 66 percent of respondents saying they received *no* income from recorded music at all while, collectively, 28 percent of their income came from live performances (Future of Music Coalition 2012; Hracs and Leslie 2014).

As the recorded music industry struggles—August 2014 marked the lowest album sales since Nielsen began tracking them in 1991—the live music industry carries on (Christman and Peoples 2014). Mortimer et al. look at concert data from 200,000 performances by 12,000 artists from 1995 to 2004 and album sales data from over 1,800 artists to find an expected inverse relationship between the drop in album sales and the rise of numbers of concerts performed, but also learn that record sales for smaller acts decreased less while concert revenue sales improved (2012, 4; see also Black et al. 2007). Touring used to be a part of the marketing for an album as a way to generate press and build an audience. Talking Heads frontman

David Byrne, in his book *How Music Works*, writes of the idea that musicians lose money on a tour is an "old lie . . . that really doesn't hold true anymore" (2012, 207). In the digital age, then, live music is a force.

It is paradoxical that place matters in the age of digital music, and, yet, touring is an intense enterprise that musicians now rely on (see: Atkins 2007; Waddell et al. 2007). This is a relevant, yet less tangible facet of the cultural geography of music which, of course, serves as an important additional link between the recorded music industry and places around the country.

Such a perspective ties music research with research on the rise of central city areas as zones for cultural consumption. As disinvestment, globalization, and suburbanization undermine the manufacturing cores of American cities, urban stakeholders turn to cultural wares and crafting experiences in order to become "entertainment machines" (Lloyd and Clark 2001). Following this line of research, Silver et al. define a scene as the physical and social spaces "devoted to practices of meaning making through the pleasures of sociable consumption" (2010, 2297; Currid and Williams 2010). While festivals are not located solely in cities, they do link with placemaking strategies and existent urban music scenes.

Festivals are meaningful social moments, bringing together a confluence of motivations (see also Jansson and Nilsson, this volume): musicians' desire to sell tickets and albums, audiences' enjoyment of music, and cities and scenes interest in development. It, therefore, makes sense to link artists' performance travels before and after festivals with particular cities. Place matters here, and linking festivals and cities near and far illustrates a wider economic and cultural ecology for cities and musicians.

Let us take, for example, the perspective of small label singer-songwriter and Newport Folk Festival alum, Erin McKeown. She noted that festivals are a way to play to two audiences: people who are already fans and new audiences she hopes to win over. For her career, however, McKeown told us how festivals work for her on an additional level:

> I was happy to have been invited [to Newport] because it meant I was having a good year. That's what I think about festivals. You don't get invited unless you have a lot of stuff happening for you. They tend to be an anchor you build a tour around . . . then you can ride on the wave of that and play other gigs.

A New England talent booker—someone who hires performers for a venue—corroborated McKeown's claims, stating that a festival act has a "better chance for success in our local market . . . we're able to exploit the media imprint of a band's success before the festival happens." He says he can confidently review the Newport festival lineup and pick several acts heading to the event, and a few others hitting the road afterwards.

Additionally: although data indicate that the economic profits might be the prime motivator for touring, there are other less tangible benefits. It is, in fact, this dynamic we will explore more here: musicians' experiences of festivals as opportunities for building careers and exchanging ideas.

UNDERSTANDING TOURING, REPUTATIONS, AND SOCIAL CONNECTIVITY IN THE FOLK MUSIC GENRE

Research on cultural production—from Howard Becker's artists in *Art Worlds* (2002[1982]) to film and television actors, directors and screenwriters (Zafirau 2008) to Hollywood musicians (Faulkner 1983) to recent research on interns in the recorded music industry (Frenette 2013, this volume)—confirms that strong network ties are invaluable for building a career in the cultural industries (Randle and Culkin 2009), for understanding cultural workers as occupational groups, and for understanding the innovations that lead to the formation of, and changes within, a genre (Peterson 1997). A tour, as it winds its way through various music scenes and social networks is another social form of cultural work. In addition to selling tickets, tours build social capital, augment cultural skills, and amplify reputations.

In this effort, it is, first, important to understand that such connections are at work well before a single note is played and can have repercussions long afterward. Aspiring musicians develop a reputation among fans but also among music industry professionals. These networks play out when festival producers use these ties to book artists. In this case, Newport Folk Festival producer Jay Sweet explained that he uses his advisory board of musicians to identify other acts to book for his event. He asked board members and local musicians John McCauley (from independent label band Deer Tick) and Ben Knox Miller (from Nonesuch/Elektra/Warner Music Group band The Low Anthem) who the festival should book from Rhode Island, and they recommended an independent band called Brown Bird. He explained that such reputations count: "That went a hell of a lot farther than a press release, or 'Hey, please listen to our link.' I trusted those people and I listened to them and they were great. My trust is 100% predicated on those bands basically testifying for another band." Sweet also uses these artists to convince talent to join the festival since their nonprofit budget cannot offer the same kinds of contracts that bigger festivals like Bonnaroo and Coachella can. He explains that his board persuades musicians to come and "hang out" with like-minded musicians, sing together, and have a good time.

Building off of Sweet's last comment there's a second point: live performances are places for potential exchanges of ideas (Jansson and Nilsson, this volume). While there is research on festivals as creative destinations for tourists and consumers (see Prentice and Andersen 2003), they are creative destinations for performers, too. There is a great deal of interaction among Newport musicians. Being on tour allows for opening and headlining bands to interact with each other, with industry professionals, and with a patchwork of cultural scene-makers as well.

In regards to folk music, Grammy award winner, Dom Flemons of the Nonesuch/Elektra/Warner Music Group band Carolina Chocolate Drops, would agree with this point. In an interview he expressed excitement over attending festivals because of the opportunities for sharing songs and stories with what he sees as a "big folk family." At Newport, artists often join other bands on stage, collaborating on a cover of an older folk song, for example. The late Pete Seeger, when in attendance, served as a kind of merry trickster popping up on different stages to sing along with various bands. As another example of the festival influencing musicians, the Capitol Records band The Decemberists (whose frontman, Colin Meloy, is also on the advisory board), produced a critically praised 2011 album that was deeply inspired by Newport Folk traditions and included vocals from Meloy's fellow advisory board member, Gillian Welch (who founded her own label, Acony Records).

Over the last few years, festival producer Jay Sweet aimed to nurture connections between musicians in other ways. There have been afterhours 'hootenanny' BBQ benefits. Indie musician David Wax described them as additional places where musicians try to puzzle through the folk canon. Older songs are reinterpreted (e.g., "Goodnight Irene," "This Land is Your Land"), while newer songs are tested (e.g., Gram Parsons' "Sin City," Leonard Cohen's "Hey That's No Way to Say Goodbye"). He says these events attempt to make "room for people to be more collaborative, and harken back to a different era."

While these stories underscore the kinds of social connections and interactions made in and around the festival, two caveats are needed. First, the unique quality of the folk/Americana music genre should be reasserted. The genre may not be generalizable because not only does it loosely span blues, rock, and country, it also comes with a unique heritage that explicitly valorizes the kind of collaboration and interaction this chapter seeks to illustrate. Second, after the 2008 economic crash, which made finding a marquee advertiser difficult and bankrupting the prior Newport festivals' owners (in under two years), the festival itself attempted to capitalize on nearby Providence's burgeoning Americana scene. As David Wax teased out the symbiotic relationship between the event and the local scene in an interview, he said that a group of bands—The Low Anthem, Deer Tick, Brown Bird, and Joe Fletcher—all deserved credit for "embracing being from Providence, trumpeting that fact, making that part of their identity, and then forming strategic connections with other bands with Providence connections." It is, then, perhaps a unique case, but one that offers a valuable perspective nonetheless.

With these stipulations in mind, we can still see a festival as the intersection of various careers, touring routes, and potential genre formation and innovation. Tours, and the festivals embedded within them, are opportunity structures, but also reputational networks which are important in the music industry as they are in any art world. Musicians aren't necessarily present in these places at the same time, but a tour and a festival performance are markers for reputations. Reputations link to local scenes. Regional talent bookers pay attention to the lineup and what media buzz surrounds acts to book bands for venues, small town record stores want to carry and promote 'hot' bands, radio stations want to play their music, and fans want to buy their albums before and after their shows. (For more on reputations in the cultural industries see Delmestri et al. 2005 and Jones 2002).

It is, then, hardly the case that touring for most musicians is the matter of going from nowhere to nowhere as per the Dylan maxim. While some high-end performers might be more isolated from other musicians, for most early and mid-career musicians touring can be a process of moving from one localized network of media, community, and cultural amenities to another similar local network. These reputations and exchanges of ideas and strategies extend beyond the festival itself, hooking up with existing music scenes on the road, tracing out this dissemination and exchange of cultural goods.

"THE NEWPORT EFFECT": MEASURING THE CONNECTIONS CREATED BY THE TOURING PATTERNS OF A COHORT OF FOLK ARTISTS, 2012 AND 2013

Although the idea of the "Newport Folk Effect" came from the media (e.g., see Harwood 2012) and not from inside the festival organization, Jay Sweet has happily embraced it. When asked for an example of this elevation in reputation coming from performing at the festival, he offered the example of Dawes (an independent Los Angeles band):

> In 2010 Dawes plays Newport on the smallest stage on the smallest day. No one's ever really heard of them. They kill. NPR—we have so much press—everyone thinks that they are incredible. (The band is fucking good, mind you, it's not about us.) But then that fall, only a few months after that—when all the kids go back to school and the whole of New England quadruples in size—they'll go and play. They've skipped [sizes of venues by] two rooms. That is 100% directly related to playing the Newport Folk Festival. That was organic, but we were conscious that we wanted to make that happen because we don't have the money to go and 'wow' bands with our offers. It's not us doing the testifying, it's the artists testifying to other artists: "Go play Newport. Do Newport and you'll own New England. The number of offers [from venues in] New England is going to go through the roof."

Sweet's quote—linked with McKeown's earlier one—points to how tours and festival performances serve as markers for reputations and building careers for this largely small- and independent-label group of musicians. Once an artist is booked at a festival, they are labeled, encircled in a kind of marketable network for regional talent buyers hoping to book similar artists. Musicians are eager to string together a tour before and after a festival to build off of success and prestige that comes with such a booking.

A result of this marker for reputations is the creation of stronger networks that are represented in how musicians tour. Analyzing the links among musicians formed by virtue of performing in the same cities in 2012 and 2013, we compared the effect of the Newport Folk Festival on the interconnectedness of folk musicians and the centrality of the cities where they performed.

At least two major qualifications are necessary for this comparison. First, careers are hardly static, and an invitation to perform at the Newport Folk Festival is unlikely to be the only variable that changed for these artists between 2012 and 2013. For example, it is possible that, as Erin McKeown noted, a festival booking means that other things were going well for a musician that year. Second, three acts had unique characteristics making their inclusion in the analysis incomparable: Jim James and Colin Meloy were both members of bands that performed in 2012 and who performed solo in 2013, and The Lone Bellow appears to not have toured in 2012. Therefore, we excluded these three artists in the analysis.

Still, there are important takeaways from this geography of genre. Our social network analysis of the touring patterns reflects both a convergence of touring in the year when the musicians performed at the festival and a binding together of different locales in a year when these bands performed at a festival. These points should be explained in greater detail.

First, playing a festival created more connections among musicians by the virtue of performing in the same cities. This is seen in the increase of performer-by-performer network density–an indicator of how many of the potential ties between musicians actually exist–from 2012 to 2013. In 2012, the performers' network had a density of 0.78. In 2013—when they performed in the festival–this increased to 0.91. This means than in 2012 78 percent of the possible ties between musicians, created by having performed in the same city at least once, existed. In 2013, 91 percent of possible total ties were there. This is also seen in the number of ties each musician had with other musicians. The average number of ties between a musician and others was 32 in 2012 and 37.5 in 2013. In 2012, no performer was connected to every single one of the other 41 acts. The highest degree, or number of ties, that performers had in 2012 was 38. In 2013, eight performers had ties with every other performer.

Second, the centrality of cities in the mapped network is concentrated in a group of cities in both non-festival (2012) and festival (2013) years, but composition of those on top changed.[2] Earlier research demonstrated a stable concentration and clustering of the recorded music industry by measuring the number of production firms (studios), or the number of employees in the music industry in a specific area, finding that New York City, Los Angeles, and Nashville—unsurprisingly—are the main centers of production of music in the United States (Scott 1999; see also Florida and Jackson 2010).

Regarding the live music industry, however, we propose that the degree centrality obtained using the cities-by-cities network projection of two mode network connecting artists and cities can provide a strong indicator of a city's importance in the folk music genre in the United States. The node degree centrality will tell us the number of connections a city has with other cities by virtue of sharing at least one performer. A high degree centrality score means that a city has many connections to other cities. Two different scenarios can make a city have a high score by this measure: A city may have a large number of performers that create ties between this city and all other cities where these artists played. A city with a high degree could have a lower number of very well connected performers that would create ties with a large number of other cities. Using location quotients or other measures of concentration would ignore the second scenario (Table 10.1).

These results show that, yes, the expected cities of New York City, Los Angeles, and Nashville appear in the top ten for a non-festival year. However: in 2013 New York falls, Nashville rises, and Los Angeles drops out of the top ten (to #14). Austin and New Orleans, cities known for their live music venues, surface on the list.

Figure 10.1, showing data in a different format, adds the next ten cities to illustrate how a bundle of cities benefit from this network of folk musicians.

Here we see that some cities rise in centrality for these musicians in a festival year (e.g., San Francisco, Nashville, Minneapolis, New Orleans) while others plummet (e.g., New York City, Seattle, Atlanta, Richmond, Asheville, and San Diego). This is to note that the significance of a city, in the geography of this genre, changes depending on the relations of the bands that play

Table 10.1 Top ten cities in the folk geography of genre, measured by network degree centrality

	2012		2013	
Ranking	City	Degree	City	Degree
1	New York, NY	0.85	San Francisco, CA	0.87
2	Chicago, IL	0.77	Nashville, TN	0.80
3	San Francisco, CA	0.77	Chicago, IL	0.79
4	Seattle, WA	0.76	Portland, OR	0.77
5	Atlanta, GA	0.74	New York, NY	0.76
6	Nashville, TN	0.70	Philadelphia, PA	0.72
7	Los Angeles, CA	0.69	Austin, TX	0.72
8	Philadelphia, PA	0.68	Minneapolis, MN	0.71
9	Portland, OR	0.68	New Orleans, LA	0.67
10	San Diego, CA	0.68	Seattle, WA	0.66

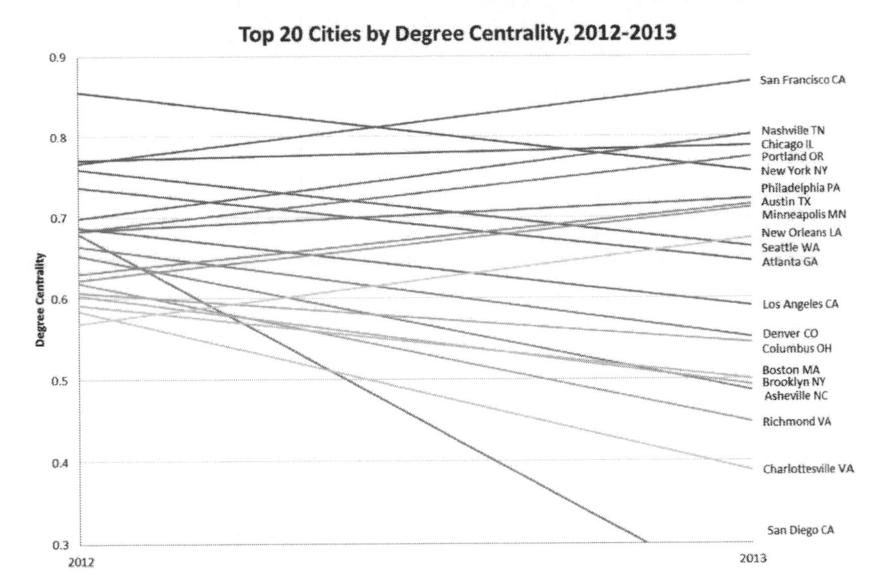

Figure 10.1 Top 20 Cities by Degree Centrality, 2012–2013

there. Only nearby Boston's drop makes obvious sense, since the Newport festival serves a proximate music market.

As a result, knowing which cities drew a greater number of similar musicians might help venues to target similar acts or local media to understand national culture better, or to help small and independent label artists to remap tours, by bending to places where similar musicians performed. McKeown, for example, explained her process of how she crafts a tour in these terms:

> There are probably 14 cities that I always go to. Even if not that many people came to the show the last time, or I can't quite get the perfect night. I'll go anyway. Seattle, Portland, San Francisco, LA, Chicago, maybe Madison, DC, Philly, Brooklyn, Boston, Northampton, Asheville, Louisville and Pittsburgh . . . In all of those places there's one or more of these things: A great radio station, a long history of playing there, a great record shop that I've done in-stores in (back when people did that), and some core group of people who have always shown up, who have "gotten it." So whatever else happens, I feel those are places I always have to get.

Understanding this geography of folk music can help an inclined musician identify locations that are more connected to the year's folk music network. And so, while Erin has her 14 cities—a few of which are included in the bundle of top folk cities in Figure 10.1 (e.g., San Francisco, Philadelphia, and Portland, Oregon)—she might also try booking a gig in Nashville when she's in nearby Asheville or Louisville, or head to Minneapolis when she's a few hours drive away in Madison.

New prospective tour stops provides musicians with a map of opportunity to target gigs, stoke exposure and promotion with specific media (e.g., radio shows, newspaper reporters, music stores, local bloggers), and tap into specific and perhaps unexpected scenes. As another musician described it in an interview:

> If your machine is working for you, [they] are looking to get in those local scenes to make every stop worthwhile. You are basically trying to tap into a local scene and even if you are not strong enough to headline a show there, perhaps you could open for a local band.

Even if a performer didn't perform in a festival, he or she might want to tour these locales to build off of the resultant folk network and sympathetic local music scene.

Of course, there are still the perennial logistics and economic considerations that serve as primary considerations for touring: the distance between gigs, concentrations of fans, venue size and availability, willingness of promoters to offer guaranteed pay, etc. And yet, understanding musician-city connections allows us to trace networks through a geography of the folk genre, a map of places and congregations of actors that make up scenes (e.g., touring and local musicians, tour managers, talent bookers, festival producers, cultural entrepreneurs, culture media professionals, and urban placemakers would all be interested in learning of the relationships of cities in this fashion) to provide what James Kitts calls a networked "opportunity structure" (2014). These pathways chart numerous opportunities for musicians, festivals, and music scenes alike.

CONCLUSIONS: THE GEOGRAPHIES OF GENRE?

In this brief chapter we have begun to unravel the relationships between touring and festivals, bands with other bands, and economic and social exchanges that might result in reputational and social capital. Such threads can tie to a number of interesting additional questions for research: 1) Are there other geographies of other genres? 2) Is there an equivalent to the "Newport Effect" in other music genres? There is likely a similar bump in reputation for performers at other festivals, but is the "Lollapalooza Effect" or the "Bonnaroo Effect" more or less powerful than the "Newport Effect?" 3) How do genre-based festivals like Newport (e.g., hip-hop, EDM, country) compare with "generalist" festivals (e.g., Milwaukee's Summerfest or Tennessee's Bonnaroo), and how do the ties between cities differ in these other instances? 4) Does the reputational mark of performing at a music festival positively affect the size and importance of the venues where acts perform? 5) Do festivals affect the touring pattern for established musicians the same way as it does for mid-career or new performers? What about major label artists as compared with "indie" musicians? 6) Does participating in a festival affect digital listenership? The answers to such questions, we contend, hold promise.

At the same time, we want to offer a few words of caution. Newport, for one, may work differently as a small locale (with little to distract musicians from interacting at the festival) that is proximate to other large northeastern cities, facts that might affect both the kinds of collaborations and connections that occur inside the festival and regional touring strategies. Additionally, folk may be an outlier, as stated earlier, since it is particularly attuned to crafting connections between musicians as compared with other genres. These concerns do not necessarily discount the value of these findings. In fact, other events might well be interested in adopting similar emplacement and tactics for their musicians. As always, further research is needed.

NOTES

1. Two mode networks (also called bipartite, affiliation or hyper networks) are networks that have two different sets of nodes. Two mode networks do not measure ties established directly between two actors, but between actors and an event. The ties in two mode networks do not exist only between nodes that belong to different sets. The two mode network used here depicts the links between performers (first mode) and cities (second mode). For more on Social Network Analysis and two mode networks, see Borgatti and Everett (1997) and Opsahl (2013).
2. We use normalized degree centrality to compare two different sized networks. Additionally, the unequal concentration of centrality in a few cities increases in the year of the festival. (While degree centrality indicates the number of ties each city had, degree centralization measures the concentration of ties in a small number of nodes.) In 2012, the city-by-city network has a degree centralization score of 0.62 showing that the ties in the network are highly concentrated in a few cities. In 2013, the year of the festival, this increased to 0.64.

REFERENCES

Atkins, Martin. *Tour Smart: And Break the Band.* Chicago, IL: Chicago Review Press, 2007.

Becker, Howard S. "The Professional Dance Musician and His Audience." *American Journal of Sociology* 5, no. 2 (1951): 136–144.

Becker, Howard S., and Robert R. Faulkner. *"Do You Know . . .?" The Jazz Repertoire in Action.* Chicago, IL: University of Chicago Press, 2009.

Black, Grant C., Mark A. Fox, and Paul Kochanowski. "Concert Tour Success in North America: An Examination of the Top 100 Tours from 1997 to 2005." *Popular Music and Society* 30, no. 2 (2007): 149–172.

Borgatti, Stephen P., and Martin G. Everett. "Network Analysis of 2-Mode Data." *Social Networks* 19, no. 3 (1997): 243–269.
Butts, Carter T. *Package sna: Tools for Social Network Analysis*. Reference Manual, 2013. http://cran.r-project.org/web/packages/sna/index.html
Carney, George. "T Is for Texas, T for Tennessee: The Origins of Country Music Notables." *Journal of Geography* 78 (1979): 218–225.
Christman, Ed., and Glenn Peoples. "Album Sales Hit a New Low." *Billboard,* August 28, 2014. http://www.billboard.com/biz/articles/news/digital-and-mobile/6236367/album-sales-hit-a-new-low
Connolly, Marie, and Alan B. Krueger. "Rockonomics: The Economics of Popular Music." In *Handbook of Arts and Culture*, Vol. 1, edited by Ginsburgh, V.A., and D. Throsby, 667–719. Amsterdam: Elsevier, 2006.
Currid, Elizabeth, and Sarah Williams. "Two Cities, Five Industries: Similarities and Differences within and Between Cultural Industries in New York and Los Angeles." *Journal of Planning Education and Literature* 29, no. 3 (2010): 322–335.
Delmestri, Guiseppe, Fabrizio Montanari, and Alessandro Usai. "Reputation and the Strength of Ties in Predicting Commercial Success and Artistic Merit of Independents in the Italian Feature Film Industry." *Journal of Management Studies*, 42 (2005): 975–1002.
Faulkner, Robert R. *Music on Demand*. New Brunswick, NJ: Transaction, 1983.
Florida, Richard, and Steven Jackson. "Sonic City: The Evolving Economic Geography of the Music Industry." *Journal of Planning Education and Research* 29, no. 3 (2010): 310–321.
Fonarow, Wendy. *Empire of Dirt*. Middletown, CT: Wesleyan University Press, 2006.
Frenette, Alexandre. "Making the Intern Economy: Role and Career Challenges of the Music Industry Intern." *Work and Occupations* 40, no. 4 (2013): 364–397.
Future of Music Coalition. "FMC Artist Revenue Streams Project." 2012. http://money.futureofmusic.org/
Grazian, David. "The Production of Popular Music as a Confidence Game: The Case of the Chicago Blues." *Qualitative Sociology* 27 (2004): 137–158.
Harwood, Garland. "The Rise of Brown Bird." *Grass Clippings Blog*, August 12, 2012. http://grassclippingsblog.com/2012/08/02/the-rise-of-brown-bird/
Hracs, Brian, and Deborah Leslie. "Aesthetic Labour in Creative Industries: The Case of Independent Musicians in Toronto, Canada." *AREA* 46, no. 1 (2014): 66–73.
Jones, Candace. "Signaling Expertise: How Signals Shape Careers in Creative Industries." In *Career Creativity,* edited by Peiperl, M.A., M.B. Arthur, and N. Anand, 209–228. Oxford, UK: Oxford University Press, 2002.
Kitts, James. "Beyond Networks in Structural Theories of Exchange: Promises from Computational Social Science." *Advances in Group Processes* 31 (2014): 263–299.
Kuhlken, Robert, and Rocky Sexton. "The Geography of Zydeco Music." *Journal of Cultural Geography* 12, no. 1 (1991): 27–38.
Lloyd, Richard, and Terry Clark. "The City as an Entertainment Machine." *Research in Urban Sociology* 6 (2001): 357–378.
Madden, Mary, and Lee Rainie. "Music and Video Downloading." *Pew Internet & American Life Project*. March 23, 2005. http://www.pewinternet.org/Reports/2005/Music-and-Video-Downloading.aspx

Mortimer, Julie H., Chris Nosko, and Alan Sorensen. "Supply Responses to Digital Distribution: Recorded Music and Live Performances." *Information Economics and Policy* 24, no. 1 (2012): 3–14.

Opsahl, Tore. "Triadic Closure in Two-Mode Networks: Redefining the Global and Local Clustering Coefficients." *Social Networks* 35, no. 2 (2013): 159–167.

Peterson, Richard A. *Creating Country Music*. Chicago, IL: University of Chicago Press, 1997.

Peterson, Richard A., and Donald G. Berger. "Measuring Industry Concentration, Diversity, and Innovation in Popular Music." *American Sociological Review* 61 (1996): 175–178.

Prentice, Richard, and Vivien Andersen. "Festival as Creative Destination." *Annals of Tourism Research*. 30, no. 1 (2003): 7–30.

Randle, Keith, and Nigel Culkin. "Getting in and Getting on in Hollywood: Freelance Careers in an Uncertain industry." In *Creative Labour,* edited by McKinlay, A., and C. Smith, 93–115. New York: Palgrave Macmillan, 2009.

Scott, Allen J. "The U.S. Recorded Music Industry: On the Relations Between Organization, Location, and Creativity in the Cultural Economy." *Environment and Planning A* 13, (1999): 1965–1984.

Seman, Michael. "How a Music Scene Functioned as a Tool for Urban Redevelopment: A Case Study of Omaha's Slowdown Project." *City, Culture and Society* 1, no. 4 (2010): 207–215.

Shelton, Robert. *No Direction Home*. New York: De Capo Press, 1986.

Silver, Daniel, Terry N. Clark, and Clemente J.N. Yanez. "Scenes: Social Context in an Age of Contingency." *Social Forces* 88, no. 5 (2010): 2293–2324.

Strait, John B. "Geographical Study of American Blues Culture." *Journal of Geography* 109, (2010): 30–39.

Waddell, Ray D., Rich Barnet, and Jake Berry. *This Business of Concert Promotion and Touring*. New York: Billboard Books, 2007.

Wynn, Jonathan. *Music/City: American Festivals and Placemaking in Austin, Nashville, and Newport*. Chicago, IL: University of Chicago Press, 2015.

Zafirau, Stephen. "Reputation Work in Selling Film and Television: Life in the Hollywood Talent Industry." *Qualitative Sociology* 31 (2008): 99–127.

11 Musicians and Temporary Spaces

The Case of Music Festivals in Sweden

Johan Jansson and Jimi Nilsson

Recent technological developments have altered the nature of where, when, and how music-related creativity, production, and distribution take place (see Arditi, this volume; Arriagada, this volume; Hracs, this volume; Speers, this volume; Watson, this volume). For the music industry, these developments have led to declining revenues from traditional business models and a thorough restructuring of the entire industry (Power and Jansson 2004). For the individual musician, this restructuring has strongly affected the conditions of creating and producing music and the prospect of making a living from it (Haijen, this volume; Hracs, this volume; Speers, this volume). Today, musicians are involved in a variety of creative and non-creative tasks which have contributed to the fragmentation of musicians' work lives in both time and space (Hracs 2012). For example, they not only spend time finding inspiration and writing/recording songs, they are also involved in distributing and promoting their music, planning tours, attending business meetings, and finding new projects and collaborators. Considering these tasks, contemporary musicians show many similarities to entrepreneurs in other industries. In particular, the restructuring of the music industry has forced many musicians to tour for longer periods between releasing new albums (Wynn and Dominguez-Villegas, this volume). Consequently, musicians spend less time in traditional settings such as workshops, recording studios, and at home, and more time in temporary settings such as tour buses, venues, mobile recordings studios, and music festivals (Hracs 2009; Menger 2006; Nilsson 2014).

These developments relate to the literature on temporary spaces which stresses that professional gatherings such as trade fairs, conventions, and festivals tend to display some of the characteristics found in permanent clusters: as platforms for networks, creativity, innovation, and labor markets (Bathelt et al. 2004; Bathelt and Schuldt 2008; Maskell et al. 2006). In addition, a relational approach encourages us to view distant places/spaces as being connected by formal and informal linkages and hence part of a complex web of cyclical events, timed and arranged in such a way that markets and innovations can be reproduced and continuously renewed over time (Power and Jansson 2008).

The overarching aim of this chapter is to examine the changing role of music festivals for Swedish musicians, ranging from full-time professional and typically contracted to a record label (and thus benefitting from their services), to independent musicians that are typically non-contracted and managing their careers themselves, and occasionally having secondary jobs. In the chapter, we will identify important spaces at influential Swedish music festivals and analyze how these spaces relate to each other and how the processes taking place within these spaces are extended beyond the actual event. The chapter is structured as follows. First, a background to the changes in the music industry is presented, with a focus on the individual musician. Second, a theoretical framework involving the concepts of temporary spaces, field configuring events, and festival circuits is offered. The empirical sections identify four "spaces" in which processes of networking, reputation building, finding work opportunities, and inspiration take place. Finally, these spaces are discussed "beyond the festival," i.e., how events such as festivals, although temporary in time and space, may have long-lasting effects.

THE CHANGING MUSIC INDUSTRY

Recent changes in the music industry and the way musicians work and communicate can be examined by starting with the impacts of technological achievements on employment standards and the organization of work patterns. The paradigm shift in music technologies represented by digital recordings, peer-to-peer (P2P) file-sharing networks, and online distribution opportunities became evident in the mid to late 1990s resulting in rapidly declining album sales (Johansson and Larsson 2009; Leyshon 2009; Tschmuck 2006). In the Swedish music industry, revenues from album sales decreased from $220 million to $105 million (in USD) between 2001 and 2008 (Johansson and Larsson 2009; STIM 2009). On the other hand, in 2011 revenues from digital sales exceeded sales of physical formats in Sweden for the first time and in 2014 digital sales of music accounted for 79 percent of total sales of music (Ifpi). These developments have led to new business models where revenues are based on a broader set of income sources (Power and Jansson 2004).

The Changing Nature of Work for Musicians

In contrast to the record label-driven music economy based on record deals between labels and musicians, many musicians today face increasing responsibilities for the management of music careers (Cummins-Russell and Rantisi 2011; Frenette, this volume; Haijen, this volume; Hracs 2009, this volume; Speers, this volume). The organizational arrangement of the new and digitized music industry is manifested in short-term project-based work and an increasing pool of self-employed and freelance workers (Coulson 2012; Grabher and Ibert 2006; Hracs 2009; Watson 2012). Although major shifts in employment standards concern music agents and the music industry, they also reflect the overall changes related to post-industrialization and discussions on the individualization of risk (Beck 1992). The termination of many long-term record deals due to lower profits from album sales (Johansson and Larsson 2009) and the associated non-contractual conditions of work consequently have resulted in transfers of risk and responsibility to individual music agents (Watson 2012). In light of such changes, new features of work organization have become a widespread standard in the contemporary music industry—precarious jobs, decreasing earnings, the addition of non-creative work, increasing risk and uncertainty, irregular work, and requirements of flexibility and spatial mobility of musicians (Cummins-Russell and Rantisi 2011; Hesmondhalgh and Baker 2008; McRobbie 2002; Neff 2005). Job offers, contracts, competitiveness, and interaction spaces are increasingly internationalized, thus creating a pool of nomadic music agents traveling between different sites in order to construct sustainable career paths (McRobbie 2002). As a result of new working conditions and the associated "just-in-time" work patterns, musicians have started to become a workforce of more mobile individuals. Therefore, musicians find it necessary to reconfigure work in time and space in order to cope with increasingly fragmented work patterns, thus improving work efficiency.

Music Festivals

With the decline of traditional album sales festivals now constitute a steady stream of revenues and account for an increasingly important element in the music industry, both for individual musicians as well as for organizers, record labels, and booking agents (Wynn and Dominguez-Villegas, this volume). Music festivals now serve as hotspots for temporary agglomerations of music actors involving transfers of information and knowledge between temporarily co-located agents. These festivals also facilitate a wide array of opportunities for artistic experimentation and development with many musicians devoting more time and effort at festivals to workshop new material. The music festivals are arranged partly from their geographical location—where each country has its own network of festivals—and temporally—where each continent has its own festival season. Globally, the festival season takes place at different times of the year, resulting in an annual circuit of festivals. Popular musicians take advantage of this seasonal diversity and carefully book their festival appearances to comprise their own extended festival "season."

In recent years, the Swedish music festival industry has experienced some thorough restructuring; traditional festivals (e.g., "Hultsfred Festival" and "Peace & Love") that were developed and operated by local grassroots organizations, have been replaced by major international organizations (e.g.,

Scorpio and Live Nation) that are now running a large part of the Swedish festival circuit. Thus, due to international competition, the organizations responsible for contemporary music festivals in Sweden are increasingly more professional. On a yearly basis roughly 30 popular music festivals are hosted in Sweden, ranging from the Bråvalla festival organized by international actor Scorpio with approximately 40,000 visitors to small-scale niche festivals organized by enthusiasts attracting a few hundred spectators.

TEMPORARY SPACES AND FIELD-CONFIGURING EVENTS IN THE MUSIC FESTIVAL CIRCUIT

A recent strand of literature within the field of economic geography has emphasized the idea of temporary spaces. In this literature, temporary gatherings such as trade fairs, conferences, and conventions are said to embody some of the characteristics found in traditional and permanent clusters, such as knowledge spillover effects, face-to-face contacts, work coordination, network and symbolic capital creation, sales and economic transactions, and staff recruitment. They also help connect clusters of local firms with global projects and markets as well as constitute a platform for collaboration networks (Bathelt et al. 2004; Bathelt and Schuldt 2008; Maskell et al. 2006). Despite their temporary character, these events are often described as a highly concentrated and condensed version of the processes normally taking place in an industry over longer periods of time. Arguably, they constitute a microcosm of a given industry. Processes of creating and re-creating industry structures take place at these temporary events resulting in long-lasting effects on the actual industry (Power and Jansson 2008).

Field Configuring Events

Temporary spaces and events bring to mind another term that also discusses important and long-lasting aspects of temporary gatherings of actors and processes, namely field-configuring events (Lampel and Meyer 2008; Meyer et al. 2005). Meyer et al. define field-configuring events as: "settings where people from diverse social organizations assemble temporarily, with the conscious, collective intent to construct an organizational field" (2005, 467). In other words, these are events that may be temporary in nature but which may have implications that not only last after the event is over, but also have the power to (entirely or partially) define a question, a field, or an industry. However, although individual organizers of events may have the ambition of creating a field-configuring event, the hierarchy between different events leads to unequal power relations (Lampel and Meyer 2008). Consequently, some events have the mandate to configure a field while others play a secondary role in reproducing existing structures. Recently, academics have argued that this way of thinking may be a useful tool for studying specific industries, not least the cultural industries where value-making processes are often associated with temporary spaces and events (Anand and Jones 2008; Rüling and Strandgaard Pedersen 2010).

Circuits and Cyclical Clusters

A focus on highly localized aspects of knowledge and value creation requires perspectives that consider regional, national, and global flows. In so doing, economic geography has drawn attention to the need to systematically link explanations of localized systems of knowledge production with an increased understanding of the connections between spatially dispersed nodes, production, and markets (Bathelt et al. 2004; Dicken et al. 2001). A relational approach helps us explain and understand the dispersed spatial structures of production and consumption and stresses how these are connected through various networks of actors, commodities, or production chains (Boggs and Rantisi 2003; Dicken et al. 2001; Power and Jansson 2008).

Although the fact that trade fairs and music festivals may constitute a microcosm of an industry is an important observation, understanding how these temporary events affect processes beyond the event itself is also noteworthy; they should not be seen as singular events as they are often interconnected and arranged in almost continual global circuits (Sassen 2002; Storper 1997). Power and Jansson (2008) state that both exhibitors and visitors in the international furniture industry organize their year by preparing and following-up on their participation in these "cyclical circuits" and industry specific events. Consequently, these efforts are not secondary to their day-to-day business where products are traditionally developed.

Music Festivals and Temporary Events

Previous literature on music festivals details the economic impact of such events for the festival itself (Andersson and Getz 2009), for the cities and/or regions where they take place (Van Aalst and Melik 2012; Wynn and Dominguez-Villegas, this volume) in terms of their social and communicative aspects (Bruggeman et al. 2012; Cummings 2008), and the importance of knowledge sharing (Abfalter et al. 2012; Kloosterman 2005; O'Grady and Kill 2013). Also, previous literature on music festivals has highlighted the importance of income and building audiences at temporary gatherings for artists and musicians (Gibson 2007).

Music festivals serve as hubs of information and many musicians consider festivals crucially important for information flows (Klein 2011). Building networks of industry contacts by exploring the temporary gatherings of music festivals serves as "substituted support" to fulfil the new roles of self-employed music actors. Musicians employing these festival strategies emphasized the issue of job seeking, e.g., new projects, recordings, and additional festival gigs. The presence of a wide range of social spaces for interaction such as bars and lounges, exhibition opportunities, product comparisons, and creative input through a wide array of live shows, and the formal as well as informal business meeting areas in festival backstage areas can, when taken together, be considered similar to the flows of activities occurring at trade fairs and conferences (Kloosterman 2005; Maskell et al. 2006; Torre 2008).

RESOURCE SPACES AT MUSIC FESTIVALS

This chapter is based on a combination of three different types of methods and material in order to examine the new roles of music festivals for music work (for a more detailed account see Nilsson 2014). First, an extensive semi-structured interview study was conducted with 26 established professional and independent Swedish musicians (from various music genres) working and participating in important and influential music festivals in Sweden. The interview guide and questions were designed to examine viewpoints and experiences of changing working conditions in the music industry. In particular, the interview guide addressed the role of music festivals for coping with contemporary work patterns. Second, participant observation conducted at a total of 13 different popular music festivals in Sweden contributed to our understanding of networking behaviors and transfers of resources between music agents at various festivals. Third, "netnographies"—online ethnographical research of correspondences made between musicians and artists before and after the music festivals in virtual online communities—served as another monitoring function on how musicians prepare and organize work processes at festivals. These different types of material have been triangulated in order to provide the highest resolution view of the different processes taking place at the temporary setting of music festivals. Although the empirical material is gathered in a Swedish context, the international characteristic of the music festival industry allows for a more general interpretation of the results.

Arguably, festivals are organized as "several spaces into one space," e.g., performance stages, a wide range of lounges, and numerous spaces for interacting with fans. In the following sections we argue that temporary events such as music festivals are growing in importance for individual musicians and artists and we will describe important "spaces" and processes taking place at the temporary event, and link these spaces and processes to what happens beyond the specific event.

A Space for Network Capital

Networking is considered a proactive strategy to enhance the opportunities for success in the new music economy. In order to adapt to the spatial changes of work, music festivals serve as spaces of opportunity to meet with established colleagues, friends, and acquaintances, and new people. Musicians engage in networking create new connections by exploring such temporary locations that festivals provide. As one respondent explained:

> Festivals have always been important but their roles have changed. It's not only about live shows anymore. Because many people in the music industry have relocated to events like festivals you need to find your way in there to get in touch with those people who can help you out
>
> ("Peter," musician 2013).

As a result of the spatial relocation of the music industry, a vast majority of the participant musicians emphasized that they consciously seek out these spaces to benefit from the many potential connections and project opportunities offered in order to create sustainable career paths. Music festivals attract the important network agents of the music industry and thus contribute to strengthening the role of festivals for various artistic work practices. In order to speed-up work efficiency and, above all, to adapt to the requirements of the short-term project economy, many musicians make use of festival spaces to find new connections while simultaneously maintaining existing relations. Music agents exchange network resources, maintain network ties at the same time as building new network relations which ultimately provide for access to information, learning, and jobs. Most importantly, these temporary clusters of music agents represent job negotiation spaces in which musicians explicitly engage in job searching by making use of many co-located network agents.

A Space for Work Opportunities

As numerous actors from the music industry (and related activities) gather at festivals, they provide excellent spaces for both making contacts with actors that offer work opportunities as well as opportunities to recruit people and musicians to specific projects (e.g., studio sessions, live musicians, band members). The interviewees emphasize that music festival spaces serve as important job mediation spaces. Building networks of industry contacts by exploring the temporary gatherings of music actors in festival spaces is one way individual music actors engage in new roles for creating artist careers. Although festivals mainly serve as opportunities to market music goods in interactions (live shows) with potential consumers (fans), the major shift in how music careers are organized has resulted in increasing attention to the role festivals play in job networking. As one respondent explained:

> I don't think we really consider them to be job centers but that's actually what they are. Sure, you don't plan go to festivals thinking "I wonder which jobs there will be for me this time" but somewhere back in your

> head it's actually what you look for. [. . .] I remember when I came home from the Hultsfred festival last summer and didn't have any jobs with me [. . .] and I was both annoyed and to some extent stressed about it [. . .] I think that says it all, how festivals are our employment agencies in a way
>
> ("Peter," musician 2013).

Moreover, festival spaces also serve as recruitment spaces, not only for music projects, but also for new types of secondary jobs. Uncertain income and fierce competition for music employment makes it necessary for many musicians to supplement artistic incomes with secondary jobs. In holding multiple jobs, many musicians preferably seek out artist-related job opportunities, for instance working as music teachers, studio technicians, and record shop clerks. Also common, are the many musicians who find their income on the non-creative labor market in bars and restaurants. However, the findings from the observation demonstrate a growing number of important non-music actors in music festival spaces searching for novel combinations of partnerships to present and market their products, thus offering new types of secondary jobs. The traditional forms of music work and secondary employment in the music industry have extended into broader creative labor markets which involve a wide range of new job opportunities, in particular music-related job opportunities. As this respondent points out:

> The most exciting stuff is all the new job opportunities you can get by just being here. I have been contracted for three music commercials this summer which means four months of full-time payment
>
> ("David," musician 2013).

Many of the participating musicians emphasized the changing nature of secondary jobs and that these new opportunities are perceived to be creative and related to "artistic work." Work in bars, grocery stores, or as music teachers can be ignored in favor of more creative jobs. The expansion of the music labor market to other creative markets has involved many new job opportunities for musicians, e.g., fashion shows, computer games, and even unexpected markets such as fitness clubs. Most importantly, these new secondary jobs are considered creative by the participating musicians although the outcome of such collaborations may not contribute to traditional artist careers.

A Space for Reputational Capital

Most of the participating musicians recognize the growing importance of music festivals for gaining access to crucial network resources and job opportunities, but such features of the music profession still rest on the preconditions of reputation (see also Wynn and Dominguez-Villegas, this volume). In fact, because of increasingly fragmented work patterns and the self-employed nature of work in the new music economy, reputation capital is necessary to access the specific work spaces and network resources which support exchanges of jobs, knowledge, and connections. As a result, many musicians highlight the importance of getting access to specific festivals since just "being there" (Gertler 2003) can boost reputational aspects of artistic careers. In the process of creating artistic brands and establishing reputation based on recurrent partnerships and project cycles, specific music agents and festival locations play more important roles in individual reputation building. Indeed, for some of the musicians in this study the growing importance of certain festivals results in the adoption of a selection mechanism for choosing specific festivals to attend. Some musicians try to monitor trends in festival reputation as well as seeking out tour schedules of specific music actors in order to find the sites and partnerships that can contribute to reputational gains. As one respondent put it:

> If the major artists in my genre are booked at some festivals I have to go there as well. [. . .] If you hook up with certain bands others may notice "ah, you know the guys in [band name], do you want to join us next week," or you will get connected with other important people from the [music] industry who will get me onto this touring circus
> ("Martin," musician 2013).

It is crucial to identify specific network connections—to "know-who"—in order to find the right skills and competencies that ultimately enhance individual artist brands through reputation. Therefore, as argued by some musicians, the success or failure of music careers in the contemporary music industry is increasingly predicated on how well musicians are able to identify festivals which attract specific music actors which possess specialized talents and competencies advantageous for gaining reputation.

A Space for Inspiration

Music festival spaces can be explained as organized for performances and creative feedback. The spaces combine numerous music agents and fans, thus being crucially important contributors for inspiration and idea generation. Simply put, three different spaces of inspiration for musicians can be identified at the festival. First, festivals allow for a combination of network interactions in, for instance, the backstage areas. Additionally, opportunities for feedback and creative input from visiting other festival spaces may be gained. Most of this input is the result of spontaneous meetings as well as more formal and planned meetings. Second, festival events also involve planned visits to other artists' shows. These visits (or monitoring) may create input for a wide range of activities, from technical stage solutions via on-stage performance to songwriting. As one respondent explained:

> Festivals are forums for meetings and feedback [. . .] where you can find inspiration by checking out other bands and meet fans spontaneously
> ("Andy," musician 2013).

Finally, festivals offer a great opportunity to get inspired from meeting up with fans—those already existing and new ones usually not accessible through regular touring schedules. As a result of being present in festival environments, musicians gain creative input and a wide array of ideas, in particular inspiration on how to combine the performance of music creativity and live shows with instant feedback from fans.

BEYOND THE FESTIVAL

The processes taking place at festivals have far-reaching consequences for both the music industry in general and individual musicians in particular. Not least, it is important to examine what is happening beyond the festival, e.g., how musicians are following up contacts made at the festival and how different festivals constitute a web of important nodes in which musicians strategically plan their participation.

The Festival Circuit

Swedish musicians view festivals as an important and recurring feature of their working lives. In order to take advantage of their participation and the spaces (described above), it is important to repeatedly visit festivals. It requires that musicians invest time, both during and after the festival, to build a fan-base and an audience, and to benefit from network capital, reputation, and work opportunities. As one respondent put it:

> The huge supply of connections is the main reason why I go to festivals where I'm not performing. Prior to the festival season I usually make a festival tour plan in order to hook up with my important network connections at different festivals during the summer. It's a way to make work more efficient today
> ("Alan," musician 2013).

Music festivals are usually scheduled with strategic distance from each other, both in time and space. This enables musicians to participate in numerous festivals throughout the annual cycle. However, unlike participation in international trade fairs, as the literature suggests, it is not up to the individual musician to allocate resources to participate in festivals. Rather, this is determined by the musician's management as well as local festival organizers, international booking agents (e.g., Live Nation), or transnational festival organizers (e.g., FKP Scorpio).

Festivals should be seen as temporary clusters as well as cyclical clusters. Each festival is characterized by overlapping spaces and these spaces overlap with similar ones at other festivals in an almost cyclical calendar. In general, business contracts are not signed at festivals, rather the contacts made at festivals often lead to concrete deals. Hence, festivals are not merely singular events with fixed beginnings and end points; rather, they are interlinked within annual circuits. Consequently, preparation for and follow-up activities, including building relationships with contacts requires considerable investment throughout the year.

The Festival as Configuring-Field Event

There is a hierarchy between different music festivals that only partially depends on size, i.e., number of paying visitors. Some festivals may be strong in specific music genres and, thus, attract the attention of musicians from representative genres. What this hierarchy means for the industry in general is that it enforces some fixed points in the calendar—events that should not be ignored. For musicians performing at the most influential and well attended festivals, a lot of time is invested in preparing before a big event. For example, it is common that they develop staging, choreography, and/or alternative versions of their repertoire specifically for these shows. Even for musicians that do not work at a specific festival, it is important to simply be there to take part of the network comprised of the operators and contacts gathered as well as gain inspiration from the performances by other artists.

The top international festivals attract the most attention and provide musicians with the widest range of opportunities. However, in recent years, traditionally strong festivals, which have usually been organized by local actors, are being replaced by international actors. These are specialized festival organizers, as well as large international booking agencies that have entered the festival circuit in order to diversify their economic activities. Both types of players have the experience that comes with being large organizations managing substantial productions with the economic strength and contacts to introduce and market the same artists at several festivals. Hence, these international actors have the power to create field-configuring festivals. On the other hand, smaller and more niche festivals still have the potential of becoming field-configuring from a non-commercial perspective, e.g., in the development of a specific genre.

As a few international actors have restructured the domestic festival circuit, it has become more difficult to assess which festivals are most influential and hence important to attend. This results in rumors and buzz about specific musicians and/or actors' presence influencing the idea of which festivals are crucial to attend. Finally, most striking is that the entire continuum of the festival calendar must be considered in order to understand how it creates and recreates the hierarchies and patterns that help set the agenda for the general music industry.

THE CHANGING ROLE OF TEMPORARY EVENTS IN THE MUSIC INDUSTRY

In relation to the main themes of the book, this chapter discussed how technological development is changing the music industry in general and for individual musicians in particular. Special attention has been paid to how musicians have been forced to become more entrepreneurial and, related to this process, also more mobile in their activities and business. Permanent spaces in the traditional music industry have been partly replaced by more fragmented spaces wherein musicians are operating. This has led to a changing role of temporary events such as music festivals. Although music festivals have always been intense "gatherings" where professionals meet and exchange ideas and information, these processes are accentuated and intensified in the contemporary music industry landscape. Consequently, we argue that there has been an increased professionalization in how individual musicians utilize the "resource spaces" provided by music festivals.

Furthermore, we have identified four "spaces" (spaces for network capital, reputation capital, work opportunities, and inspiration) that exist within music festivals in which processes relevant to both the industry and individual musicians are taking place. We have also discussed how music festivals should not be analyzed as single events, but rather interpreted in relation to each other. It is particularly important to understand that festivals exist "beyond" the event itself in the sense that what is happening at the temporary event has an impact also when the festival is over. For example, musicians must follow up and develop relationships with contacts made at the festival. In addition, it is also important in a rapidly changing festival scene to clearly identify the major (and most influential) festivals that have the potential to become "field-configuring"—noting that the festival circuit is constituting the configurable element. This research illustrates that in the digital age of music production and consumption, it is important for artists and others employed in the industry to understand that the temporary spaces music festivals represent are an important "permanent" feature of the musician's life, rather than an additional business.

REFERENCES

Abfalter, Dagmar, Raphaela Stadler, and Julia Müller. "The Organization of Knowledge Sharing at the Colorado Music Festival." *International Journal of Arts Management* 14 (2012): 4–15.

Anand, N., and Brittany C. Jones. "Tournament Rituals, Category Dynamics, and Field Configuring: The Case of the Booker Prize." *Journal of Management Studies* 45, (2008): 1036–1060.

Andersson, Tommy, and Donald Getz. “Festival Ownership. Differences Between Public, Non-Profit and Private Festivals in Sweden.” *Scandinavian Journal of Hospitality and Tourism* 9 (2009): 249–265.

Bathelt, Harald, Malmberg Anders, and Peter Maskell. “Clusters and Knowledge: Local Buzz, Global Pipelines and the Process of Knowledge Creation.” *Progress in Human Geography* 28 (2004): 31–56.

Bathelt, Harald, and Nina Schuldt. “Between Luminaires and Meat Grinders: International Trade Fairs as Temporary Clusters.” *Regional Studies* 42 (2008): 853–868.

Beck, Ulrich. *Risk Society*. London: Sage, 1992.

Boggs, Jeff, and Norma Rantisi. “The ‘relational turn’ in Economic Geography.” *Journal of Economic Geography* 3 (2003): 109–116.

Bruggeman, Jeroen, Daniela Grunow, Mark A. Leanders, Ivar Vermeulen, and Jeroen Kuilman. ”Market Positioning: The Shifting Effects of Niche Overlap.” *Industrial and Corporate Change* 21 (2012): 1451–1477.

Coulson, Susan. “Collaborating in a Competitive World: Musicians’ Working Lives and Understandings of Entrepreneurship.” *Work, Employment and Society* 26 (2012): 246–261.

Cummings, Joanne. “Trade Mark Registered: Sponsorship within the Australian Indie Music Festival Scene.” *Journal of Media and Cultural Studies* 22 (2008): 675–685.

Cummins-Russell, Thomas, and Norma Rantisi. “Networks and Place in Montreal’s Independent Music Industry.” *The Canadian Geographer/La Géographe Canadien* 56 (2011): 80–97.

Dicken, Peter Philip Kelly, Kris Olds, and Henry Yeung. “Chains and Networks, Territories and Scales: Towards a Relational Framework for Analyzing the Global Economy.” *Global networks* 1 (2001): 89–112.

Gertler, Meric S. “Tacit Knowledge and the Economic Geography of Context, or the Undefinable Tacitness of Being (there).” *Journal of Economic Geography* 3 (2003): 75–99.

Gibson, Chris. “Music Festivals: Transformations in Non-Metropolitan Places, and in Creative Work.” *Media International Australia* 123 (2007): 65–81.

Grabher, Gernot, and Oliver Ibert. “Bad Company? The Ambiguity of Personal Knowledge Networks.” *Journal of Economic Geography* 6 (2006): 251–271.

Hesmondhalgh, David, and Baker Sarah. “Creative Work and Emotional Labour in the Television Industry.” *Theory, Culture and Society* 25 (2008): 97–118.

Hracs, Brian J. “Beyond Bohemia: Geographies of Everyday Creativity for Musicians in Toronto.” In *Spaces of Vernacular Creativity: Rethinking the Cultural Economy*, edited by Edensor, D. et al. London: Routledge, 2009: 75–88.

Hracs, Brian J. “A Creative Industry in Transition: The Rise of Digitally-Driven Independent Music Production.” *Growth and Change* 43 (2012): 443–462.

Ifpi, “Musikförsäljningsstatistik helåret 2014”. http://www.ifpi.se/dokument-och-statistik?cat=2014 [Accessed June 9 2015], 2015.

Johansson, Daniel, and Markus Larsson. “The Swedish Music Industry in Graphs—Economic Development Report 2000–2008.” The Royal Institute of Technology, 2009.

Klein, Robert R. “Where Music and Knowledge Meet: A Comparison of Temporary Events in Los Angeles and Columbus, Ohio.” *Area* 43 (2011): 320–326.

Kloosterman, Robert. “Come Together: An Introduction to Music and the City.” *Built Environment* 31 (2005): 181–191.

Lampel, Joseph, and Alan D. Meyer. "Guest Editors' Introduction: Field-Configuring Events as Structuring Mechanisms: How Conferences, Ceremonies, and Trade Shows Constitute New Technologies, Industries and Markets." *Journal of Management Studies* 45 (2008): 1025–1035.

Leyshon, Andrew. "The Software Slump?: Digital Music, the Democratisation of Technology, and the Decline of the Recording Studio Sector within the Musical Economy." *Environment and Planning A* 41 (2009): 1309–1331.

Maskell, Peter, Harald Bathelt, and Anders Malmberg. "Building Global Knowledge Pipelines: The Role of Temporary Clusters." *European Planning Studies* 14 (2006): 997–1013.

McRobbie, Angela. "Clubs to Companies: Notes on the Decline of the Political Culture in Speeded Up Creative Worlds." *Cultural Studies* 16 (2002): 516–531.

Menger, Pierre-Michel. "Artistic Labour Markets: Contingent Work, Excess Supply and Occupational Risk Management" In *Handbook of the Economics of Art and Culture*, edited by Ginsburgh, V.A., and D. Throsby, Amsterdam: Elsevier, 2006: 765–811.

Meyer, Alan D., Vibha Gaba, and Kenneth Colwell. "Organizing Far from Equilibrium: Nonlinear Change in Organizational Fields." *Organization Science* 16 (2005): 456–473.

Neff, Gina. "The Changing Place of Cultural Production: The Location of Social Networks in a Digital Media Industry." *Annals of the American Academy of Political and Social Science* 597 (2005): 134–152.

Nilsson, Jimi. "The Music Geographies of Artistic Practices in the Swedish Music Industry." Kulturgeografiska Instituitionen; Uppsala Universitet, 2014.

O'Grady, Alice, and Rebekka Kill. "Exploring Festival Performance as a State of Encounter." *Arts and Humanities in Higher Education* 12 (2013): 268–283.

Power, Dominic, and Johan Jansson. "The Emergence of a Post-Industrial Music Economy? Music and ICT Synergies in Stockholm, Sweden." *Geoforum* 35 (2004): 425–439.

Power, Dominic, and Johan Jansson. "Cyclical Clusters in Global Circuits: Overlapping Spaces and Furniture Industry Trade Fairs." *Economic Geography* 84 (2008): 423–448.

Rüling, Chales-Clemes, and Jesper Strandgaard Pedersen. "Film Festival Research from an Organizational Studies Perspective." *Scandinavian Journal of Management* 26 (2010): 318–323.

Sassen, Saskia. *Global Networks, Linked Cities*. New York: Routledge, 2002.

STIM. *STIM Årsredovisning 2009*. Stockholm: STIM, 2009.

Storper, Michael. *The Regional World*. New York: Guildford, 1997.

Torre, André. "On the Role Played by Temporary Geographical Proximity in Knowledge Transmission." *Regional Studies* 42 (2008): 869–889.

Tschmuck, Peter. *Creativity and Innovation in the Music Industry*. Dordrecht: Springer, 2006.

Van Aalst, Irina, and Rianne Melik. "City Festivals and Urban Development: Does Place Matter?" *European Urban and Regional Studies* 19 (2012): 195–206.

Watson, Allan. "Sociological Perspectives on the Economic Geography of Projects: The Case of Project-Based Working in the Creative Industries." *Geography Compass* 6 (2012): 617–631.

Part V

Distributing

12 Exploring the "360 Degree" Blur

Digitization, Sonic Capital, and the Strategic Orientations of Electronic Indie Labels

Hans-Joachim Bürkner

Recent waves of digitization have altered popular music production and distribution within a short period of time. Physical musical formats have experienced a tremendous economic decline, while digital formats and live performances have come to the fore (Bourreau et al. 2008; Hracs 2012; Leyshon 2009; Wynn and Dominguez-Villegas, this volume). Consequently, the focus of value creation has shifted from the physical format to the music maker and to digital distribution channels (Bockstedt et al. 2006; Leyshon et al. 2005; Mortimer et al. 2012). For those involved, the music market is less transparent than ever and the former mass market has turned into a "mass of niches" (Burkhalter 2013, 11, ref. to Anderson 2006). Market disorder makes many stakeholders abandon older production and distribution strategies, engaging instead in open-ended, trial and error activities. Independent musicians, producers, and labels in the electronic dance music (EDM) sector have been versatile explorers of the challenges and options brought about by digitization. More broadly, this shift has prompted professional and academic experts to talk about new strategic "360 degree" concepts. This means that producers, artists, labels, distributors, and other stakeholders try to control as many different aspects of value creation as possible (Tschmuck 2013). This is to "make up" for the decline in emphasis on physical format sales. Relevant activities range from local club performances, digital track production, vinyl and CD production, digital online distribution of tracks and albums to event management, booking, and the merchandizing of by-products.

Media scholars have been quick to assume that a general restructuring of markets and modes of production is taking place (Tschmuck 2013; Winter 2013a, 2013b). However, this desire to claim paradigmatic shifts might be premature, both in theoretical and empirical terms. For independent artists and labels, a 360 degree orientation might even be a poor option. Hence, it is still unclear if we are facing a transitory phase of "trial and error" activities or lasting outcomes of sustainable market strategies. As it stands, more close-up empirical observation of emerging production models and their context is necessary.

Referring to the production of EDM, this chapter undertakes a critical revision of the 360 degree assumption. It asserts that digitization does not turn the production scene completely upside down. Based on empirical evidence, it shows that the diversification of trial-and-error routines follows implicit rules created by limited sets of individual and collective orientations, preferences, and pre-set artistic or economic interests. Hence, artists, producers, and labels develop strategies that allow them to stick to their original orientations while they adapt to shifting technologies and related articulations of demand. The concept of "sonic capital" is introduced as a way of understanding how these artists, producers, and labels adapt to these changes.

THE 360 DEGREE THESIS

Over the past 15 years, the digitization of music production and distribution has massively affected music markets (see for instance Brandellero and Kloosterman, this volume). The traditional pop music market dominated by major labels and media corporations as well as independent DIY production and its relationship to music scenes has changed considerably (Bockstedt et al. 2006; Hracs 2012; Kruse 2010; Leyshon et al. 2005). While physical formats lost their former significance as items of economic value creation and generators of income, the digital production and distribution of music has expanded. Even popular music based on intense support by local scenes has been affected by the general trend towards social communication and economic value exchange via the Internet (see Virani, this volume). This has become particularly apparent in EDM where local scenes still serve as a social, economic, and symbolic backing for the work of musicians, DJs, labels, producers, and promoters, etc. (Denk and von Thülen 2012; Kühn 2011). More so than in other fields of music production, scenes acquire the function of a collective cultural intermediary (c.f., Hracs 2015), curating the generation of taste, reputation, and expertise. Meanwhile, local EDM scenes have largely expanded into the Internet, populating new distribution channels (e.g., commercial and non-commercial distribution platforms), chat forums, blogs, social media (MySpace, Facebook, etc.), or mainstream media platforms such as YouTube.

For the individual artist or label, the Internet facilitates access to global scenes and social networks (Sargent 2009), combining physical or live music production with online distribution, marketing, and reputation building. Existing constraints, caused by the need to compensate for income losses from declining sales of physical formats, could be balanced by digital formats and Internet distribution as well as revenue from live events, booking, and publishing.

Media scholars have recently included the digitization-driven proliferation of market-oriented strategies under the catchy notion of "360 degree production" (Tschmuck 2013; Winter 2013a). Early approaches to the phenomenon, operating under the notion of "360 deal," had been restricted to the analysis of major record labels and their successful attempts at extending value creation and income to collateral revenue streams such as merchandizing and publishing (Marshall 2013). Labels have sought to compensate for decreasing record sales following the MP3 revolution (Sterne 2012) and the popularity of file-sharing and free online music streams by negotiating new contracts with artists. Such contracts allow for the valorization of a range of musical activities beyond the sale of records and digital files. Indeed, this propelled popular music stars such as Robbie Williams, Madonna, and Jay-Z to higher levels of stardom than mere branding or marketing alone (Gervais et al. 2011; Marshall 2013).

Although originally referring to big enterprises in the music business, and to their specific ways of reorganizing revenues, the 360 degree idea has recently been reframed by media theorists (Tschmuck 2013, Winter 2013a) and social scientists (Wong Chi Chung 2010). Now, 360 degree orientations are expressly discussed as a feature of altered strategies developed by small stakeholders such as individual musicians, DJs, producers, and independent labels. Heterogeneous musical formats, Internet-based distribution and curation, social media communication with a focus on music, Internet fandom, and net-supported live music events seem to have created a new multiplicity of occasions for music production which appeal to agents of differing professionalism and aspirations (Arriagada and Cruz 2014; Arriagada, this volume; Johansson et al., this volume; Leyshon et al., this volume; Wynn and Dominguez-Villegas, this volume; Virani, this volume). Whereas in the "analog" age a small number of models of production and value creation prevailed—implying a clear division of labor and simple market structures—digitization seems to have created a chaotic field of infinite possibilities for virtually everyone. Former boundaries between individual activities, types of agents, and organizational forms have been blurred (Tschmuck 2013). DIY musicians and small independent labels in particular have gained wider scopes of action, for example, by having access to direct distribution via the Internet (Wong Chi Chung 2010). Essentially, 360 degree theorists assume that "anything goes" for all artists and producers now because they can conduct a number of money-making activities that they would have normally avoided in the past. Even DIY artists trying to preserve their reputation based on non-commercialism seem to have been drawn into this undertow of increasing diversification.

This new trend of imagining almost everything as potentially relevant to music production has created confusion. Former production-oriented concepts of value creation (those centered on the production of physical formats) appeared to have become less relevant once the 360 degree idea emerged. This is problematic since technological change (like digitization as well as social dynamics like the evolution of music scenes) have always contributed to the restructuring of music markets; the only difference being that musicians and fans are now faced with a plethora of resources, options, and constraints. This being said, current studies show that many stakeholders have entered a phase of trial and error, trying to find a new balance between artistic aspirations and the need to make money (Wong Chi Chung 2010). This involves a great deal of individual and collective learning. However, DIY learning is never unspecific (Lankshear and Knobel 2010; Perry 2011); there is good reason to assume that agents follow trails which have been pre-structured by their particular ambitions, qualifications, capabilities, preferences, social environments, and various experiences.

Particularly for DIY musicians, the 360 degree orientation might turn out to be a dubious option. Indeed, one observation is that the thesis generally suggests conflict-free adaptations to market change. However, the contrary may also be true: Stakeholders might struggle to survive (see also Hracs, this volume). The DIY careers of DJs are especially endangered where they often end up in precarious economic situations (Cohen and Baker 2007; Reitsamer 2011). It is still unclear how material, personal, and conceptual limitations, as well as particular challenges inherent to market niches, restrain agents from enjoying "free choice" and calculable success. Deliberately changing from one choice in the 360 degree set of options to another might not be realizable, at least not immediately, due to a lack of qualifications, knowledge, or experience. Therefore, it would be more realistic to assume that actors engage in a search for opportunities and alternatives, but that these are not as wide-ranging as the 360 degree thesis suggests.

SONIC CAPITAL AS A RESOURCE FOR COPING WITH MARKET CHANGE—AND AS A MEANS OF VALUE CREATION

The issue of adapting to rapid changes in music scenes, digital technologies, and disruptive markets is developed here against the backdrop of the concept of sonic capital. Devised as a variant of Pierre Bourdieu's category of cultural capital (Bourdieu 1984, 1986), it allows for theorizing the specific types of knowledge and strategic capacity that are necessary to mold shifting economic niches, business concepts, and distribution channels. Focusing on a social meso-level relevant to the specific economic field of independent music production, it addresses the question of how social resources are acquired by economic agents as a way of: coping with technological change, developing ideas and innovations, and using their ideas and products (Bürkner et al. 2013, 26). The notion of sonic capital particularly helps to explain the flexible reconfiguration of cultural and economic value creation emerging from strategic reorientation. It refers to the fact that in music production and consumption, cultural value creation (such as aesthetic taste or artistic reputation) combines with economic value creation (Lange and Bürkner 2010). This combination requires special qualifications, professional and social capabilities, and resources.

Sonic capital is a capacity acquired by professional agents and users/consumers by creating, modifying, distributing, and consuming musical goods.

This capacity is tied to specific types of knowledge which enable agents to influence the quality, contexts, and procedures of musical production, and consumption (Bürkner et al. 2013). In contrast to Bourdieu, the concept of sonic capital incorporates field-specific knowledge which is not universally accessible. Often it can only be acquired in particular "communities of practice" (Amin and Roberts 2008). Agents need access to practical knowledge and implicit (tacit) knowledge (Polanyi 2009). These are mainly developed by observing, copying, experimenting, and "learning by doing" (Westerlund 2006). However, while the communities of practice approach tends to exclude consumers, sonic capital largely draws upon the expert, scene-specific, knowledge of a well-informed and experienced audience. Such knowledge is also shared by artists and producers.

Of course, this is not a new phenomenon. Subcultural musical communities have worked on this basis from the beginnings of popular music. Also the recent technology-driven changes in music production have been addressed by media scholars as a result of increased producer-consumer collaboration. The concept of the "prosumer," as established by Tschmuck (2013) and Winter (2013a, 2013b), includes Internet communication between artists and consumers. Hence, the process of musical creation and production may be influenced by the preferences and tastes prevalent among an audience or scene. Having created categorical ambivalence, the term "prosumer" has also been applied to the phenomenon of home recording and the subsequent release of amateur music via the Internet (many of them specialized in EDM). Home recording obviously inspires the passive consumer to become a producer himself (Cole 2011; Winter 2013a).

What makes sonic capital a focused analytical category beyond the rough idea of prosuming or professional learning-by-doing, is its transformative capacity. Sonic capital can be converted into other types of capital, especially social, cultural, economic, and symbolic capital (Bürkner et al. 2013). Artists and producers build professional and social networks, contribute to scenes and milieus, and acquire music-related knowledge. They shape symbols of membership to scenes, engage in cultural and economic value creation, generate income, and accumulate a surplus of recognition and prestige which enables them to influence their field of interest. They also employ habitus formation as a means of positioning themselves and facilitating the conversion of capital types.

Sonic capital transcends Bourdieu's concept by explicitly referring to the inherently subcultural nature of economic niches and scenes. Leading protagonists, especially in the field of EDM, often develop a pronounced anti-commercial and anti-establishment (DIY) habitus which refers back to the origins of EDM scenes. This was when they were still part of local scenes and sometimes obscure youth underground cultures (see Denk and von Thülen 2011). There is a specific way to demonstrate coolness and a non-conformist lifestyle which translates into controversial attitudes towards production and economic success—between strict anti-commercialism and hybrid variations of "coolness and success" (Reitsamer 2011). Value creation thus can become subordinated to habitus and scene-conforming self-representation.

It can be said that in all its conversions and associations, sonic capital remains clearly visible as a distinct type of capital (Bürkner et al. 2013). Because the field of music production triggers specific activities (e.g., musical invention), socialities, contexts of action, and institutions, the emerging conversions are not universal—they arise in context-specific representations and channeled manifestations. Particularly when meeting the challenges of digitization, sonic capital may work as a capacity which enables and guides the search for accessible solutions.

ELECTRONIC LABELS AND THEIR STRATEGIES: TRIAL AND ERROR IN THE CITY OF BERLIN

Empirical Approach and Sampling

The case has been selected from an empirical database made up of qualitative interviews with stakeholders of EDM production conducted in the city of Berlin during the summer of 2012. Having served as a global center of techno and house production from the 1980s onwards, the city has remained relevant in spite of the stylistic and generational evolution of the genre (Bader and Scharenberg 2010; van Heur 2010). EDM is mainly created in and around local techno clubs which serve as urban nodal points of consumer scenes and networks of artists/producers (Lange and Bürkner 2010). Following a clear locational pattern, many clubs are embedded in neighborhoods such as Neukölln, Kreuzberg, or Friedrichshain. These locales contain scene-specific infrastructures such as bars, cafés, bookshops, record stores, informal concert venues, recording studios, label offices, etc. (Heinen 2013). This socio-economic-spatial structure has been addressed as a specific assemblage of inner-city music clusters (van Heur 2009). Club tourism, gentrification, and the popularization of techno has altered the strategic orientation of many clubs from subcultural exclusiveness of the DIY type to semi-commercial globalized openness (Bader and Scharenberg 2010). However, many of them have retained their original aspiration to appear as exclusive trendsetters and breeding grounds for DJs.

One particular aspect of building up an exclusive reputation has been a close affiliation of clubs to prestigious independent house and techno labels, often run by resident DJs or scene-bound producers. Such linkages have often been symbolized by spatial proximity: label offices or important record shops are located near the club or at least within the same neighborhood.

The interview sample consists of local stakeholders engaged in such scene-based and neighborhood-related production of EDM. Nine interviews were conducted with label managers, producers, and DJs. Respondents range from managers of prestigious, globally renowned, labels, operating on the basis of fixed organizational models, to less formalized types of organization. They include: personal labels run by individual DJs for reasons of visibility and accountability, independent micro-net labels specializing in stylistic niche production (Galuszka 2012; Weijters et al. 2014), and individual performers trying to address economic niches by developing small down-to-earth live performances as well as producing digital tracks. The sample represents a number of typical strategic orientations in the field.

Content analysis was applied to identify the main perspectives that stakeholders have developed against the backdrop of persistent market turmoil and oscillating digital-analog reference making. It considered the uncertainties connected to trial and error routines as well as production concepts that have been developed under these specific conditions. For the purposes of gaining a closer insight into these trial and error strategies, including their effects on production models, I will focus on an insightful single case. It assembles a number of common activities developed by many small scene-based labels combining mainstream DJing and performing as mentioned above (see Bürkner 2013).

The Case of Independent Small Label Production Combined with DJing

Frankie M-Cult (pseudonym given by the author) is a DJ and producer of digital tracks who runs a small house label. Together with a partner he also performs live shows in local techno and house clubs. Their focus is on analog electronic sound production which alternates with DJ sets. They also share a small recording studio in the trendy inner-city neighborhood of Kreuzberg, Berlin, which they occasionally let to other DJs and producers. Their response to digitization is twofold: on the one hand, they try to stick to analog sound conventions and track production routines which end up in vinyl pressings used for live mixes. On the other hand, they pre-devise parts of their tracks digitally (i.e., on PC/notebook equipment) and mix them via digital sequencer software (e.g., Ableton Live) to the sounds they produce with traditional analog sound generators (synthesizers, drum machines, sequencers).

In recent years Frankie has been experimenting with a number of self-owned, short-lived labels which specialized in different techno sub-styles, most of them operating without any considerable economic success. The present label is performing better. It serves a dual purpose: It follows a non-commercial rationale by directly taking up Frankie's original tracks which he wants to publish without any aesthetic compromise. Essentially, he wants to capture the energy of his live shows on a digital track which is then released by the label unencumbered—thereby preserving its integrity and his ethos. This is the logic by which Frankie defines the center of all his artistic ambitions and activities. Additionally, the label is oriented more towards cultural value creation than commercial success. It showcases a number of external artists (DJs) who want to gain visibility and a better standing in the live event business. The main aim is to build the artists' reputation so that they would be able to acquire better paying club jobs and climb up the "DJ ladder of prestige." This strategy is advantageous for the label too—by gradually becoming able to contract renowned DJs, the label gets a better reputation within the scene. This function of serving as a stirrup for club gigs, live events, and other purposes is dominant; commercial sales of tracks and physical formats are not given much attention because cash flows are usually very low.

At first sight, this individual strategy reflects a general structural trend in scene-based EDM (Kühn 2011). Economic value creation and exchange do not focus on record stores—whether physical or online—anymore. Their importance has been reclassified somewhere between clubs, a variety of low-cost download portals, various live events (particularly festivals), the booking of DJs and performers, and the merchandizing of by-products, etc. (Lange and Bürkner 2010, 2013). Track production has mutated from being an end in itself to a means. This is exemplified by DJs who use tracks published by prestigious labels as door-openers and stepping stones to well-paid live jobs—knowing full well that their value in terms of record sales is continually declining (Bürkner 2013).

However, Frankie did not copy his strategy from overtly commercial models. He found out the exact positioning of the label by experimenting, i.e., by trying out a number of promising label concepts which allowed him to keep up his original aesthetic aspirations. From the beginning, the commercial side has been marginal. Therefore, the present label's orientation and internal organization does not follow a fixed business plan. Its dual structure has developed in a more or less contingent way. In its evolution, musical ambition and indebtedness to a local scene played the most important structuring role. These ambitions, roughly based on a DIY attitude towards music making, were developed by Frankie during his former career as an independent rock musician—long before he entered the techno/house scene.

What appears to be contingent at first sight, and an outcome of unsystematic trial and error, reveals a distinct internal logic as soon as it is observed from the perspective of the very process of track production. To Frankie, the individual track is the basic point of reference for all corollary or follow-up activities. These activities include 'analog' as well as 'virtualized' elements. These comprise pieces of work that have been acquired by digital sound processing as well as using the Internet for production, distribution, and scene-based consumer feedback. Figure 12.1 gives an overview of the analogous/analog and virtualized (digital) elements involved.

Reading the figure from left to right, a sequential impression of the production of tracks—and the items involved—can be gained. The analog side of track production and distribution (in the lower half of the scheme)

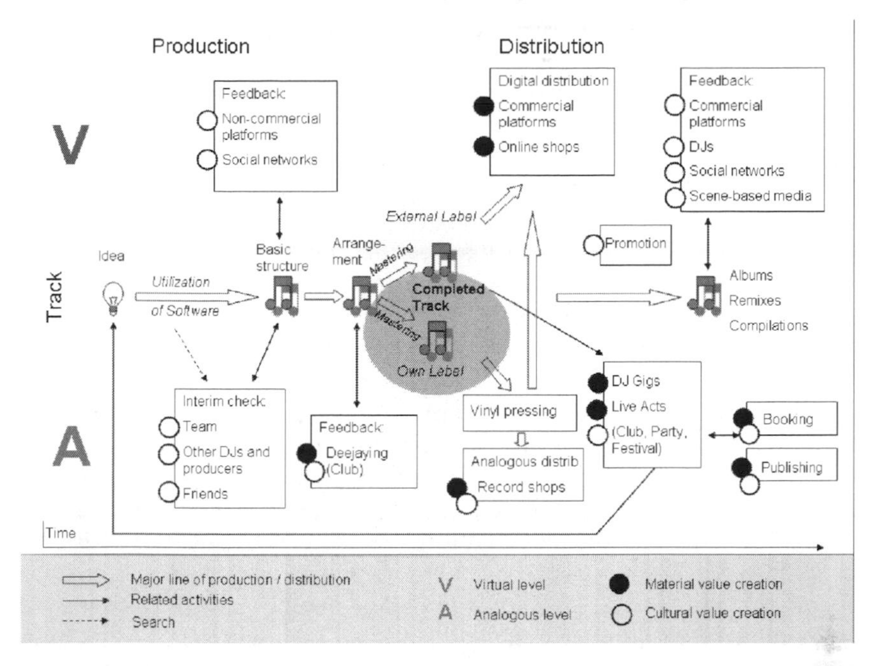

Figure 12.1 Track production: small label combined with mainstream DJing. Source: Bürkner (2013, 80). By permission of transcript Verlag 2013.

seems to be fixed in that it contains a lot of well-known routines such as DJing in the club for the purpose of developing new ideas, or getting immediate (mostly non-verbal) feedback. There is also a strong clue to vinyl production for reasons of ensuring taste and sound quality, the tracks on vinyl being one of the most important sources of live mixing in the club performance.

The virtualized side is only occasionally touched by the process of digital track production itself; during production hardly any feedback from Internet-based social networks or non-commercial platforms is taken in to advance production. Digitization, however, comes in strongly as soon as distribution begins. From this moment on, non-commercial as well as commercial platforms are supplied with digital file materials. Also, feedback from commercial platforms (via DJ download charts) or occasional social network media and specialized chat forums, is recognized to a larger extent. Nevertheless, in many productions this does not substantially influence follow-up projects or the invention of new tracks.

Sonic Capital in Track Production

In this empirical case, sonic capital has been accumulated according to routines of learning by doing, and by selective conversions of social capital.

What is evident is that the utilization of social capital has only partially been influenced by reactions to the digital challenge.

In contrast, social capital suitable for being converted into sonic capital is mainly offered by the local scene. Conversion happens in the analog making of music, i.e., while working in the club or at party events. Therefore, the DJs/label managers try to keep as close to the scene as possible. It is the intensity of face-to-face experience and the excitement of the crowd during a live performance which give primary feedback about the quality of a track.

High-valued tracks contribute to the reputation of the performers and DJs, to the reputation of the club, and to the reputation of the label which documents such music. This mutual escalation of positive valuations is at the core of cultural value creation in this specific field (see also: Kühn 2011; Lange and Bürkner 2010). At the same time, it propels the quest for good solutions when making and publishing music.

Their continual activities as DJs and performers help to refine their artistic skills and develop implicit knowledge about the aesthetic rules of mixing. They also put digital track production (which mostly accompanies DJing) into perspective. Not every pre-established track which goes into a mix catches the dancers. Paradoxically, it is often the DJ's favorite track or critic's choice which does not excite the crowd. This dialectic of digital track production and analog performance is not simply an outcome of "prosuming" (Cole 2011). Rather, it is a vital source of new skills and updated professional knowledge. They are field-specific in the sense that they cannot be generated outside of situational social and economic conditions, implying much intuition and tacit knowledge. At the same time they guide the protagonist's way through the variety of options when placing his "products."

It is also obvious that Frankie's former professional knowledge, which he acquired as a rock musician, still influences his present approach to electronic music production. This adds something special to the way he accumulates sonic capital. It is his natural tendency to prefer the live production of music in front of an audience which strongly influences the design of individual tracks, as well as the orientation of the label. Similar to a band musician, he shares a high level of tacit knowledge with his partner when performing live. They also preserve this intimate mutual understanding when they work together on a track in the studio. There is an inherent logic of creativity involved which has been formed by personal experience, shared by congenial partners, backed up by a co-evolving scene, and documented by making use of available technical tools. Trial and error strategies based on such sonic capital follow a personalized, contingent pathway of development. Although they contain elements of "muddling through," the individual parts blend into a discernible strategy in the end. This is mostly through repeating satisfying or successful procedures and removing unsuccessful or irrelevant ones, thereby habitualizing the application of available sonic capital in the very process of production.

Outside the live set, taste generation and cultural value formation usually happen within a network of friends and other artists/producers. It also takes place in social hubs such as "analog" record stores in the neighborhood or during occasional talks with clubgoers and other scene members. It is also in the larger surroundings of live activities that Frankie identifies a personal learning process. He has learned to read indications of ongoing cultural value creation from the feedback he receives from journalists and DJs. The big names in the musical evaluation business contribute much to further reputation building and taste formation, which often has a positive effect on economic value creation. In particular, vinyl sales of a track tend to go up after influential experts have given their opinion. Feedback from digital platform users also charges published tracks with cultural value. However, for Frankie there often is no visible material effect of such opinion-giving due to low returns from digital online sales.

Within the specific arrangement of activities established by Frankie, there is a strong conservative element which restricts his choice of trial-and-error options. This becomes evident as soon as he reflects on his vinyl sales. Although Frankie has recently been unable to sell sufficient numbers of records, this format is still the bedrock of his artistic and professional ambitions. It contributes to the image of the label, the preservation of an insider culture and the co-evolution of a local scene. To him it appears as if the general shift towards digital track production and distribution has been enforced by the conditions of the big players of the market, while most stakeholders would prefer something different. He reports cases of "re-analogization," citing owners of digital labels who returned to exclusive vinyl production after some time because in this way they were better able to shape interesting sub-genres and stylistic niches. He would still agree to the old in-scene proposition that analog techno tracks can only develop their full sonic and cultural potential on vinyl records. Building on this conviction, he would not engage in too many new activities which might distract him from the focus on vinyl production inherited from his professional past.

Frankie has some hopes of a limited return to economic value creation through a vinyl revival. However, it is clear that the focus of income generation will remain on the club gigs and live acts that he and his partner realize on the basis of associated track production, label publishing, and other sources of reputation building. Additionally, Frankie employs a number of other potential sources of economic value creation which periodically enhance the scope of his activities. Most of them are social resources converted into contextualized sonic capital:

- Involvement in other labels' compilations and remixes, mostly organized by good friends in the local production scene. This has turned out to be favorable both in reputational and economic respects.

- Occasional engagement in the organization of parties and events. This proved to be too time and labor consuming to expand it to a regular activity; it also distracted Frankie too much from his original interest in music making. The necessary conversion of social capital into sonic capital could not be achieved.
- Partial engagement in booking DJs for clubs and live performances. While this activity created new social capital by networking and trust building, both sonic capital and social capital could not be successfully converted into economic capital. This was because booking activities generated too few financial returns when counted against working hours and time lost for Frankie's own musical activities.

Most of the activities and methods of economic value creation Frankie tried did not conform to his original artistic aspirations and his habitus as a creative performer. Consequently, he reduced them to a minimum or gave them up completely. Only the expanding collaboration with other labels and producers on special projects, such as compilations or (analog and digital) albums, proved to be rewarding, in cultural, social, and economic terms. Trial and error, thus, only partially enhanced the scope of his activities. However, trying to find a way to combine digital and analog track production and take benefits from digital distribution (for the purpose of increasing reputation and creating chances to be booked as a performer) definitely improved his position on the market.

CONCLUSION: "TRIAL AND ERROR" DOES NOT INEVITABLY LEAD INTO 360 DEGREE MODELS

The case study interpreted above clearly displays a number of basic characteristics of the strategic workings of sonic capital. These are:

- A strong orientation of stakeholders towards local scenes and related social capital building.
- Visible efforts to enhance access to club performances, festivals, and other live events.
- A trend towards preserving DIY attitudes, convictions, and routines–making them a filter of the selection of digitized options.
- Selective adaptation of digital formats and channels of distribution.
- Digital track production as a way to elevate one's reputation and acquire better paid live jobs.

This case study reveals the characteristic trial and error logic present in altered independent label strategies after the digital revolution. It re-frames the question of how inevitable the 360 degree assumption really is. In fact, although the constraints set by digitization and the search for additional or alternative occasions of value creation kept him busy, Frankie did not develop a full 360 degree concept. Instead he focused on a few well-considered activities after a period of trial and error. They were easy to develop because he acquired the necessary sonic capital via intensified accumulation and conversion of available social capital. It is part of a pathway of personal and organizational development. It is based on scene-compliant cultural value creation and a corresponding artistic DIY philosophy. Frankie simply kept following his original "analog" orientations and made the digital options he acquired conform to them. DJing and live performing served as the primary drivers of reorientation, and also as testing areas of the changes he made.

Instead of a general "anything goes" attitude that is suggested by the 360 degree idea, focused pathways of strategic development have to be assumed—at least for small independent labels. Since in the field of EDM production it is the local scenes of producers and consumers which provide important social capital, stakeholders conceive their individual pathways in a scene-compatible way. While major labels apply a strict economic logic of redirecting revenue flows—largely neglecting the social aspects of music production (Marshall 2013)—independent scene-based labels, artists, and producers have to mobilize social capital in order to update their sonic capital and take benefits from digital change. Only through the conversion of social into sonic capital can emerging strategies contribute to innovative niches, linking well-established scenes to new modes of marketing and distribution.

REFERENCES

Amin, Ash, and Joanne Roberts. "Knowing in Action: Beyond Communities of Practice." *Research Policy* 37, no. 2 (2008): 353–369.

Anderson, Chris. *The Long Tail: Why the Future of Business Is Selling Less of More.* New York: Hyperion, 2006.

Arriagada, Arturo, and Victor Cruz. "Music Fans as Mediators in the Age of Digital Reproduction." In *The Ashgate Research Companion to Fan Cultures*, edited by Duit, L., K. Zwaan, and S. Reijnders, 149–162. Farnham, Surrey, and Burlington, VT: Ashgate, 2014.

Bader, Ingo, and Albert Scharenberg. "The Sound of Berlin: Subculture and the Global Music Industry." *International Journal of Urban and Regional Research* 34, no. 1 (2010): 76–91.

Bockstedt, Jesse C., Robert J. Kauffman, and Frederick J. Riggins. "The Move to Artist-Led On-Line Music Distribution: A Theory-Based Assessment and Prospects for Structural Changes in the Digital Music Market." *International Journal of Electronic Commerce* 10, no. 3 (2006): 7–38.

Bourdieu, Pierre. *Distinction: A Social Critique of the Judgement of Taste.* Cambridge, MA: Harvard University Press, 1984.

Bourdieu, Pierre. "The Forms of Capital." In *Handbook of Theory and Research for the Sociology of Education*, edited by Richardson, J.G., 241–258. New York: Greenwood Press, 1986.

Bourreau, Marc, Gerhard Gensch, and Francois Moreau. "The Digitization of the Recorded Music Industry: Impact on Business Models and Scenarios of Evolution." Working Papers in Economics and Social Sciences ESS-08-01. Paris: Telecom Paris, 2008. http://papers.ssrn.com/sol3/Delivery.cfm/SSRN_ID1092138_code362009.pdf?abstractid=1092138&mirid=3

Burkhalter, Thomas. *Local Music Scenes and Globalization: Transnational Platforms in Beirut*. Routledge studies in Ethnomusicology 3. New York and Milton Park: Routledge, 2013.

Bürkner, Hans-Joachim. "Trackproduktion als Trial and error? Wertschöpfungsvarianten in der elektronischen Clubmusikproduktion zwischen Digitalisierung, Internet und lokalen Szenen (Track Production as Trial and Error? Variants of Value Creation in Electronic Club Music Production Between Ditialization, Internet and Local Scenes)." In *Akustisches Kapital: Wertschöpfung in der Musikwirtschaft (Sonic Capital: Value Creation in the Music Industry)*, edited by Lange, B., H.J. Bürkner, and E. Schüßler, 45–98. Bielefeld: transcript, 2013.

Bürkner, Hans-Joachim, Bastian Lange, and Elke Schüßler. "Akustisches Kapital: Perspektiven auf veränderte Wertschöpfungskonfigurationen in der Musikwirtschaft (Sonic Capital: Perspectives on Changed Configuration of Value Creation in the Music Industries)." In *Akustisches Kapital: Wertschöpfung in der Musikwirtschaft (Sonic Capital: Value Creation in the Music Industry)*, edited by Lange, B., H.J. Bürkner, and E. Schüßler, 9–41. Bielefeld: transcript, 2013.

Cohen, Bruce M.Z., and Sarah Baker. "DJ Pathways: Becoming a DJ in Adelaide and London." *Altitude* 8 (2007). http://thealtitudejournal.files.wordpress.com/2008/07/4_cohenbaker_final_completeep.pdf

Cole, Steven J. "The Prosumer and the Project Studio: The Battle for Distinction in the Field of Music Recording." *Sociology* 45, no. 3 (2011): 447–463.

Denk, Felix, and Sven von Thülen. *Der Klang der Familie: Berlin, Techno und die Wende (The Sound of the Family: Berlin, Techno and the Fall of the Wall)*. 2nd ed. Berlin: Suhrkamp, 2012.

Galuszka, Patryk. "The Rise of the Nonprofit Popular Music Sector: The Case of Netlabels." In *Music, Business and Law: Essays on Contemporary Trends in the Music Industry*, edited by Kärjä, A.V., L. Marshall, and J. Brusila, 65–90. IIPC Publication Series 5. Helsinki: IASPM Norden, 2012. Available http://iipc.utu.fi/mbl/galuszka.pdf

Gervais, Daniel J., Kent M. Markus, and Lauren E. Gilmore. "The Rise of 360 Deals in the Music Industry." *Landslide* 3, no. 4 (2011): 1–6.

Heinen, Christina. *"Tief in Neukölln": Soundkulturen zwischen Improvisation und Gentrifizierung in einem Berliner Bezirk (Deep in Neukölln: Sound Cultures in a Neighbourhood of Berlin Between Improvisation and Gentrification)*. Bielefeld: transcript, 2013.

Hracs, Brian J. "A Creative Industry in Transition: The Rise of Digitally Driven Independent Music Production." *Growth and Change* 43, no. 3 (2012): 442–461.

Hracs, Brian J. "Cultural Intermediaries in the Digital Age: The Case of Independent Musicians and Managers in Toronto." *Regional Studies* 49, no. 3 (2015): 461–475.

Kruse, Holly. "Local Identity and Independent Music Scenes, Online and Off." *Popular Music and Society* 33, no. 5 (2010): 625–639.

Kühn, Jan-Michael. "Arbeiten in der Berliner Techno-Szene: Skizze der Theorie einer Szenewirtschaft elektronischer Tanzmusik (Working in Berlin's Techno

Scene: Draft Theory of the Scene Economy of Electronic Dance Music)." *Journal der Jugendkulturen*, no. 17 (2011): 52–59.

Lange, Bastian, and Hans-Joachim Bürkner. "Wertschöpfung in der Kreativwirtschaft: Der Fall der elektronischen Klubmusik (Value Creation in the Creative Industries: The Case of Electronic Club Music)." *Zeitschrift für Wirtschaftsgeographie* 54, no. 1 (2010): 46–68.

Lange, Bastian, and Hans-Joachim Bürkner. "Value Creation in Scene-based Music Production: The Case of Electronic Club Music in Germany." *Economic Geography* 89, no. 2 (2013): 149–169.

Lankshear, Colin, and Michel Knobel. "DIY Media: A Contextual Background and Some Contemporary Themes." In *DIY Media: Creating, Sharing and Learning with New Technologies*, edited by Knobel, M., and C. Lankshear, 1–26. Routledge Studies in Ethnomusicology 44. New York: Peter Lang, 2010.

Leyshon, Andrew. "The Software Slump? Digital Music, the Democratisation of Technology, and the Decline of the Recording Studio Sector within the Musical Economy." *Environment and Planning A* 41, no. 6 (2009): 1309–1331.

Leyshon, Andrew, Peter Webb, Shaun French, Nigel Thrift, and Louise Crewe. "On the Reproduction of the Musical Economy After the Internet." *Media, Culture and Society* 27, no. 2 (2005): 177–209.

Marshall, Lee. "The 360 Deal and the 'new' Music Industry." *European Journal of Cultural Studies* 16, no. 1 (2013): 77–99.

Mortimer, Julie H., Chris Nosko, and Alan Sorensen. "Supply Responses to Digital Distribution: Recorded Music and Live Performances." *Information Economics and Policy* 24 (2012): 3–14.

Perry, Shannon A.B. "This Is How We Do: Living and Learning in an Appalachian Experimental Music Scene." Appalachian State University, 2011. http://libres.uncg.edu/ir/asu/f/perry,%20shannon_2011_thesis.pdf

Polanyi, Michael. *The Tacit Dimension*. Reprint. Chicago and London: University of Chicago Press, 2009.

Reitsamer, Rosa. "The DIY Careers of Techno and Drum 'n' Bass DJs in Vienna." *Dancecult: Journal of Electronic Dance Music Culture* 3, no. 1 (2011): 29–43.

Sargent, Carey. "Local Musicians Building Global Audiences." *Information, Communication and Society* 12, no. 4 (2009): 469–487.

Sterne, Jonathan. *MP3: The Meaning of a Format*. Durham: Duke University Press, 2012.

Tschmuck, Peter. "Das 360°-Musikschaffen im Wertschöpfungsnetzwerk der musikindustrie (360 Degree Music Creation in the Music Industry's Network of Value Creation)." In *Akustisches Kapital: Wertschöpfung in der Musikwirtschaft (Sonic Capital: Value Creation in the Music Industry)*, edited by Lange B., H.J. Bürkner, and E. Schüßler, 285–315. Bielefeld: transcript, 2013.

van Heur, Bas. "The Clustering of Creative Networks: Between Myth and Reality." *Urban Studies* 46, no. 8 (2009): 1531–1552.

van Heur, Bas. *Creative Networks and the City: Towards a Cultural Politic Economy of Aesthetic Production*. Bielefeld: transcript, 2010.

Weijters, Bert, Frank Goedertier, and Sofie Verstreken. "Online Music Consumption in Today's Technological Context: Putting the Influence of Ethics in Perspective." *Journal of Business Ethics* 124, no. 4 (2014): 537–550.

Westerlund, H. "Garage Rock Bands: A Future Model for Developing Musical Expertise?" *International Journal of Music Education* 24, no. 2 (2006): 119–125.

Winter, Carsten. "Die Entwicklung der Medien als 'Ursachen' und als 'Wesen' musikbezogener Wertschöpfung (The Development of Media as 'Cause' and 'Nature' of Music-related Value Creation)." In *Akustisches Kapital: Wertschöpfung in der Musikwirtschaft (Sonic Capital: Value Creation in the Music Industry)*, edited by Lange, B., H.J. Bürkner, and E. Schüßler, 321–347. Bielefeld: transcript, 2013a.

Winter, Carsten. "Media Development and Convergence in the Music Industry." In *Media and Convergence Management*, edited by Diehl, S., and M. Karmasin, 261–281. Berlin, Heidelberg: Springer, 2013b.

Wong Chi Chung, Elvin. "The Working of Pop Music Culture in the Age of Digital Reproduction." PhD Thesis, University of Hongkong, 2010.http://hub.hku.hk/bitstream/10722/61019/3/FullText.pdf?accept=1

13 More Than Just Bytes?

Responses to Digitization in the Paris Cluster of World Music Production

Amanda Brandellero and Robert C. Kloosterman

"World music" is a controversial expression which, since its popularization in the 1980s, has been used to refer to the variety of the world's music cultures (*Encyclopædia Britannica Online*, 2016) and has ranged in its focus from non-Western traditions to the marketing of "danceable ethnicity and exotic alterity" (Feld 2000, 151; Guilbault 2006). Thus, far from constituting a uniform "music genre," world music encompasses a variety of musical styles and traditions, from flamenco to fado, as a glance at *Billboard*'s World Music charts will show (see also Taylor 1997). Historically, Paris has positioned itself as an important cluster of world music production and consumption, with a particular focus on the music of Francophone North and West Africa (Brandellero and Pfeffer 2011). Paris-based record labels were instrumental in broadening the focus of world music, "bridging the gap between immigrant and indigenous European markets" (*Encyclopædia Britannica Online*, 2016). Like almost everyone else in the music industry (Leyshon et al. 2005), makers of world music are now faced with technological changes, more specifically the impacts of digitization. These changes have, in principle, enlarged the market for music by coming up with new easily reproducible and cheap (digital) formats and related audio gadgets. Moreover, they have lowered barriers of entry for aspiring music makers by decreasing the costs of music production (cheaper musical instruments and recording equipment) and those of distribution through the Internet (see Arditi, this volume; Haijen, this volume; Watson, this volume).

However, the impact of the Internet and new technologies on locally concentrated networked production systems or clusters has been interpreted in various ways (see also Virani, this volume). While some argue that it helps primarily to reinforce the local networks (Hauge and Hracs 2010), others argue instead that it strengthens global connections (van Heur 2009). In world music specifically, the effect of the digital revolution on production has been downplayed, because of the costs and unequal distribution of technologies in the world, which means that music production, distribution, and exchange is concentrated among the wealthiest sections of society (Manuel 2013).

This chapter explores the impact of digitization on the makers of world music within the Paris cluster. It considers how actors within the Paris cluster of world music production and consumption respond to the arrival of digital formats and Internet distribution and the ways in which digitization affects the circulation of world music. The chapter begins by discussing the collaborative and networked nature of production in the music industry. After unpacking the structure of the Paris world music art world, as a complex and multi-levelled scene, the chapter concludes by presenting the broader implications of our findings with respect to the relationship between types of art worlds and digitization. Based on in-depth interviews with key actors in the field, we explore how some actors within that cluster perceive digitization as helping to provide access to larger markets (and perhaps higher profits), while others fear the erosion of the layered experience world music gives, as a portal to other cultures and traditions.

METHODOLOGY

We conceptualize the Paris cluster of world music not just as an economic geographic entity but also as an "art world," a socio-spatial configuration encompassing "the network of people whose cooperative activity, organized via their joint knowledge of conventional means of doing things" which tends to generate, share and reproduce certain aesthetic views (Becker 1984, x). Taking this approach, we reveal a complex ecology of actors comprising record labels, stages, dedicated media, and musicians within the cluster (Brandellero 2011). Producers of world music are conceptualized as a particular type of "ethnic entrepreneur," who cater to specific markets with each of these segments requiring a distinct set of resources, aesthetic strategies, and social embeddedness (Basu and Werbner 2001; Kloosterman 2010). This horizontal differentiation across market segments based on aesthetic aspects implies that there are distinct art worlds within one cluster of cultural production. In this chapter, we argue that understanding the internal structure of the Paris world music cluster and its distinct art worlds is crucial to grasping the differential challenges of and responses to digitization therein.

Our research builds on 33 in-depth interviews conducted in 2007 with key actors in the field including record label managers, venue programmers, record shops, journalists, and musicians. This was a time when the city of Paris, having identified the world music cluster as a priority cultural sector, set up and funded a project to help businesses in the field make the transition to digitization. It was, hence, a time of reflexivity and questioning about the nature and direction of the cluster, and an opportunity to grasp the challenges and opportunities raised by digitization (Brandellero and Calenge 2008). Respondents were identified through the French world music business directory Planètes Musiques (CIMT 2007), and interviews were supplemented with ethnographic participant observation. In order to respect the privacy of these individuals, all interviews have been anonymized in the text.

THE NETWORKED NATURE OF THE MUSIC INDUSTRY

Given the oversupply of musicians, making money by making music is anything but given and only a few see their music actually turned into a commodity sold on a market or, in other words, commodified. Even then, making money and earning a living is difficult as markets for cultural products are typically near saturation point, unpredictable, and highly volatile (Caves 2000). Like many other cultural industries which feature uncertainty and market volatility, the typical organizational format of the music industry is vertically disintegrated, although spatially clustered (Scott 2000, 2004, 2012). The endemic risk is spread among a number of small firms through vertical disintegration, while spatial clustering generates agglomeration economies through proximity, allowing lower transaction costs between different parts of the production network. In addition, spatial clustering fosters the emergence of both a specialized labor pool and a dedicated infrastructure creating external economies of scale. These clusters also function as spaces of socialization and habituation for producers and consumers in which "common points of reference" (Scott 2000, 31) or shared frameworks of aesthetic interpretation are generated.

Recent work on the music industry provides a useful typology of the vertically disintegrated stages of the production of music. Leyshon et al. (2005) define four stages consisting of distinctive, yet overlapping networks of the production process within the music industry from its conception to its access by consumers. These networks represent stages through which musical creativity flow and eventually become commodified and sold on markets. The network approach suggested by Leyshon and colleagues highlights the varying combinations of actors, institutions, and places intervening in the translation of music from creative impulse to products exchanged in markets, characteristic of the collaborative nature of art worlds.

The production of music thus occurs through the interaction of multiple inputs, institutional set-ups, actors, and localized geographies active within creative fields (Power and Hallencreutz 2002; Scott 1999). Moreover, these networks are spatially embedded and crystallized in specific locations, such as recording studios (Watson et al. 2009, this volume) or wider urban environments (Bürkner, this volume; Haijen, this volume; Hracs, this volume; Seman 2010; Virani, this volume). The boundaries between professionals and amateurs are fluid and changing (Hracs et al. 2011). The dedicated infrastructure may comprise physical components such as venues, record shops, and recording studios, but also includes key actors and intermediaries such as gatekeepers, tastemakers, and critics (Hracs et al. 2011).

An essential part of such a vertically disintegrated, localized, and embedded music production complex is the filtering mechanism. To deal with the almost merciless state of uncertainty, cultural industries had to develop mechanisms to pick potential successes among the endemic oversupply of cultural products and combat the "nobody knows" property or the inability to predict the consumers' appraisal of the quality of a product (Caves 2000). According to Blanning (2008, 227), "[o]f the great hordes of aspirants, very few ever find their way into the recording studio, let alone to the charts, but so great are the material rewards and so glamorous is the lifestyle awaiting those who succeed that there has never been a shortage of people trying." As music, like other products in the cultural industries, tends to be taste-driven (Currid 2007), the selection processes that call into question the aesthetic qualities of the music and the standards against which judgement is passed, are part of wider "regimes of value" (Appadurai 1994). As Appadurai notes, the value coherence may change depending on the commodity and the social arenas in which it is transiting (Ibid.). The creation of aesthetic systems can be an "industry in its own right," developed and maintained by specialized professionals such as critics (Becker 1984,131–132; Van Rees 1987). Every cluster of cultural production, accordingly, has to develop aesthetic systems to assign value, select winners and losers, and suggest taste hierarchies to reduce uncertainty among its producers (see also Bürkner, this volume). This gives rise to a vertical differentiation based on socially constructed notions of worth (Yogev 2010), but we also can observe a horizontal differentiation along taste lines within clusters where layered or plural aesthetic systems have emerged (Anderson 2004). By moderating entry to the market, gatekeepers influence the content of products (Yogev 2010). The evaluation of cultural products is highly dependent on—in this case musicians'—adoption of "a repertoire of socially acceptable practices which are culturally, morally and even economically distinct" (Ibid.: 516–17). Hence, the candidacy of products to commodification and the value they gain in exchanges is partly dependent on the positioning of artists and their music within a network of relations and conventions.

THE PARIS WORLD MUSIC CLUSTER

In a cluster of world music production such as Paris we can expect to find a networked ecology of actors, one or more filtering mechanisms, and related aesthetic conventions. Additionally, because of the specific nature of world music, we can expect actors to draw on a unique cultural repertoire or, more generally, the cultural capital related to a particular background or region (Basu and Werbner 2001). This combination of their rather unique cultural capital and a particular background imbues their music with specific aesthetic qualities as well as with an aura of authenticity (Nettl 2013). Building on ethnic entrepreneurship studies, we can identify three potential markets for world music. One is based on a market of co-ethnics (Rusinovic 2006), which we define as "community music" (i.e., linked to the ethnic communities based in Paris); a second targets a niche market of cognoscenti outside of their ethnic community, termed here as "traditional music" (reflecting production of a more ethno-musicological nature); and a third "breaks out" into more mainstream markets (Engelen 2001), which we term "mainstream world music" (including hybrid sounds, occasionally borne out of cross-fertilization of musical traditions occurring in large metropolitan areas). These categories are not suggested fixed, immutable; rather, we suggest they are three "market clouts" with distinct networks of production and consumption within the wider Parisian world music cluster. Each of these markets is linked to a distinct art world with its own characteristic configuration of aesthetic criteria, gatekeepers, audiences, and, as we will argue in the next section, different responses to digitization.

DIFFERENT ART WORLDS AND THE IMPACT OF DIGITIZATION IN THE WORLD MUSIC SCENE IN PARIS

The study of the production of world music in Paris reveals the presence of different opportunities and markets for ethnic music. Paris, alongside London and New York, is the main center of production, marketing, and distribution of world music globally, with a particular specialization in music from the African continent (Brandellero and Pfeffer 2011). The Parisian cluster combines a dense web of actors, working in more or less formalized relationships. Our interest is in how world music, which in principle could originate from anywhere in the world (Connell and Gibson 2003, 2004; Guilbault 2006; Taylor 1997), comes to be commodified through markets in Paris. We contend that the Parisian cluster of world music cannot be understood as a monolithic aesthetic system, but instead has to be unpacked into three distinct art worlds with their own market orientation, aesthetic values, and, crucially, different responses to digitization. These three distinct art worlds within one cluster of music production—community-based music, traditional music, and mainstream world music—will be analyzed below.

Community Music

Community-based music is centered on the production and marketing of music by and from co-ethnics. "There are many things happening at the level of (ethnic) communities in Paris" proclaimed one record label director "which do not appear on the radar of the average Parisian" (interview 17). This particular form of ethnic or migrant entrepreneurship in the music industry has been dubbed "bootstrap capitalism" by Dipannita Basu and Pnina Werbner (2001) in their analysis of how African-American artists in the United States have been able to pull themselves up the social ladder through making and selling a specific music genre. Like African American artists in the United States, makers of world music have started their own businesses in the music industry to a large extent by deploying their unique (ethnic) cultural capital while typically coming from an economically disadvantaged position. Community-based music: a spectrum of products more or less anchored in the ethnic repertoire, thick fabric of small ethnic businesses, compartmentalized markets, and low barriers of entry but in dead-end markets.

The community niche offers a spectrum of products, more or less anchored in the ethnic repertoire of the specific community in question. Production here is highly compartmentalized along ethnic and nationality lines, with only few genres (for example the "ndombolo" originating in the former Zaire) crossing boundaries; "I've had many contacts with local musicians of African origin and it's true, it's very, very segmented. African music, it's very different audiences, depending on ethnic origin and we shouldn't put everything together" (interview 28). Here we find a range of contemporary music inspired by Western rhythms to more tradition-inspired sounds, thus placing the niche in between ethnic and non-ethnic products. The customer base is strongly linked to their own community and its cultural capital, although the geographical scale shows wider networks of connection across the transnational diaspora. Information communication technologies (ICTs) have facilitated this contact for artists and music producers alike—record shop owners spoke of customers from other parts of the world getting in touch over the Internet to purchase music (interview 31). Community record shops in particular were seen as part of the life of certain Parisian neighborhoods with a stronger history of immigration, such as the XVIII arrondissement. A local festival organizer emphatically spoke about their vibrancy: "It's great that it's there [the community record shops and producers], I find, because at least they still have a real popular culture that belongs to them and that evolves in time, like all other popular cultures" (interview 3).

However, the reality of digitization means that only the "real fans" are still buying CDs, as free digital copies rapidly spread online (interview 31). This makes the job of discovering new talent in the country of origin more difficult, as producers can offer few financial incentives to a record deal (interview 31). This was clear from the fact that record shops were receiving fewer or no promotional copies of product for months (interview 30). As a result, some music producers were shifting their attention from new artists to "heritage" artists, thus re-mastering old recordings and converting them to digital formats (interview 33), while others were shifting their business focus to different merchandise altogether (interview 30). Far from the mainstream distribution channels and hardly hit by music digitization, it is becoming increasingly difficult for community producers to sustain their activities and contribute to the discovery of new artists and their growth (interviews 31, 30, 33). The future lies in live music and festivals, where it is often easier to receive public subsidies as part of a growing city prioritization of cultural diversity (interview 3). While record sales might flop, for some there is optimism because of the multiplication of local festivals (interviews 3, 2).

Traditional Music

While community music is anchored in the life of Parisians of migrant backgrounds and part of their attachment to their country of origin (interview 30), traditional music, in the words of Alain Weber—Quai Branly Museum's music programming advisor—should remain connected to its original social function and reality, while any departure from "art for art's sake" is treated as a denaturation of music (Minimum 2006). Migrant music is in this context often deemed as "second rate" traditional music (Aubert 2005, 12). It is the task of ethnomusicologists to take audiences on a voyage of musical discovery. Here, the direct link to ethnic capital is fundamental to the valuation of music, insofar as it enhances its aura of authenticity. Underlying this valuation is a dynamic of "fetishization whereby cultures that are perceived as untouched by commodification are sought out and brought to the fore—where eulogies are commonplace" (Connell and Gibson 2003, 157).

The focus here is on the traditional as opposed to the modern or contemporary. As a result, in the ears of some critical listeners, "music does not travel well . . . The further away from its place of origin, the less value it has" (interview 34). In order to "discover" this traditional music, Paris-based record labels and venue managers rely on a network of experts. A record label director stated that "in the early years, I developed a network of friends more knowledgeable than myself on this or that culture, they alerted me to certain things" (interview 32). In the same vein, the Théâtre de la Ville employs a series of expert consultants who scour the world in search of "new traditions" to populate the venue's prestigious world music weekly program. On the consumption side, traditional music is seen as being "pre-globalized," thus likely to "spark the curiosity" of audiences worldwide (interview 32). Traditional music is seen as offering a window on a culture, on a people, and its target audience as being interested not just in the sound, but also the pedagogic experience proposed.

Private record labels specializing in traditional music are rare, and in most cases they are connected to public institutions. This is the case of the Maison des Cultures du Monde, with its label Inédit, and the public Radio France and its Ocora label. As one private record label owner explained, traditional music does not sell much; it is the province of connoisseurs. When trying to get his company started, he first opted for acts which would make good sales, in order to stabilize the company financially, before moving on to "a real authenticity, avoiding folklore, avoiding falling into tourism [. . .] a requirement of artistic quality and authenticity [. . .] and rarity, meaning we tried to have some world premieres, which we managed a couple of times.

We did a complete Chinese opera, with a trilingual booklet, and a series on Siberian music. These releases don't have much competition" (interview 32). What clearly emerges is a separation between cultural and commercial interests. As the director of a public institution with a focus on world cultures and music stated, "we don't work in show business [. . .] we don't make money with cultural heritage [. . .] culture is not a commercial product" (interview 34). Functioning primarily as "micro-enterprises," labels in the traditional music field were already working on the basis of limited sales (interview 32).

Digitization was seen as changing the nature of the product these companies offer and the way they are circulated, rather than casting a doubt on sales and profits. "When I release an album, it comes with a 28-page booklet plus a 40-page PDF [containing information on the artist]. When downloading, you won't get this. [. . .] My aim has always been to sell a cultural product" (interview 32). This statement underlines the importance of contextualization in this particular art world which hampers outright digitization.

The same can be said for live performances which constitute an essential component of traditional music. A venue programmer explained that he realized in time the importance of direct contact with artists. "I realized that people who didn't know world music at all, people who came [to my venue] and discovered gypsy or Indian music, they were incredibly touched. [. . .] I thought to myself, well, that's it. It's the artist's presence that really makes people get the spirit of world music, there is a presentation, because when Chinese artists play [. . .], when Indian artists play, they aren't wearing jeans [. . .] there is a sacralization of music" (interview 5).

Mainstream World Music

Away from the ritualistic and sacred field of traditional music, Paris hosts a number of labels, venues, and artists active in world music who are not bound to communities of co-ethnic or experts. Music production here does not answer the tastes of a specific community, be it based on ethnicity and/or expert listeners, but strives for wider audiences and hybrid sounds. The opposition between heritage/tradition and modern/contemporary music is shunned, while the emphasis is placed on living culture (Lecomte 2005), but also on the accessibility of music for wider audiences (interview 14).

Just like with traditional music, the link with live performances is important here, although for different reasons. A record label owner told us about having barely survived the 1992 transition to CDs, when his vinyl records were being sent back to him from the shops, unsold (interview 2). At the time of fieldwork, FNAC and large supermarkets were the main distributers of music to mainstream audiences, and were beginning to downsize their stocks and shelf space for CDs. Some labels relied on Harmonia Mundi for a specialized retail service for jazz and world music, both via its own shops and online. All record labels felt the pinch as a result of the downsizing of their distribution deals, and were finding alternative ways to sell their CDs. Voicing a common strategy, one label manager said, "Nowadays we are invisible, we only sell records when we put on a show, which means we have to organize tours just to sell CDs" (interview 2, 20). Smaller venues were seen as replacing labels and A&R staff in the discovery of new acts, "what do producers do now they can't make CDs anymore? They start organizing concerts, in big venues. [. . .] we play a role in the discovery [of artists], but we also work on their development [. . .] we network, we professionalize them, because foreign artists aren't necessarily familiar with French regulation" (interview 6).

The founder of a media company specializing in world music explained how getting local music producers on board for the "Internet revolution" was similar to a process of "evangelization," as many non-believers failed to grasp the transformative power of the web (interview 7). After a successful bid to the City of Paris administration, Paris Mix, a local development initiative centered on world music and digitization, was set up in 2008. Over the years, the initiative has promoted the visibility of world music production in the urban environment, through a series of musical routes and events, but it has also helped local actors embrace digital technologies and the web through a series of "Music and Internet" workshops.

DISCUSSION AND CONCLUDING REMARKS

Music has become near ubiquitous as the historian Tim Blanning has observed in his book *The Triumph of Music* (2008). This holds even truer in the digital age when music is transposed into bytes. Not just on the radio, in a café or restaurant, an elevator, or a supermarket, but now also on a smart phone or a tablet—music seems to be everywhere. Technological change has played a role in extending the market by coming up with digital formats and related audio gadgets, but has also, it seems, lowered barriers of entry for aspiring music makers by decreasing the costs of music production (via inexpensive musical instruments and recording equipment) and those of distribution through access to the Internet. In addition, technological change has seriously eroded intellectual property rights as digital formats can now be easily copied and distributed. We have looked at how a specific segment of the music industry has responded to the challenges of digitization. Our vantage point is the world music cluster located in Paris which offers a pertinent case, given its complex geography entailing the diffusion of "local" sounds to "global" audiences (Connell and Gibson 2003; Guilbault 1993). Our main finding is that within one localized production of world music or cluster, we can encounter quite different coherent art worlds facing diverse challenges of digitization. While we note a certain level of movement of artists, audiences, and producers across the borders of these three art worlds,

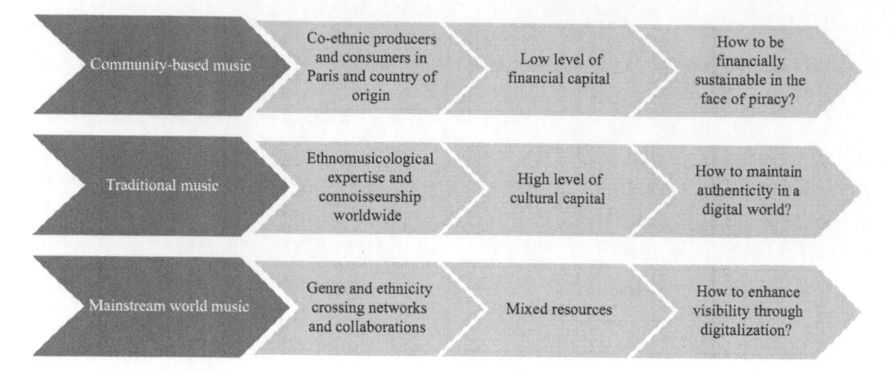

Figure 13.1 World music art worlds in Paris and their digitization challenges

it seems likely that the art worlds themselves and their market clouts will remain fairly stable.

Figure 13.1 illustrates how the Parisian cluster of world music production can be divided into three distinctive art worlds. Each world with its own market orientation, type of taste makers, composition of the audience, and crucial resources in terms of often intertwined financial, cultural, and social capital. Each art world faces rather different challenges regarding digitization thus requiring key actors, the producers of music, to adopt specific entrepreneurial strategies which suit their market orientation and its aesthetic criteria.

First, communities of migrants will demand (and produce) music catering to their co-ethnics and this will primarily involve live performances sustaining the community-based art world. Secondly, producers of traditional music will be able to rely on a particular segment of the market, namely those who are interested in music precisely because they are looking for something that will distinguish them from a mainstream audience (see Hracs et al. 2013). Notably, world music appears to give such a distinction by offering a (perceived) authentic cultural experience partly founded on a particular kind of cultural capital shared by the community of cognoscenti which frames and positions the music and its makers, creating distance from the mainstream. Moreover, blatant commodification and border-crossing through digitization may erode the authentic aura attached to the music in this market segment and, thus, undermine the appeal for these cognoscenti (c.f. Bourdieu 1984; Sandel 2012). Thirdly, mainstream markets will still be out there, attracting and tempting producers of world music within the cluster to use other forms of distribution—e.g., digitization—and transcend circumscribed and localized markets.

Notwithstanding the apparent in-built stability of the three art worlds within the Parisian world music cluster, they all have to respond to digitization by adapting their respective business models. Among the community music actors we noted a diversification of activities, branching out into the provision of other (often non-cultural) products. In the traditional and mainstream world music worlds, we noted a turning to live music in particular as a source of revenue and audience development, but also a call on public funding to help preserve music as an expression of the diversity of world cultural heritage.

Digitization affects the strategies of the key actors with respect to format, distribution, marketing, and packaging. The continuity of distinct art worlds, however, hinges on the social reproduction of audiences with their respective tastes and preferences for how the music should be experienced. The community-based and traditional music art worlds will be reproduced as long as communities of co-ethnics and cognoscenti are present, respectively. Their dependence on live performances will limit the impact of digitization. The greatest impact will occur in mainstream markets where we may observe, on the one hand, a decrease in income because of lack of intellectual property rights protection. On the other hand, we may also observe an extension and upscaling of markets beyond the local and national and an exploration of new sources of income (e.g., advertising, banners on the Internet). The mainstream market is, however, at least partly dependent on the other two art worlds of world music for inspiration and ideas which can then be adapted, diluted, commodified, and digitized for a much larger audience. As a result, a successful and sustainable music cluster in an era of digitization consists of a complex ecology of different art worlds—distinct, but overlapping art worlds . . . stable, but dynamic art worlds. Lastly, such a sustainable ecology also comprises both art worlds that are partly shielded from digitization and those that are thoroughly digitized.

REFERENCES

Anderson, Chris. "The Long Tail." *Wired Magazine* 12, no. 4 (2004): 170–177.

Appadurai, Arjun. "Commodities and the Politics of Value." In *Interpreting Objects and Collections,* edited by Pearce, S., 76–91. London: Routledge, 1994.

Aubert, Laurent. "Prélude" In *Musiques migrantes*, edited by Aubert, L., 11–16. Geneva: Musée d'ethnographie, 2005.

Basu, Dipannita, and Pnina Werbner "Bootstrap Capitalism and the Culture Industries: A Critique of Invidious Comparisons in the Study of Ethnic Entrepreneurship." *Ethnic and Racial Studies* 24, no. 2 (2001): 236–262.

Becker, Howard Saul. *Art Worlds.* Berkeley, CA: University of California Press, 1984.

Blanning, Timothy. *The Triumph of Music: The Rise of Composers, Musicians and Their Art.* Cambridge, MA: Harvard University Press, 2008.

Bourdieu, Pierre. *Distinction: A Social Critique of the Judgement of Taste.* Cambridge, MA: Harvard University Press, 1984.

Brandellero, Amanda, and Pierric Calenge. *Le fonctionnement des filières des musiques du monde: Une approche par les individus et les réseaux.* Paris: Paris Mix, 2008.

Brandellero, Amanda, and Karin Pfeffer. "Multiple and Shifting Geographies of World Music Production." *Area* 43, no. 4 (2011): 495–505.

Caves, Richard. *Creative Industries: Contracts Between Art and Commerce.* Cambridge, MA: Harvard University Press, 2000.

CIMT. *Guide annuaire Planète Musiques. Musiques traditionelles et du monde en France.* Paris: Irma.

Connell, John and Gibson, Chris. *Sound Tracks. Popular Music, Identity and Place.* London: Routledge. 2003

Connell, John and Gibson, Chris. "World Music: Deterritorializing Place and Identity." *Progress in Human Geography* 28 no. 3 (2004): 342–361

Currid, Elizabeth. *The Warhol Economy: How Fashion, Art, and Music Drive New York City.* Princeton: Princeton University Press, 2007.

Encyclopædia Britannica Online, s. v. "World Music", accessed February 10, 2016, http://www.britannica.com/art/world-music.

Engelen, Ewald. "'Breaking In' and 'Breaking Out': A Weberian Approach to Entrepreneurial Opportunities. *Journal of Ethnic and Migration Studies* 27 no.2 (2001): 203–223.

Feld, Steven. "A Sweet Lullaby for World Music." *Public Culture* 12, no. 1 (2000): 145–171.

Guilbault, Jocelyne. "On Redefining the 'Local' Through World Music." In *Ethnomusicology A Contemporary Reader,* edited by Post, J., 137–146. New York: Routledge, 2006.

Guilbault, Jocelyne. *Zouk: World Music in the West Indies.* Chicago: University of Chicago Press, 1993.

Hauge, Atle, and Brian Hracs. "See the Sound, Hear the Style: Collaborative Linkages Between Indie Musicians and Fashion Designers in Local Scenes." *Industry and Innovation* 17, no. 1 (2010): 113–129.

Hracs, Brian, Jill Grant, Jeffry Haggett, and Jesse Morton. "A Tale of Two Scenes: Civic Capital and Retaining Musical Talent in Toronto and Halifax." *The Canadian Geographer/Le Géographe Canadien* 55, no. 3 (2011): 365–382.

Hracs, Brian, Doreen Jakob, and Atle Hauge. "Standing Out in the Crowd: the Rise of Exclusivity-Based Strategies to Compete in the Contemporary Marketplace for Music and Fashion." *Environment and Planning A* 45, no. 5 (2013): 1144–1161.

Kloosterman, Robert. "Matching Opportunities with Resources: A Framework for Analysing (Migrant) Entrepreneurship from a Mixed Embeddedness Perspective." *Entrepreneurship and Regional Development* 22, no. 1 (2010): 25–45.

Lecomte, Henri. "Deux ou trois choses que je sais d'elles . . . " In *Musiques migrantes*, edited by L. Aubert, 131–44. Geneva: Musée d'ethnographie. 2005.

Leyshon, Andrew, Peter Webb, Shaun French, Nigel Thrift, and Louise Crewe. "On the Reproduction of the Musical Economy After the Internet." *Media, Culture and Society* 27, no. 2 (2005): 177–209.

Manuel, Peter. "Music Cultures of Mechanical Reproduction" In *The Cambridge History of World Music*, edited by Bohlman, P.V., 55–74. Cambridge: Cambridge University Press, 2013.

Nettl, Bruno. "On World Music as a Concept in the History of Music Scholarship." In *The Cambridge History of World Music*, edited by Bohlman P.V., 23–54. Cambridge: Cambridge University Press, 2013.

Power, Dominic, and Daniel Hallencreutz. "Profiting from Creativity? The Music Industry in Stockholm, Sweden and Kingston, Jamaica." *Environment and Planning A* 34, no. 10 (2002): 1833–1854.

Rusinovic, Katia. *Dynamic Entrepreneurship; First and Second-Generation Immigrant Entrepreneurs in Dutch Cities*. Amsterdam: Amsterdam University Press, 2006.

Sandel, Michael J. *What Money Can't Buy: The Moral Limits of Markets*. New York: Macmillan Publishers, 2012.

Scott, Allen. *The Cultural Economy of Cities; Essays on the Geography of Image-Producing Industries*. London, Thousand Oaks, and New Delhi: Sage Publications, 2000.

Scott, Allen J. "Cultural-Products Industries and Urban Economic Development: Prospects for Growth and Market Contestation in Global Context." *Urban Affairs Review* 39, no. 4 (2004): 461–490.

Scott, Allen. *A World in Emergence; Cities and Regions in the 21st Century*. Cheltenham and Northampton: Edward Elgar, 2012.

Seman, Michael. "How a Music Scene Functioned as a Tool for Urban Redevelopment: A Case Study of Omaha's Slowdown Project." *City, Culture and Society* 1, no. 4 (2010): 207–215.

Van Rees, Cees. "How Reviewers Reach Consensus on the Value of Literary Works." *Poetics* 16, no. 3 (1987): 275–294.

Taylor, Timothy Dean. *Global Pop: World Music, World Markets*. New York: Routledge, 1997.

Watson, Allan, Michael Hoyler, and Christoph Mager. "Spaces and Networks of Musical Creativity in the City." *Geography Compass* 3, no. 2 (2009): 856–878.

Yogev, Tamar. "The Social Construction of Quality: Status Dynamics in the Market for Contemporary Art." *Socio-Economic Review* 8, no. 3 (2010): 511–536.

14 Emotional Landscapes and the Evolution of Vinyl Record Retail

A Case Study of Highland Park, Los Angeles

Tyler Sonnichsen

Depending on which storylines one follows, opening a record shop in the twenty-first century is either admirably courageous or questionably foolish. As with much entrepreneurship in the globalized digital age, the reality lies somewhere in between. Selling anything for a living has never been simple, particularly an item widely viewed as archaic or even obsolete. Adding a new brick-and-mortar outlet for vinyl records onto the globe often not only creates or expands public space for music lovers, but also enhances a place's cultural and economic geography (see Seman 2010).

Regardless, despite ostensibly widespread mainstream ambivalence, sales of vinyl records have reached their highest numbers in decades. According to Nielsen Soundscan, 6 million vinyl records sold in the United States in 2013, a 500-percent increase since 2007. The 2014 sales statistics made moves to dwarf even that of 2013 at a 40 percent gain (Bernasek 2014). Coupled with the so-called "vinyl revival," a re-emergence of independent brick-and-mortar music retailers has not been a coincidence.

Record shops, like most specialized retail locations, are all "highly textured place[s] with multiple layers of meaning" (Cosgrove 1989, 119) and "full of internal conflicts" (Massey 1994, 155). Whereas many could view a small shop that specializes in punk records as a vital "subcultural marker . . . where people congregate and a sense of community pervades" (Gracon 2011, 215), others in the same vicinity could see the store as a nuisance, perhaps generating noise pollution with loud music outside the shop and luring an unattractive clientele to the area. Record shops as places unto themselves are often not even universally beloved by vinyl junkies; certain shops that cater to one demographic (e.g., oldies and jazz fans) may draw the ire of collectors who specialize in a different genre and cannot find certain desired items. It would seem impossible for any retail space to evenly cater to every demographic; depending on a host of factors (gender, race, class, sexual identity, tastes, political beliefs) most individuals' senses of the place regarding interpersonal connections and emotional constructs will vary (Massey 1994).

Certain examples from this study, however, suggest that newer locations are making a conscious effort to address the social dynamics in order to create the most inclusive spaces attainable. This chapter examines this contemporary phenomenon in light of three proximate vinyl outlets in Los Angeles that have succeeded against many odds by honing in on that thriving collectors' and hobbyists' market through contrasting yet similar means. This overarching narrative falls within three phases: First, a brief cultural context will be given for the significance of the revival of vinyl record sales over the past decade. Second, the elements that propel these shops will be discussed, touching upon the value of emotional geographies (see: Pile 2010; Thien 2005), the private "home" dynamic within public space, and interpersonal connection and co-construction thereof. Third, each of the three stores will be examined and reconnected to this overarching narrative. The breakdown includes background on the stores Wombleton Records, Mount Analog, and Gimme Gimme Records obtained through informal interviews with the stores' founders, participant observation by the author, and content analysis of their respective online presences. This chapter will address and contextualize the elements, aside from simply consumer interest in vinyl in itself, that make these stores successful and resilient in a still-challenging market. While each store has a unique approach, all three channel the importance of respecting their customers' emotional connection to place (both real and imagined), reiterating the vitality of physicality and place in the contemporary marketing of physical media.

THE CULTURAL MEANING OF VINYL IN THE TWENTY-FIRST CENTURY

Over the course of the 1980s, the CD's rise to eclipse the vinyl record "removed the aura of mass-production from vinyl" (Yochim et al. 2008, 187), thereby rearticulating a subcultural sense of kinship with analog media. The interaction between humans and technology suggested a more fulfilling relationship with vinyl than was possible with CDs, or as would appear toward the end of the century, MP3s and Internet-streaming audio. These objects "contain layers of value not offered by digital downloads and mass-produced" digital media (Hracs et al. 2013, 1151). Many who started purchasing vinyl over the past decade are living proof of a void in music consumption that relatively few realized had existed until recently. CD sales have fallen in double-digit percentages for almost five years consecutively, while vinyl records are selling in their greatest numbers in over two decades (Knight 2012). Even MP3 players, once a bastion of the digital revolution, have largely fallen in the consumer market in favor of Smart Phones, often used for streaming audio (Hall 2012). A comprehensive amount of literature and scholarship is available on the dynamics of collecting and the cultures surrounding it (see: Clouse 2008; Dougan 2006).

Understanding the ways in which humans channel their emotions and passions through tactile things can be paramount in illustrating the picture of economic and artistic interaction. There is something deeper to this resurrected micro economy than the quasi-humorous narrative of the self-righteous hipster fetishizing an antiquated format to "be different." Despite what particular cultural forces suggest, there is no such thing as a "typical" record collector, particularly now as cultural studies and social science refuse to let themselves be bound to what lies on the surface. Vinyl record collecting, related to this idea, "converges with those anti-consumerist ethics which tie the collector's investment in the obscure to the bohemian's refusal of the blatantly commercial" (Straw 1997, 636). In other words, spending excessive time and money on being a vinyl junkie is simple to justify as an intellectual pursuit:

> Consumers are not necessarily the dupes of the capitalist record industry as many high cultural critiques of popular music would suggest, but can often subvert these commodities to support lifestyles that cut against the grain of conventional society
>
> (Leyshon et al. 2005, 182).

While vinyl record collecting remains a niche market, it is a vibrant one that has warranted a prodigious number of ethnographic (Shuker 2010), sociological (Hayes 2006; Shuker 2010), anthropological (Vaher 2008; Yochim et al. 2008), and economic (Hesmondhalgh 1998; Plasketes 1992; Sirois and Wasko 2011) studies. However, few studies exist on the role of place in the development of emotions that guide the record collector. A vastly overlooked and yet integral element of the record collecting subculture has been the ways in which places (both real and imagined) and the emotional attachments that collectors have to them. Literature has applied vinyl consumption to the sociological and psychological dialogue on identity construction through accumulation; records are objects that are:

> multifaceted, dynamic, and filled with certain intangible qualities . . . such as emotional encounters with the historical past [that] will almost always escape a valuation system that works to render all things measurable and comparable
>
> (Clouse 2008, 15).

In fact, a limited number of studies (e.g., Vaher 2008) expound upon the intersections between emotions, place, and music records. However, the vinyl industry relies more closely than perhaps they even realize on emotional geographies.

THE NEW SPATIAL DYNAMICS OF RECORD RETAIL

These interstitial relationships between collectors' attachment to place (both real and imagined) that the records elicit and the places through which the records flow are equally prescient in the analysis; the "pleasure of . . . places derives from the consumption of goods and services that somehow stand for or signify that place . . . that are somehow unique or at least culturally specific to that place" (Urry 2005, 79). When it comes to how collectors arbitrate their own selective inquisitiveness, certain fantasies about time and place come to bear. In terms of published media (records specifically), "there are . . . extramusical reasons for searching out the first [pressing]: it locates us there, at the point of origin" (Osborne 2008, 279). This is the point (in time and place) of origin upon which humans naturally fixate, especially antiques and other objects that are older than we are, because "the moment of creation cannot be reproduced" (Baudrillard 2006, 81).

Even some who frequented record stores prior to the realization of the Internet as a conduit for both non-tactile digital music and mail-ordered analog music made their visits more infrequent. For certain individuals, that arterial conduit removed the necessity of physical contact and social negotiation that was once inherent in the acquisition process (Massey 2005). Even during the era when corporate-owned chains dominated or played a key role in the subcultural landscape, no two record stores were identical, although certain purposefully anachronistic aspects of record stores grew to be standardized:

> When teenage shoppers grew up to be record store employees and eventually owners, many reached back to their initial experiences for inspiration. And rather than tap into the modern world, young people who go into the business in the 21st century often base their vision on tales from their parents and older relatives about what made record stores great in the [past]
>
> (Calamar and Gallo 2010, 7).

An understanding of shopping motives requires the consideration of satisfactions which shopping activities provide, as well as the utility obtained from the merchandise that may be purchased (Tauber 1972). Additionally, as certain products and services fall back into the public taste and esteem, these trends are usually concentrated within particular socio-demographic segments of society, often allied with certain sets of established values, beliefs, and interests (Mark 2003). Emotion, giving way to enthusiasm, becomes crucial for both salespeople and consumers:

> It is through the proximity of others of like-mind—whether real or imagined—that enthusiasm produces the 'surfaces' and boundaries' that enable the individual to identify as a group member. The emotional affiliation of the member to the group is thus rewarded with feelings of belonging wherever they are
>
> (Geoghegan 2013, 41).

When long-standing record shops close, eulogists often lament them as "another victim of the Internet, the economy, and changing tastes in music and shopping" (Applebome 2012), furthering this propensity to ascribe human qualities to analog media (see Chivers Yochim and Biddinger 2008). When Tower Records went bankrupt in October 2006, customers offered condolences as if "a close friend had died" (Calamar and Gallo 2010, 10), exemplifying the way in which record stores took on the characteristics of the fetishized products within. *New York Times* feature writers Peter Applebome and Ben Sisario emotionally eulogized two long-standing record shops in that region (Ronnie I's and Bleecker Bob's, respectively) within one month of each other at the beginning of 2012.

The realities of why record shops close are difficult to simplify and attribute squarely to economy or technology-bred rationales. The final two Virgin Megastores were shuttered on June 14, 2009 in Times Square and Hollywood; real estate companies who owned them shut them down. It was not necessarily poor sales; the big commercial stores dug their own graves by overreaching, poor management, and unsustainable overseas expansion (Calamar and Gallo 2010). These media megastores, all opened well after the ascent of the compact disc, never specialized in vinyl, and beyond a certain degree, neither do the remaining music-centered high-volume retail outlets under independent operation like Amoeba (Los Angeles and San Francisco bay area), Rasputin's (Berkeley, California), or even Manifest (Charlotte, North Carolina).

To classify any unified reading of any emotional geography of a certain space (or codified class of space) would be impossible (see Ettlinger 2004). One longstanding shop going out of business may greatly upset a longtime customer, yet it may be virtually meaningless to somebody who has never shopped there. Regardless, when culturally significant retail locations are "disrupted, so too are the identities [developed] within" (Morrice 2013, 35). Journalists like Applebome and Sisario convey sentiments interrelated with Western consumption practices to elicit emotions of loss and grief pursuant to the disappearance of venerable record shops. One does not need to collect records to understand the financial hardships that record shops face as an inevitable byproduct of catering to a niche market for hobbyists. Hobbies typically center on products or services, and "stores that offer hobby-related goods serve as a focal point for people with similar interests to interact" (Tauber 1972, 48). Cultural economy and cultural industries "are dialectic in that economic practices have been thoroughly culturalized and culture is an economic commodity" (Lukinbeal 2004, 307). The vinyl industry's niche appeal, particularly when it comes to collectors who frequent record shops, drives a heavy concentration within highly populated, highly educated areas, often referred to as "cultural clusters."

These clusters of artistic and literary outlets often play key roles in the revitalization of urban areas (see: Currid and Williams 2010; Ley 2003; Seman 2010). Lower rents attract both educated middle-class denizens and independent retailers seeking to cater to this demographic. Consequently, similar specialized retailers like record shops tend to open in close proximity to one another, providing a convenient gauntlet through which vinyl lovers can spend a weekend afternoon traversing multiple storefront locations. This phenomenon is common in several major cities; Washington, DC's heavily gentrified Adams-Morgan neighborhood boasts four small record shops (Crooked Beat, Red Onion, Joint Custody, and Smash!) within a five-block walk down 18th St NW. While the greater Los Angeles area boasts a wide array of storied independent record stores of various sizes and cultural impacts, this chapter focuses on three smaller, independent retailers located within walking distance of one another in the Highland Park neighborhood of northeastern Los Angeles.

THE YOUNG RECORD SHOPS OF HIGHLAND PARK

The first of the three storefronts considered here will be Wombleton Records, a boutique-style storefront specializing in imported British vinyl and the first vinyl shop of its ilk to open in Highland Park, in 2010. The second is the topographically-named Mount Analog, opened in July 2012 a short walk from the Highland Park Metro station on N. Figueroa Street. The final store is Gimme Gimme Records, a freestanding shop relocated to Los Angeles in 2012 after eighteen years on New York's Lower East Side.

Whereas the stores that line 18th St in DC have opened their doors at various times over the past ten years, all three of the Highland Park shops have opened within the past five, emphasizing the appeal of the revitalizing neighborhood and the shared need to locate near a centralized consumer base (Currid and Williams 2010). While Highland Park has grown more affluent over the past decade and transformed into "an outpost of hipster cool" (Lazo 2012), the shops' close proximity to one another also draws record collectors to their neighborhood from varying distances around the greater Los Angeles area.

Each of the three storefronts carries a unique, carefully deliberated aesthetic that guides both the dynamics of the commercial space as well as influencing the social consumption habits of customers. All three of these shops are similar in size, stock volume, and pertinent business practices. Continuing a timeless tradition that Milt Gabler started in the 1940s at the Commodore Radio Shop (Calamar and Gallo 2010), all three play music in their stores, a practice that transforms both the interior and exterior spaces, enticing potential customers to enter, and enticing active customers to approach the audibly present artists or genre. The recordings played in-store are always for sale and almost always on vinyl.

On my first visit to Gimme Gimme Records, a spinning record by the 1990s Georgia band Olivia Tremor Control put me in the mood to seek out other records by bands with a similar sound. If Gimme Gimme didn't have a specific record I was looking for, the chances were that I could find it at one of the other two shops. As they are all unique in specific genre specialty, they are not in noticeable competition and support each other through word-of-mouth and links on their respective websites and announcements in their email newsletters:

> Dan [Cook]'s experience in NYC found that clusters of record stores in a single area made that area a go-to for vinyl fiends, which is why he chose York Blvd., close to the great stores of Wombleton, Permanent Records, and Mount Analog' (gimmegimmerecords.com/aboutus; Links to each shop's website were provided).
>
> In the past year or so, great new local shops have opened hither and tither making our neighborhood an internationally reknowned [sic] one-of-a-kind vinyl shopper's paradise unlike anything this side of Shinjuku. At Wombleton we're excited to be a part of the zeitgeist and would like to officially welcome Mount Analog, Strictly Grooves, [and Gimme Gimme Records] to our neck of the woods
>
> (Marshall 2012).

Notable how both proprietors here finely leverage commonly held perceptions of other, better-known financial and commercial districts on diametrically opposite geographic sides of Los Angeles (New York City and Tokyo, respectively). This is common cross-culturally, as those involved in particular pockets of a cultural economy frequently cite these "economies of scope" that stem from the ability to take advantage of other related and co-located activities (Florida et al. 2010, 12). All three of the shops upon which this chapter focuses bring something unique to Highland Park shoppers' experiences which cannot be reproduced virtually. Following are individual backgrounds and descriptions of Wombleton Records, Mount Analog, and Gimme Gimme Records that illustrate their physical strengths against the waves of an increasingly virtual industry.

CASE STUDY 1: WOMBLETON RECORDS

Opened in September 2010 by Canadian transplant Ian Marshall, Wombleton Records is perhaps the most prototypical example of rearticulating a specific place of any record shop in Los Angeles. The shop is replete with Edwardian design that suggests a recreation of a British-style salon. Marshall cites the King's Road commercial district of London as a key aesthetic influence:

> [I thought], What about a place that sold those records I was so high on, looking like the clothing places we went into [on UK trips] in the King's Road area? That kind of London approach, which is [essentially] Parisian by ancestry.

London and Paris would both be on a short list of not only the top tourist destinations in the world, but the most instrumental places in the construction of quintessential Europe in the public memory. International cities that function as centers of both commerce and popular culture, Paris especially, have long since produced standardized iconographies of themselves that are "abundant, systematic and cheap," and provide the world with simple imaginary and symbolic representations of themselves (Schor 1994, 252). Shared senses of place are based on mediation and representation; even those of us who have not been to these places have some sense of "sets of meanings produced in films, literature, advertising, and other forms of mediation" (Cresswell 2004, 1), particularly music and music-based artwork and environs. Marshall decided not to decorate the walls with record covers, instead opting for simple thematic and expensive wallpaper in the interest of directing the shoppers' attention to a finely manicured vinyl selection. He and his wife, Jade, who co-own Wombleton, consciously chose to feminize the record shopping experience, countering traditional "patriarchal bourgeois design" trends (Baudrillard 2006, 13) in the interest of catering to a significantly female customer base. True to form, Wombleton's Edwardian interior design suggests an idealized London (or Paris) salon reflective of "not what the past was really like, but what its customers like to think it was like" (Windsor 1994, 55). Considered together, the Marshalls' simulacrum is perhaps the prototypical example of using collective imagination and memory to sell records, arranging foreign iconographies with a "mental sonic utopia . . . communicated back to the broader audiences interested

Figure 14.1 Interior at Wombleton Records in Highland Park, Los Angeles. Photo courtesy of Ian Marshall.

in popular music and cultural history" (Vaher 2008, 344). Because a vast majority of their stock is hand-picked European imports, housing these objects in a culturally appropriate setting seems a necessity, particularly to justify certain prices.

As intended, this intersection of idealized place and the conglomeration of fetishized objects lends itself to a heightened endowment of cultural and social capital for customers. Whether these customers profess to be experts in the genres or regions of music represented on their shelves is somewhat inconsequential; in a sense, walking through the door imbues customers with certain "high levels of social and cultural capital" (Hracs et al. 2013, 1157) necessary to find and obtain these rare artifacts of sonic geography. The shop charges premium rates for records personally imported and curated. Members of the Wombleton mailing list receive photos of these records, laid out side-by-side in enticing high-resolution photographs, the lead-in text emphasizing that these are "ORIGINAL PRESS—COUNTRY OF ORIGIN" records (Marshall 2013, emphasis his). Marshall himself indulges in this idealized sense of being and recalibrating this style of "cultural anamnesia" (Vaher 2008, 350):

> It just seems to correlate that a German band on a German pressing [from the record's year of recording] sells for more . . . [People] like to think 'what would the friends of this band have access to? . . . For me, every time I dig up a record and look at it and listen to it and unfurl it, I'm engaging in some kind of fantasy about a time and place and sound and everything . . . some [reissue] that came out [decades later in a different country] . . . I'm transported not to Germany in 1971, I'm transported to Seattle or Portland in 2006.

When assembling a mental map, collectors prize coherence over accuracy. An item imbued with authenticity, as an original press from the artist's country of origin "is capable of constructively representing that amalgam of sentimental interpretations of history that constitutes modern . . . nostalgia" (Windsor 1994, 54).

CASE STUDY 2: MOUNT ANALOG

Where Wombleton relies heavily on an idealized sense of specified place, Mount Analog thrives off idealized conceptions of abstract space. Several record shops in contemporary Los Angeles began as outgrowths of the owners' already-operational vinyl imprints. Like Vacation Vinyl in nearby Silver Lake, Mount Analog started after co-owner Mahssa Taghinia grew a label (Finders Keepers) up from a small mail-order reissue service. She and her partner Zane Landreth captured a prime, affordable retail space on a gentrifying patch of N. Figueroa Street, a short walk from the Highland Park

Metro station. They opened their storefront in late summer, 2012. According to Landreth, varying geographic factors led them to open Mount Analog where they did:

> We're both really good friends with the [art] gallery that's next door . . . seeing how well their events did, I think that's what drew us to the space. It was also huge and really cheap. We both have a lot of friends that are out here, and that are moving East [within LA] . . . and [are] going to continue to do so.

Accordingly, both the existence and subsequent success of Mount Analog has relied heavily on their familiar and proximate customer base. While Highland Park has been primarily Hispanic since the racially motivated era of white outmigration (Pulido 2000, 26), the area's increasing dedication to serving a changing populace has laid a foundation for networks like the ones that converge in the shop. As in the social and economic elements that molded Highland Park into a home base for Landreth and Taghinia within Los Angeles, tacit social and economic benefits (Currid and Williams 2010) to locating their shop where it is have prevailed. Having the location most convenient (of the three shops discussed here) to the Highland Park Metro station, for example, have made Mount Analog most easily accessible to the Angelinos without cars or who simply wish to avoid traffic and parking. Destinations with relative ease of access, especially in troublesome commuting cities like Los Angeles, may adopt positive emotional associations for those who wish to avoid or minimize such hassles.

Landreth and Taghinias' personalized business sense reflects varying theories on the connection between humans and analog musical objects, particularly emphasizing the role of records and tactile media in establishing and enhancing interpersonal relationships within the home space:

> It was like how you go over to a friend's house, when you always wind up flipping through their records and looking through their books . . . we wanted that familiarity to be translated into our retail space. And I think we've done a pretty good job of making people comfortable in here, and . . . [not] pushing you through some sort of factory or a Costco experience. I want you to be able to come in, and listen to records, and hang out with the records, and interact with the records, and interact with the other people that are in here buying the records.

This inclusionary record shopping experience is largely the end goal of two overlapping spatial dynamics. The first involves creatively engineering a de facto "home away from home" for customers through designing "recognizable architectural persona and patterns of behavior of [certain amenities]" (Tuan 1992, 37). The second dynamic focuses on recreation of places (idealized, imagined, and concrete) to supplement the clientele's emotional attachment to the music itself. These dynamics overlap because both emphasize collecting consumers' emotional geographies as best as possible and "synthesizing those emotions into design" (Ettlinger 2004, 27). Certain shops in question, particularly those that have opened since the sales and manufacture resurgence in the vinyl industry (approximately 2004 through this writing), may lean more heavily toward one of these two dynamics than the other, but they still address both sides of this post-structural coin in the interest of maximizing their client base, particularly given the dominance of MP3 and streaming technology and reinterpretation of the relationship between music lovers' control of space and vice versa (see: Bull 2005; Magaudda 2011). Additionally, by placing the human customers on the same level with the records, he exemplifies this subcultural trend of coveting the intangible, abstract quality that record lovers frequently wed to humanity itself and place in opposition to the unforgiving corporate world (Yochim et al. 2008, 188). These anti-corporate sentiments that pervade among purveyors and adherents of vinyl culture "are integrated into how the store functions, which connects to an independent store atmosphere" (Gracon 2011, 213) and aims to attract potential customers who share similar values. They treasure their ability to define themselves against "nonplaces [that] are marked by a plethora of texts, screens, and signs which facilitate mediated relationships between people and places rather than direct ones" (Cresswell 2004, 6).

CASE STUDY 3: GIMME GIMME RECORDS

While Wombleton and Mount Analog both employ their customers' collective imaginations of place in time to drive business, both originated largely as Los Angeles-bred institutions. Gimme Gimme Records, the youngest of the three shops, began in New York City two decades ago and transplanted itself to Los Angeles, transforming itself into an institution of the latter city while retaining the spatial sensibilities it developed in the former. When Gimme Gimme opened in New York, many retail locations that refused to stock compact discs, while often considered foolish for sticking with then-marginalized analog formats, actually succeeded at cornering that subset of customers who wished to keep purchasing their music on vinyl and reported surprisingly good sales at the end of the 1980s and into the 1990s (Plasketes 1992). Dan Cook fully admits to the antagonism he originally faced for his loyalty to wax. Gimme Gimme, like Mount Analog, places emphasis on the anti-corporate retail space as a home or a refuge from the surrounding urban landscape. Cook's storefront during the shop's operation on New York City's Lower East Side stood out in contrast with other buildings on its block: its sharp green awning and yellow lettering invited customers in past the gritty brownstone that sat on top and the intimidating police precinct that sat next door.

"Like any other built feature in the environment, music has a form, function, and a spatial presence that merits the attention of geographers" (Huefe 2002, 34). Perhaps more importantly, "music is appreciated because it is a magical summing up of the patterns of life; the first function of music is to produce a feeling of security for the listener or the musician" (Carney 1998, 3). Home is often cited as a symbol of universal attachment and can vary in scale from one's house or any safe space of congregation to one's country of origin (Cresswell 2004, 5). Isolation (detachment) can be common in the large modern city, "though a stranger with a modicum of resources can find comfort in place and culture . . . in the recognizable architectural persona and patterns of behavior of [certain amenities]" (Tuan 1992, 37). Cook's shop spent years providing this comfort for vinyl fans in New York, and it continues to do so in Los Angeles. Visually, he has continued employing a vibrant color scheme that lies in stark contrast to the predominantly brown, beige, and asphalt Highland Park landscape.

While Marshall has taken to enticing Wombleton customers using photographs of his freshly unpacked rare records laid out in a patchwork, Cook has taken his Internet interactivity with fans to the next level. In videos posted to the Gimme Gimme Facebook page on February 20 and 23, 2013, Cook simulated a first-person view of somebody flipping through his new arrivals bin. Not only did this advertise the desirable records he had just placed for sale, but it in a way transposed one of the sensations of visiting the physical store and interacting with the tactile merchandise. This emphasis on interactivity elicits the emotions that accompany the physical acts of crate-digging and otherwise perusing record bins, inspiring potential shoppers to pay Gimme Gimme a visit, whether or not they saw any specific item in Dan's video. The sensation of the lived experience here almost trumps the specified pursuit of the item.[1] Keeping any shop open for twenty years is challenging, and Cook's ability to keep Gimme Gimme afloat for two decades between two cities reiterates that. What this suggests is that music may not be an outlier, but simply a valid component of the conversation about all retail outlet goods.

CONCLUSION

All three of the stores' websites match the patterns, designs, and general color schemes that formulate the aesthetic of their respective shops. Wombleton and Mount Analog both utilize imagined geographies in the virtual spaces of their Internet presence to appeal to potential customers. The Wombleton website touts those behind the store as "purveyors of rare pop vinyl treasures from around the world and beyond!" Mount Analog's owners, despite lifting the name from René Daumal's para-surrealist 1952 novel of a similar title (which they keep a copy of on display by the register), emphasize their store as a haven for "the creative idealist . . . the everyday curious and adventure seeker" in their promotional language. In fact, their website is even called ClimbMountAnalog.com, pushing the imagined geographies implied in their synthetic aesthetic as an enticement to potential consumers. The owners and clientele themselves, as key purveyors of Psych rock and other outsider genres of music, are "engaged in an ongoing enterprise of vernacular scholarship, working to bring a highly chaotic period in musical history under control, into manageable knowledge" (Straw 2000, 168). To reduce the collective form and function of Gimme Gimme and any contemporary vinyl retail outlets would be to forsake an infinite list of intangible variables that lead vinyl junkies, window-shoppers, and the simply curious through the door, but from an emotional geographic perspective, many of these design developments seem completely conscious and deliberate. On one side, style and substance trends in independent record shops emphasize universal attachment to a "home away from home," a tribute and articulation of the nostalgic and pragmatic tradition that, tantamount to the vinyl format itself, the record shop should be "a space that constitutes custom, tradition, and emotion" (Gracon 2011, 207). On the other side, the dynamic amongst these Highland Park shops emphasizes the reinvention and interpretation of various emotional geographies attached to places both real and imagined. It is important to acknowledge that, despite the inclusive aspirations of these retail spaces, not all people would necessarily feel comfortable or at home in these atmospheres (Gracon 2011, 219). However, newer shops such as these do consciously address issues of exclusive space and reify the post-structural sympathy that musical tolerance "is operationalized as the complement of musical exclusiveness-not its opposite" (Bryson 1996, 886). In the post-modern age, it may take a certain collective, romantic fantasy about time and place to entice customers to even leave their homes and enter a record store, much less spend money on musical artifacts. The relatively recent barrage of new, independent vinyl retailers and their growing, loyal customer bases are proving that this can be effective in post-modern Los Angeles, and cultural centers around the world are following suit. While not every world city has the same population, expendable income on a grand scale, or cultural capital of a Los Angeles, New York, Tokyo, or London, new vinyl proprietors are using models developed in those cores and expanding them to embrace and enhance smaller markets.

NOTE

1. In the time since I conducted this research in Highland Park, I have noticed an increasing number of record shop clerks generating similar online content, including a pair of which I had alluded to in Adams-Morgan, DC. To find the earliest timestamp on a "new arrivals" video like this may be impossible, but Cook's was the first I noticed.

REFERENCES

Applebome, Peter. "A Doo-Wop Shop Prepares to Close, Signaling the End of a Fading Genre." *The New York Times*, A24, March 1, 2012.

Baudrillard, Jean. *The System of Objects*. Translated by James Benedict. London: Verso, 2006.

Bernasek, Andrew. "Two Numbers: Vinyl Records are Back." *Newsweek Online*, November 6, 2014. Accessed February 24, 2015. http://www.newsweek.com/2014/11/14/two-numbers-vinyl-records-are-back-282604.html

Bryson, Bethany. "Anything but heavy metal': Symbolic Exclusion and Musical Dislikes." *American Sociological Review* 61, no. 5 (1996): 884–899.

Bull, Michael. "No Dead Air! The iPod and the Culture of Mobile Listening." *Leisure Studies* 24, no. 4 (2005): 343–355.

Calamar, Gary, and Paul Gallo. *Record Store Days: From Vinyl to Digital and Back Again*. New York: Sterling, 2010.

Carney, George. "Music Geography." *Journal of Cultural Geography* 18, no. 1 (1998): 1–10.

Clouse, Abby. "Narratives of Value and the Antiques Roadshow: A Game of Recognitions." *The Journal of Popular Culture* 41, no. 1 (2008): 3–20.

Cosgrove, Denis. "Geography Is Everywhere: Culture and Symbolism in Human Landscapes." *Horizons in Human Geography* (1989): 118–135.

Cresswell, Tim. *Place: A Short Introduction*. London: John Wiley & Sons, 2004.

Currid, Elizabeth, and Sarah Williams. "Two Cities, Five Industries: Similarities and Differences within and Between Cultural Industries in New York and Los Angeles." *Journal of Planning Education and Research* 29, no. 3 (2010): 322–335.

Dougan, John. "Objects of Desire: Canon Formation and Blues Record Collecting." *Journal of Popular Music Studies* 18, no. 1 (2006): 40–65.

Ettlinger, Nancy. "Toward a Critical Theory of Untidy Geographies: The Spatiality of Emotions in Consumption and Production." *Feminist Economics* 10, no. 3 (2004): 21–54.

Florida, Richard, Charlotta Mellander, and Kevin Stolarick. "Music Scenes to Music Clusters: The Economic Geography of Music in the US, 1970–2000." *Environment and Planning. A* 42, no. 4 (2010): 785–794.

Geoghegan, Hilary. "Emotional Geographies of Enthusiasm: Belonging to the Telecommunications Heritage Group." *Area* 45, no. 1 (2013): 40–46.

Gracon, David. "The Independent Record Store as a Site of Cultural Resistance and Anti- McDonaldization—A Case Study of the House of Records." In *The Business of Entertainment,* Vol. 2, edited by Sickels, R., 205–221. Santa Barbara, CA: Praeger, 2011.

Hall, James. "MP3 Players Are Dead." *The Daily Telegraph Business Insider Online*. December 26, 2012. Accessed June 14, 2015. http://www.businessinsider.com/mp3-players-are- dead-2012–12

Hayes, David. " 'Take Those Old Records Off the Shelf': Youth and Music Consumption in the Postmodern Age." *Popular music and society* 29, no. 1 (2006): 51–68.

Hesmondhalgh, David. "The British Dance Music Industry: A Case Study of Independent Cultural Production." *British Journal of Sociology* 49.2 (1998): 234–251.

Hracs, Brian J., Doreen Jakob, and Atle Hauge. "Standing Out in the Crowd: The Rise of Exclusivity-Based Strategies to Compete in the Contemporary Marketplace for Music and Fashion." *Environment and Planning A* 45, no. 5 (2013): 1144–1161.
Huefe, Edward. "Music Geography Across the Borderline: Musical Iconography, Mythic Themes, and North American Perceptions of a Borderlands Landscape." Masters Thesis. California State University, Long Beach, 2002.
Knight, Meribah. "A CD-Only Music Store that Plays to Its Own Beat." *The New York Times*. April 14, 2011. Accessed May 10, 2012. http://www.nytimes.com/2011/04/15/us/ 15cncdigital.html?_r=0
Lazo, Alejandro. "Highland Park Becoming Gentrified." *Los Angeles Times Blog*. March 11, 2012. Accessed May 10, 2012. http://latimesblogs.latimes.com/lanow/2012/03/highland- park-gentrifying-.html
Ley, David. "Artists, Aestheticisation and the Field of Gentrification." *Urban Studies* 40, no. 12 (2003): 2527–2544.
Leyshon, Andrew, Peter Webb, Shaun French, Nigel Thrift, and Louise Crewe. "On the Reproduction of the Musical Economy After the Internet." *Media, Culture and Society* 27, no. 2 (2005): 177–209.
Lukinbeal, Chris. "The Rise of Regional Film Production Centers in North America, 1984–1997." *GeoJournal* 59, no. 4 (2004): 307–321.
Magaudda, Paolo. "When Materiality 'bites back': Digital Music Consumption Practices in the Age of Dematerialization." *Journal of Consumer Culture* 11, no. 1 (2011): 15–36.
Mark, Noah P. "Culture and Competition: Homophily and Distancing Explanations for Cultural Niches." *American Sociological Review* 68.3 (2003): 319–345.
Marshall, Ian. "Thurs Oct 25—Germany New Arrivals Sale & Our 2nd Anniversary Party, 8pm." Message to the Wombleton Records emailing list. 25 Oct 2012.
Marshall, Ian. "**Wombleton's Weekend Sale** Sat March 30th & Sun March 31st! Up to 50% off all items." Message to the Wombleton Records emailing list. 28 March 2013.
Massey, Doreen. *Space, Place, and Gender*. Minneapolis: University of Minnesota Press, 1994.
Massey, Doreen. *For Space*. London: Sage Publications Limited, 2005.
Morrice, Stephanie. "Heartache and Hurricane Katrina: Recognising the Influence of Emotion in Post-Disaster Return Decisions." *Area* 45, no. 1 (2013): 33–39.
Osborne, Richard. "The Record and Its Label: Identifying, Marketing, DividingCollecting." *Popular Music History* 2, no. 3 (2008): 263–284.
Plasketes, George. "Romancing the Record: The Vinyl De-Evolution and Subcultural Evolution." *The Journal of Popular Culture* 26, no. 1 (1992): 109–122.
Pile, Steve. "Emotions and Affect in Recent Human Geography." *Transactions of the Institute of British Geographers* 35, no. 1 (2010): 5–20.
Pulido, Laura. "Rethinking Environmental Racism: White Privilege and Urban Development in Southern California." *Annals of the Association of American Geographers* 90, no. 1 (2000): 12–40.
Schor, Naomi. "Collecting Paris." In *The Cultures of Collecting*, edited by Elsner, J., and R. Cardinal, 252–274. Cambridge, MA: Harvard University Press, 1994.
Seman, Michael. "How a Music Scene Functioned as a Tool for Urban Redevelopment: A Case Study of Omaha's Slowdown Project." *City, Culture and Society* 1, no. 4 (2010): 207–215.

Shuker, Roy. *Wax Trash and Vinyl Treasures: Record Collecting as a Social Practice.* London: Ashgate Publishing, Ltd., 2010.

Sirois, André, and Janet Wasko. "The Political Economy of the Recorded Music Industry: Redefinitions and New Trajectories in the Digital Age." *The Handbook of Political Economy of Communications* (2011): 331–357.

Straw, Will. "Sizing Up Record Collections." *Sexing the Groove: Popular Music and Gender* (1997): 3–16.

Straw, Will. "Exhausted Commodities: The Material Culture of Music." *Canadian Journal of Communication* 25, no. 1 (2000): 183.

Tauber, Edward M. "Why Do People Shop?" *The Journal of Marketing* 36.4 (1972): 46–49.

Thien, Deborah. "After or Beyond Feeling? A Consideration of Affect and Emotion in Geography." *Area* 37, no. 4 (2005): 450–454.

Tuan, Yi-Fu. "Place and Culture: Analeptic for Individuality and the World's Indifference." In *Mapping American Culture,* edited by Franklin, W., and M. Steiner, 27–49. Iowa City: University of Iowa Press, 1992.

Urry, John. "The Place of Emotions Within Place." In *Emotional Geographies*, edited by Davidson, J., M. Smith, and L. Bondi. Burlington: Ashgate Publishing, 2005: 77–83.

Vaher, Berk. "Identity Politics Reco(r)ded: Vinyl Hunters as Exotes in Time." *Trames* 12.3 (2008): 342–354.

Windsor, John. "Identity Parades." In *The Cultures of Collecting*, edited by Elsner, J., and R. Cardinal, 49–67. London: Reaktion Books, 1994.

Yochim, Emily Chivers, and Megan Biddinger. "'It kind of gives you that vintage feel': Vinyl Records and the Trope of Death." *Media, Culture and Society* 30, no. 2 (2008): 183–195.

15 Music Rights

Towards a Material Geography of Musical Practices in the "Digital Age"

Andy C. Pratt

This chapter is concerned with copyright and music. Its stress on the material geographies and practice challenges the norms of debate that have been dominated by concern with the immaterial and the virtual. The chapter argues that such conceptual and practical focus on de-materialization has obscured, or distracted, analyses to such an extent that it has rendered invisible the geographical. Not surprisingly, debates have been dazzled by technological changes, to the extent that they have—erroneously—displaced other concerns. The premature announcement of the "death of distance" being a case in point. The chapter argues for the need to turn our attention to the social and spatial embedding of musical practice if we are to fully comprehend its emergent forms in the "digital age." This chapter is positioned against the notion of a "digital age": a term that is associated with teleological theories of development. Moreover, it is a term that has deep roots in the writings of conservative futurists (Bell 1973, Toffler 1980), and much of the contemporary "technology commentariat" spun out from *Wired* magazine (Kelly 1998). A telling critical exposition of such writing can be found in the exploration of the "Californian Ideology" (Barbrook and Cameron 1996).

Copyright and music are often used in the same sentence, and the issue of piracy and downloading has become the stuff of moral panics. By focusing on consumption and distribution, and the (disembodied) digital, we have become disconnected from the materiality of musical production. Debates about the consumption of music, where focus is on an exclusive concern with the online purchase and distribution of music, are a legitimate concern, but not when they lead to the exclusion of the production of music. We have accepted the organizational erasure of intermediaries (see Lange, this volume), and the idealization of a peer-to-peer world, as if it were a naïve neo-classical economic textbook. A further "invisibility" in neo-classical economics and debates about the digital age concerns spaces, institutions, and people.

A related neglect concerns work on the labor and organization of music making, and the dynamics of performance and audiences (see: Haijen, this volume; Hracs, this volume; Speers, this volume). The framing of the debate in contemporary normative literature thus immediately pre-presents this second position that is concerned with the material and affective as analogue, Luddite, or backward looking.[1] To be sure, I want to support a different perspective that acknowledges labor in the digital age; but I will argue that this can only be successfully achieved by re-conceptualizing the two positions as joined and interwoven. This chapter seeks to connect the two dimensions (the social and material, and the digital and immaterial) in a novel manner: a way that it is not simply additive, but is transformative of both sides. The key element is how we conceptualize copyright (Kretschmer and Pratt 2009). Normative views, if they acknowledge it at all, view copyright as an autonomous, "bolt on," characteristic of music; I will argue that it is better seen as a relational feature, one that re-constitutes both music and place.

Polarized debates about copyright tend to flounder on atomistic idealizations of the legal relations of music: first, via a concern with the mechanisms and business models presumed by a particular legal construct, and, secondly, in terms of the blame attributed to individuals associated with moral failure[2] (usually characterized by the youth, and those residing in the Global South). Both positions presume that copyright is universal and indisputable. It is this underlying assumption that the chapter contests. In short I argue that copyright is relational, taking its meaning from its context (social, economic and spatial): that is, opposed to an absolute position that excludes context. Conceptualized thus, we re-open the possibility of geographies of copyright and musical practice which have recently been severed. Music practices that we may observe take place in, and are constituted by, a legal framework,[3] such that we assume them to be natural. This point is analogous to driving a car on a road, it is not "natural," or always correct, to drive on either the right or the left, but is a norm constituted by particular legal codes. Under such codes, and practices, certain rights (let alone security) are created for those who operate in compliance with them.

I argue that laws constitute the practices, not simply regulate them. The law is not an idle bystander, but an active participant as it shapes, and is shaped by, history and social norms. In this chapter I seek to admit a place for the (otherwise excluded) spatial and temporal changes in music making, their practices and technologies, as well as the international flows. Examination of these various ways of music making in turn shows how they generate particular geographies of music. Such geographies and practices are not separate from the digital; they are intimately bound up with it, each being co-constitutive of the other. A critical element is the territorial variation of legal jurisdictions: in particular, the degree to which laws on the statute books in any place are implemented.[4] This analytic space, I argue, opens up a rich empirical field of copyright in and across different places, and the organizational and political mechanisms, and spatial configurations of music. It is this that I argue is a better framework for analysis, one that sees an intimate and recursive relationship between people, place, and social and economic institutions. In short, an approach that brings the digital age back to earth: specific times, places, and practices.

The structure of the chapter is as follows: I first introduce the idea of copyright and ownership in music: what it is, what can be owned, and how local institutions shape it. In the second and third parts I elaborate the issues and some practical consequences through exploration of first ownership, and second, trade. I explore these through the lens of the two types of "rights" in music: moral and mechanical. I further show how these are interwoven and embedded in space.

BASICS: WHAT DO WE OWN?

De-Materialization

We often take the idea of ownership for granted, it is banal; it is only contested if we have an obvious transgression: a theft. Such a demonstration of proof is tricky enough with a material object, let alone an immaterial one. In such a case, how do you prove that the object "stolen" is yours? What is it that you actually "own"? That it has been in your possession; you have the receipt maybe? We tend to think of the ownership of music in this way eliding the intellectual and material dimensions of the "thing." Recent debates about piracy echo such a simple good-bad distinction, one where there is a natural right or wrong. The aim of this section is to unsettle this binary of right and wrong, or at least its apparently normative values. The aim is to highlight a new dimension to the legal geographies of music that are produced through the operation of copyright regimes, and their concomitant concepts of property rights. A necessary first step is to acknowledge the multiple claims of legal rights concerning music.

In the last decade we have witnessed one round of debates about the "death of geography" and digitization (see Pratt 2000). Considered analysis has shown this to be a fallacious and sloppy argument concerned with abstract and idealized possibilities divorced from material practices in the world (Cairncross 1998). Beyond a knee-jerk corrective we can sketch a new line of debate that offers a more hybrid position, as opposed to a polarized viewpoint. The particular focus of many commentators, in part that to which other authors in this book are responding, is the dematerialization of production and consumption: co-authors are seeking to re-ground these concerns literately and figuratively (see: Watson, this volume; Leyshon et al., this volume). My contribution is complementary, but slightly different: it is focused on the notion of the "rights" of music, who can use them and in which forms. More generally, I want to show that the "legal" is not just a context, but also an active shaper of music production and its modes of consumption, and the means of production of its distinct geographies. It is these situated socio-economic-legal conditions that define and fix the local forms of "digital" practice (and its emergent forms).

Intellectual and Material Rights

Many people have rightly highlighted the challenge of digitization to many practices, especially those of music. When they do so, it is often shorthand for new business models, such as the "long tail," and new means of communication instantiated in the immaterial software download versus the physical distribution of the material product of a record or a CD (Wikström 2009). What is less discussed is the fact that we are not dealing with material things, but with electrical impulses, and that the "rights" associated are intellectual as well as, or instead of, material ones. Moreover, we are codifying who and what can be owned, or who is deemed responsible for a creative act. For example, is sampling a drumbeat a creative act, different from that of the original drummer? Who should have the rights to the sample? And how should the income be divided? Much of our common sense and everyday practice is constructed around "things"; we have common codes for referring to them (length of our possession, or, we have a receipt), locating them, and transacting them. Even then, we know that they can be the source of legal dispute (for example, did the seller own the object that we purchased). The problem is that when we discuss the digital we commonly use the same analogies. But, the analogy should be reversed. What we miss is the fact that the material object—by its brute physicality—stands in for the "legal" thing. Traditionally, we have referred to the vinyl disc or CD, as the "carrier" of the rights; however, in legal terms the MP3 is also a carrier. The rights question does not change, although apparently the carrier has "dematerialized." Here we are in danger of a philosophical debate about "thing-ness." But it can be appreciated that if you take the physical object out of the equation, all that you have are the rules of "ownership," in this chapter what I refer to as intellectual property (again, the very language refers us back to a physical analogue).

Why does all of this matter? Let's take the example of a CD (for those old enough to remember them; or substitute any carrier of the IP, or any service to distribute it). I use the CD as an example as it's the last direct physical transaction of music that we have. In this sense we use the material concepts and translate them to the real of the digital and something goes awry. In the case of a CD it is bought in a shop, and then legally you own it; don't you? You may be surprised what you actually own: some plastic and paper. The information encoded on the CD is protected, and you have purchased a right to use it; you do not own it. Likewise with an MP3 download or a streamed file: even though it's digital you don't own the IP. The right to use it (the IP) is delimited by strict conditions such as not playing it to other people (in whatever media), and not copying it (that would even include singing it), only to play it on specific machinery, and in some cases only in particular legal territories. For this right you have paid a fee, or a rent. It is a "right" that the originator can withdraw at any time. It is immediately apparent that the slippage between legal nicety and common practice creates a norm of technical "law breaking."

This might be troubling, or confusing, but does it really matter? I want to show that it matters for the geography of music, and how we conceive it. However, thus far I have only considered the rights to use or trade the music: Who owns it, and who created it? For example, it is perfectly possible and indeed likely, that the rights to play, or reproduce, a piece of music are owned by person A in country 1, and person B in country 2. There's an apparent paradox! Can two people own the same thing: yes, but separated by territory. As I will explain, this will take us in other apparently mind-boggling directions. However, it lies at the core of what it means to be a living and working musician, how you make a living from your composition. My core point will be to show that the ownership question is not obvious; in fact, it is a socially situated and negotiated thing. Related, these negotiations are embedded in particular territorial legal systems, which are different. So, there is an obvious geography of copyright. Moreover, the trade or exchange between one system or territory and another can lead to distinct inequalities. Simply, if you take your music into another legal jurisdiction, you may have no rights to use it.

By using the example of what we might "own" of a CD, I hope that I have begun to problematize ownership and the material. We naturally tend to assume that ownership is a totalizing and universal fact: both in terms of the "ownership" and the "thing." As the CD (or any other carrier) example shows, we are in fact offered rights of use only; these rights actually shape the "thing": the music on the CD, what it is, and what we can do with it (for example, different versions of the same album, or different albums, released in various countries). The common misunderstanding of ownership leads us down the false path of thinking that we can choose what we do with any object that we own, and, moreover, if we separate the thing from the material that we have somehow liberated it. As some digital libertarians have it: "data wants to be free." They are, in other words, constructing data/music as independent and somehow outside of control. This is not what the legal framework suggests. Common discourse about music rights tends to be reduced to technologies and materialities. This chapter is arguing for a more subtle relationship, hence the unease with such terms as the "digital age" and "digitization" when not used in a specific and situated manner.

The mechanical rights, or what we may normally view as the trade and consumption side, are important; but they miss a critical production and moral dimension. In the remainder of the chapter I will show that the concern with digitization has only assumed to impact on this aspect highlighting dis-intermediation, and the ideal state of autonomous producer. I will explore these two sides of the same music "coin" in the following sections: consumption and production. In both cases I will highlight the fact that scale and geography are constituent parts of music. I will do this by adopting the legal codification of moral and mechanical rights. Furthermore, I will show that there are distinct temporal, scalar, and spatial dimensions to both.

MORAL RIGHTS

Moral rights are what we normally associate with the "author." In copyright law that is the person "identified as the author," and the integrity of whose work is protected. That is, you can't copy it and claim it for yourself; you can't tamper with it, change the second verse and call it your own. An author can claim a "royalty," a rent essentially, on others using the work identified with the author (under specific terms). These notions are widespread, but not universal, and they are interpreted differently under particular legal jurisdictions. This royalty percentage may seem small, and it is for regular sales; but in a temporal monopoly (that is the particular kind of monopoly that the organizational form of the music charts represents: namely being the No.1 music that week), it can net huge gross sums.

Micro-Scale

What is it that the artist has created, can be attributed to them, and what can thus be sold? And, how can its ownership be designated? In the legal world the term used is "the work." The work is the music (and words) uniquely authored by the artist. If the work is reproduced and distributed, a second property, or division of the property, is created. That is the work, and its physical "carrier" (the recording), or the sheet music (the mechanical rights discussed above). Initially, it was the work codified as notes on a stave, and sold as sheet music: the author's original, and the copied item. On sale of the sheet music the artist got an income based on the royalty—the rent for the use of the work based upon sales. Note that this is different to the regular calculation of the margin between production costs and selling costs of a regular product (which, to complicate matters, sheet music is simultaneously). There were not constraints on the reproduction of the music (today that would be prosecuted as copying: even singing "Happy Birthday"). Historically, it was just the physical sheet music; in fact the possibility of reproduction on a piano was its raison d'etre and the business model. Times change, today those rights are retained and protected. Again, this emphasizes the situated nature of rights and how they affect the conditions under which we perform and listen to music (which will be, necessarily, place and time specific).

The slippage between common practice, or production systems, and the law generate problems. Essentially, the same system adopted from classical music carried on into popular music, and critically, the same case law and precedent. However, sales of records, and the income, quickly exceeded that of sheet music. Copying performance became an issue that rights holders wanted to protect. However, a more significant shift in musical practice complicated matters. From the mid-1960s, the popular music performance artist increasingly wrote their own compositions; however, many popular music artists didn't read or write music. This created two challenges: first, collective informal authorship; and, second, the "work" was not transcribed.

An artist's performance in the studio is either paid as a one-off fee, and/or a small proportion of the mechanical rights (or reproduction), not the moral rights (authorship; which normally carry a greater percentage revenue of royalties). Band members thus have to prove or assert authorship rights from an assumed sole authorship to instead reflect what was in practice an improvised collective construction. Many compositions emerged from a collective improvisation of the band. A step further and we entered the era of music composition in the studio where there might be many more potential "authors." Nominal authorship was often attributed to the singer, as a convenience. Moreover, if inspiration had been lifted (plagiarized) from another song, especially "folk" music, it was re-attributed to the current performer. A well-documented case concerns Led Zeppelin, who "miss-credited" themselves for music that they did not write. After court cases, the writing credits were "adjusted" on later re-issues of the albums, and revenues redirected to Delta Blues songwriters such as Willie Dixon. This was not an exceptional case (Vaidhyanathan 2003).

Bently (2009) offers another dimension to the analysis by showing how classically trained ethnomusicologists are often called as expert witnesses in court; they not only view authorship in a normative fashion, but also reproduce the "legitimacy" of non-orchestral instruments: for example, that saxophone is "ephemeral," and drums "not an element of a musical work." Thus, Bently points to an interpretation of legal cases as showing up how not only that copyright does not work (for the artists), but neither does it recognize the labor of making music.

The changing technologies of recording and the practices that developed around them further complicated the picture. Gander (2010) shows in his analysis of studio producers and engineers, a similar battle has taken place in recognition of "authorship" of the production, recording, and "the mix"–not a right generally recognized in the law. On the contrary, in the classical conception the "technical" work of the studio is further from the "creative essence" and does not count. In the digital age the nature and history of "the mix" is even more critical. Technically, it is possible to save every take, and every mix, in the recording process. Producers are wary of providing record companies with this—history. Producers are normally paid a flat fee for their services (instead of a royalty, which would imply that they were an artist). The digital history potentially allows a "remix" of producers' work–in principle, a challenge to the moral rights of the producer (if they were recognized). In an extra legal action the common response is that "possession" is 9/10th of the law. Thus, it has become usual for these "stems"[5] to be retained by the producer, only passing on the processed (and irreversible) final mix. This serves to further illustrate the extended and collective nature of "authorship" of a "work" of art, and the tensions between the material and legal realms and how they are continually multiplied.

Macro-Scale

There is a basic rational economic requirement for markets to function: that payment flows from the purchaser to producer. The system of royalties is a rent on the use of music. In practice the challenge is how to collect the rent and get paid. Generally, it is rolled up with the selling price, and then returned to a "collecting society" who redistributes the income to the rights holders based upon an audit of sales. The institutional requirements of an efficient and effective logging, claiming, and distributing of royalties has been a challenge in the Global North; the costs of institution building in the Global South are often prohibitive. These institutions—collecting societies—are run and owned by artists. They are costly and complex to organize. The incentive is the "carrot" or a stream of income, but this also requires an effective "stick," the development of a specialized legal infrastructure to prosecute piracy. The failure of these institutions to operate and articulate an operational legal framework is a major practical barrier. Empirically speaking, in much of the world songwriters do not receive royalties. The specification of the details of the above paragraph would fill a book alone, and it would be obsolete tomorrow. Hence, my strategy here is to avoid collapsing debates into technologies, focusing instead of the way that rights are mediated through locally and temporally specific institutions and technological forms. This is a conceptualization that can then be applied empirically to cases.

The consequence in the Global South is that the copyright system is broken and few people respect "rights." Indeed, one might argue that it is not "rational" to do so under such conditions. Instead an alternative, parallel market develops based upon live performance, where income for artists can be secured from the audience direct as moral and mechanical rights may be practically irrelevant to this business model. An organizational consequence is that musicians must over-exploit themselves and use up their creative stock of music without fully exploiting it. The organizational success of the western pop model is based upon monopoly profits from a "hit," and the restriction of releases of material so that the last penny is extracted from audiences before a subsequent release. One of the benefits of the monopoly model is that—for the few—incomes are higher, and that due to the protection of rights, a continuing income can be had from music, usually via "replay rights" (Bagdikian 2004). However, as can be appreciated, it is a profoundly geographical question as to whose interest this system works for.

The well-publicized "world music" stars seem to be a contrary example, succeeding by breaking out of the Global South system and into the Global Northern one (see Brandellero and Kloosterman, this volume). In reality they are using a parallel system (see next section). Once they gain recognition in the North, they secure legal rights (limited to Northern territories), and form companies to channel profits into banks based in the North.

It is far from straightforward to create a flow of money to the Global South. Moreover, it is often the case that music by Southern artists recorded and released in the North, is legally not available for distribution in the South. If Southern artists want their music to circulate in their home countries they will have to engineer a local legal agreement, and battle to secure protection of their rights (Pratt 2007). As noted above, in many cases an artist regards legal protection as irrelevant.

A further point about the relational legality of copyright touches on a more fundamental point. The Northern copyright system assumes a singular ownership of authorship. In some countries this is an alien concept; community or collective rights are recognized, but the concept of an individual right is not valid. There is clearly a fundamental problem of resolving an individualistic ontology of copyright, with a collective one. Thus, it is not a "disrespect" or a "moral failure" to recognize rights but to see them in a different economic, social, and political formation, and consequently, what they can control: Music and stories often belong to a community.[6] Moreover, as also noted above, it is not "rational" to support a copyright system that locally does not deliver benefits, or respect or local values. This continues to be a fundamental contradiction with the principles of universalist property regimes.

MECHANICAL RIGHTS

The reproduction rights of music are a product of mass popular music consumption and the social transformation of youth. Million seller records, with favorites that change by the week, became big business; it is a very successful business model. From a naive point of view the model of selling records, as the product, seems like any other field of manufacture; however, as noted above, this obscures the making of music itself. Although, as noted above, the rights are not simple, they echo the "rental" model: The fee we pay as individuals to play the music, or broadcasters to do so, or to trade in the replay rights. Who "controls" the rights of a piece of music in this case are recognizable. The point to note here is that by using digital only transactions a number of "middle men" are potentially cut out (disintermediation) of the equation, seeming to put the author in control. As we have noted above, this is seldom achieved in reality.

Micro-Scale

As the music companies own the reproduction rights, they can "re-exploit" their music libraries to their heart's content (as long as the contract was written favorably). Consumers can be encouraged to buy the same product several times packaged in new formats: a vinyl record, a CD, and an MP3 of the same music. The costs to the record company ("pressing" the CD, legal and management costs, artist development, recording, promotion, etc.) come to as much as 40 percent of the sales cost; however, the actual costs are less than half of this, the remainder is the cost of "risk."[7] The 50 percent retail and distribution and physical costs could all go back to the artist, but generally the music company, or other agents, manage to retain a large proportion.

This is the sphere of possibility that so much of the "digitization" literature focuses on, often projecting the idealized case where the artist sells direct to the consumer. This is seldom the case, despite the fact that so many routes to market are possible. The dominance of platforms such as iTunes, and Spotify,[8] highlight the emergence of digital intermediaries who, as ever, pass a small proportion of the retail fee to the artist. Added to which is the completely skewed market in cultural goods, of which music is a prime example, built upon a "winner takes all" model that fits neatly with oligopoly (Frank and Cook 1996). Just three companies dominate the music industry; it is primarily these companies that make a deal with the digital platforms.

Markets are configured and promoted by charts and commentary, the digital platforms (which configure availability, and more importantly visibility), and accompanying social media operations to promote and rapidly turn over stars, driving the market to concentration and monopoly profits. In the physical distribution years, this concentration was vital to the functioning of the business and efficient stock control and waste minimization. Today, although the physical necessity does not exist, there continues to be institutional rigidity; both the "industry" and the "audiences" are acculturated to monopoly artists. The new digital platforms are in a win-win situation with the occasional "slow burn," or "long tail" success of the back catalogue, and the monopoly profits from national, short-term stars. The obverse is that selling a few copies of anything will not make a sustainable livelihood for a musician.

Macro-Scale

The industrialization of music—its mass reproduction, consumption, and insertion into trans-local systems of exchange—created a new realm, as well as new barriers. As I have noted, music needs a "carrier"–the vinyl disc, compact disc, or digital file. Music traded in a physical form was effectively regulated after the fashion of most physical goods: The cost and time of reproduction, and (technically inferior) copies were a barrier on transgressions. Copyright issues were seen as more or less co-existent with the material object. Thus, the structuring and regulatory factors were practiced through trade–the movement of goods. Tariff barriers and national borders had to be negotiated, and taxes paid.

With digitization it has been often assumed that the link between the physical object and the musical work was severed and that none of these material encumbrances would apply any longer. Therefore, different business models would be devised to capture the added value; again, a common proposition has been disintermediation where the artist deals direct with the consumer; practice is somewhat messier.

The first aspect that we need to appreciate is the role of institutional inheritance, or path dependency. The path to market of music has traditionally passed through a highly organized and centralized music industry. It was organized on the logic of moving goods, goods for which demand fluctuated wildly, and had considerably diminished value after a time period. As I have noted, new digital platforms (and companies) have substituted but not replaced the distributional and marketing forms established in an analogue age. It would be more accurate to say a re-intermediation has taken place around digital platforms.

Even in the analog age the national and regional differences of music making and consumption were often overlooked. Negus' (1999) work offers a strong counter to this normative view. He shows that music markets are organized around a number of national territories, each structured around particular genres, release dates, and marketing campaigns. National markets were, and are, differentiated; we do not all like the same music, nor produce the same music. Music successful in one territory was seldom successful in another. Moreover, despite the emergence of popular music (dominated by a European-North American form), a number of other genres have not only persisted but also prospered. Music companies structured their activities and organized their markets (which included vertical and horizontal integration, media and performance, as well as retail). The internationalization of the music business had significant post-Fordist characteristics whereby niche markets were developed, and an example is the proliferation of "charts" associated with genre and location (Negus 1999). The structural objective is volume and turnover.

This path dependency matters because although physical distribution of music has declined, music companies (and their replacements, the digital platforms) still bear a structural legacy of the genres and territories. The music industry is still struggling with the idea of the first "global" release of music (all countries at the same time). Despite the theoretic potential, the reality still remains one of national systems. The (once physical) path and market structure of dependency is also one at the same time a legal one, too. International music distributors will not operate in some countries (most of the world), not due to lack of demand, but because they cannot control distribution and copyright. These countries are literally "off the international map" of music; they are relegated to a secondary system that is insulated from the "international" system (see previous section).

The result is far from a digital global free market dream; rather, it is an empirical story of a combined and uneven music industry development of (mainly) nations of the Global South (and their significant musical heritage). One of the reasons that these countries are "locked out" is their "non-compliance" with international copyright conventions. In practice, most countries have signed up to international conventions; however, the problem is that they have insufficient resources to police them, or more critically to make sure that the copyright industries function.

CONCLUSIONS

I have argued that we need to pay closer attention to the issue of copyright with respect to music. Popular accounts of the digital age and music have rested on a symbolic erasure of production, and with it the geographies of production. Conceptually speaking, the normative position suffers from technological reductivism, immaterialism, teleology, and universalism. The answer is not to simply offer a polar opposite point of view. Rather, I have argued for the need to examine the relationship between the social (legal, economic, and political) and the technical (digital). The example that has been explored in this chapter concerns one such mediation: the field of copyright (again one that is seldom viewed as a mediation, but as a law).

I have argued that we cannot read off musical practices from a technological map, nor draw a direct line between moral and mechanical rights or between the material and immaterial. We need to resist treating copyright as a "natural" thing, or as stable or having unitary meaning, something that can be added in as a new "factor." I have sought to sidestep the well-travelled road of the death of copyright, music, and geography. These are all important debates, but I argued that they misconstrue both the causes and the processes of change. Instead, I have shown that the subtle relationship of making and remaking music under particular local (legal, technical, and artistic) conditions offers a more nuanced account.

The realm of copyright is not universal or unitary as it is often presented; in fact, it is local and fragmented. Despite a similar legal coding of the law in many jurisdictions, the interpretation and practice of its application is various, attenuated by the organizational capabilities of collecting societies, audience, and musicians, as well as the state. These factors have a direct relationship to the income and legal capacity of regional and nation states. Particular forms are forged within these historically and spatially situated conditions.

Accordingly, by default, we have paid too much attention to the consumption of music, passing over the conditions of its production. The debates about immateriality and mechanical rights had led to a neglect of what is in essence a moral and cultural value debate. I have stressed that this is not a polarized, either-or distinction; rather, it is a complex hybrid.

With these complex matrices laid bare we can observe a rich diversity of music practice: the variety of different ways that it is possible to create and disseminate music. These practices are the raw material of the geographies of music, its forms and performances. In this sense music as a creative practice is a product of a locale, but not exclusively and not simply in its expression, but in terms of its organizational practices–practices which in turn shape and are shaped with a range of institutions that can be enabling or resistant to travelling beyond the local.

NOTES

1. Indications of other silencing has been evidenced in the re-examination of the role of "craft and graft" in cultural work (Sennett, R. 2008), as well as the vast literature on the "maker movement" Dougherty, D. (2012).
2. Copyright transgressions are subject to moral sanction: They are "bad"—"copyright is theft" when combined with developmentalist discourse that constitutes a story of "moral failure" of whole peoples—constructed as disrespect for an atomized and commoditized notion of ownership.
3. Legal frameworks, and social institutions, are, of course, embedded in places and practices.
4. This echoes a point that Sassen (2013) makes with respect to sovereignty and globalization: It is always local and requires local legal decisions.
5. Software code files produced by Pro Tools, which is the market-leading software used for mixing music.
6. See, for example, the West African Griot or storyteller tradition (Eyre 2000).
7. In music the ratio of "misses" to "hits" is high, and in any business model this has to be accounted for in total costs.
8. Despite commercial differences, these services perform a similar function of distribution and licensing of the content.

REFERENCES

Bagdikian, Ben H. *The New Media Monopoly,* 7th ed. Boston, MA: Beacon, 2004.

Barbrook, R, and Andy Cameron. "Californian Ideology." *Science as Culture* 6, no. 1 (1996): 44–72.

Bell, Daniel. *The Coming of Post-Industrial Society*. New York: Basic Books, 1973.

Bently, Lionel. "Authorship of Popular Music in UK Copyright Law." *Information, Communication and Society* 12, no. 2 (2009): 179–204.

Cairncross, Frances. *The Death of Distance: How the Communications Revolution Will Change Our Lives*. Boston: Harvard Business School Press, 1998.

Dougherty, Dale. "The Maker Movement." *Innovations* 7, no. 3 (2012): 11–14.

Eyre, Banning. *In Griot Time*. London: Serpents Tail, 2000.

Frank, Robert H., and Philip J. Cook. *The Winner-Take-All Society : Why the Few at the Top Get So Much More Than the Rest of Us*. New York: Penguin Books, 1996.

Gander, Jonathan. "Performing Music Production: Creating Music Product." PhD Diss., King's College London, 2010.

Kelly, Kevin. *New Rules for the New Economy*. London: Fourth Estate, 1998.

Kretschmer, Martin, and Andy C. Pratt. "Legal form and Cultural Symbol." *Information, Communication and Society* 12 no. 2 (2009): 165–177.

Negus, Keith. *Music Genres and Corporate Subcultures*. London: Routledge, 1999.

Pratt, Andy C. "New Media, the New Economy and New Spaces." *Geoforum*, 31 no. 4 (2000): 425–436.
Pratt, Andy C. "The Music Industry and Its Potential Role in Local Economic Development: The Case of Senegal." In *Creative Industries and Developing Countries: Voice, Choice and Economic Growth*, edited by Barrowclough, Diana, and Zeljka Kozul-Wright, 130–145. London: Routledge, 2007.
Sassen, Saskia. *Losing Control?: Sovereignty in the Age of Globalization*. New York: Columbia University Press, 2013.
Sennett, Richard. *The Craftsman*. New Haven: Yale University Press, 2008.
Toffler, Alvin. *The Third Wave*. London: Collins, 1980.
Vaidhyanathan, Siva. *Copyrights and Copywrongs: The Rise of Intellectual Property and How it Threatens Creativity*. New York: New York University Press, 2003.
Wikström, Patrik. *The Music Industry: Music in the Cloud*. Cambridge: Polity Press, 2009.

Part VI

Promoting and Consuming

16 Unpacking the "Digital Habitus" of Music Fans in Santiago's Indie Music Scene

Arturo Arriagada

Technology is central to the configuration of a music marketplace but attention is typically focused on producers and the means of distribution. Much less is known about the role consumers play and how fans use digital technologies to participate, shape, and co-produce music scenes (see also Leyshon et al., this volume). This chapter is about the practices of a group of music fans who create and maintain websites about music scenes, with special emphasis on Santiago's indie music scene. These fans spend a lot of time in front of their computers, programming, surfing the web, uploading content on their websites, redesigning them to include new applications, as well as managing Facebook and Twitter accounts and exchanging links, pictures, and various types of content. They do the same thing using their mobile phones, communicating with the audiences they build through their websites. Digital communications technologies are present everywhere in their everyday lives. It is, therefore, impossible to understand how they structure their lives without observing the centrality that the Internet, mobile phones, flows of information, and links, clicks, "tweets," or "likes" have in their daily activities. These technologies enable individuals to situate themselves in networks where different flows of objects and symbols (Appadurai 1986) circulate regarding their interests, particularly around music.

In this context the websites produced by a group of music fans in Santiago emerge as spaces where global and local flows are organized, mediated, and represented. These flows are varied and websites include everything from music to fashion goods and brands as well as musicians' identities. The sites and their creators have attracted the attention of different fields of cultural production, particularly the field of advertising, to become spaces where brands can be promoted. Marketing agents have become part of the scene's activities (advertising them, as well as organizing marketing events where some of the scenes' bands play). Again, the websites and their creators are key actors connecting the scene with other fields of cultural production, as well as developing niche markets through their use of technology and cultural knowledge, collaborating in the design and promotion of those events. These forms of exchange thereby institutionalize values, music scenes, careers, and lifestyles. In some ways, Santiago's indie music scene, as a creative industry, is produced by the practices of production, consumption, and circulation of flows by the creators of websites, as well as its representation in those spaces (Arriagada and Cruz 2014; Tironi 2009).

This chapter examines how digital technologies, particularly information and communication technologies (ICTs), become artifacts that help a group of music fans to be situated in networks of information and cultural flows. It is based on eight months of fieldwork (2011) in Santiago (Chile), using an ethnographic approach, following the everyday practices of the creators of eight music websites in Santiago through which global and local cultural flows are mediated, organized, and circulated. It also explores how music websites operate as spaces through which music fans objectify their positions within those networks, as well as representations of the scene and its flows. On the one hand, they do this through a set of practices, e.g., establishing connections with others and with flows through different digital devices. On the other hand, producing websites about local and global music scenes, they develop a set of dispositions towards cultural flows and digital technologies.

MUSIC FANS, DIGITAL TECHNOLOGIES, AND THE DEVELOPMENT OF A "DIGITAL HABITUS"

Tironi (2009, 2011) argues that Santiago's music scene is made up of multiple spatialities, such that its identity is being permanently redefined. One of the reasons for this is that "the 'buzz' of the scene, which, far from being enacted through the immediacy and closeness of face-to-face interactions, is performed virtually, via decentred, distanciated, technologically-mediated and global communications" (Tironi 2011, 225). Thus, the scene as a whole cannot be approached as a fixed entity, comprised of fans with fixed roles, nor can it be considered autonomous from other fields in processes of cultural production. On the contrary, the scene (and perhaps even the term itself suggests a coherence which is lacking) exists as a result of a varied set of technologically mediated interactions between different entities—musicians, fans, producers, record labels, corporate brands, and advertisement agencies (see also Virani, this volume). The fluidity of the Santiago scene is due in large part to the Internet, and websites are the key means of making and connecting this diversity of activity to a range of locales and, perhaps more importantly, to market agents (see also: Johansson et al., this volume; Virani, this volume).

Through their practices in the making of the websites, a group of music fans define the scene in terms of who is doing interesting things worthy of being considered by audiences (making cultural distinctions), and establish social categories in order to make such distinctions (for a useful overview of the work on fans, see Leyshon et al., this volume). They act as curators, giving meaning and value to the scene's cultural goods, mediating identities, tastes, and lifestyles, and converting them into valuable objects of consumption (see also Lange, this volume). They are, therefore, constructing the boundaries of the scene with regard to the actors, goods, and spaces that are involved in its creation (Arriagada 2014). In this context, according to Tironi (2009, 2011), although he is interested in the spatiality of Santiago's indie music scene, as a social entity it becomes valorized, amongst other exchanges, as a result of the "buzz" around the music, musicians, and places that make it available for consumers. This means looking at the different types of mediations involved in the making of the websites, especially at information and communication technologies and cultural flows that are available on the scene. Similarly, the different strategies through which the circulation of flows are performed by website creators enable them to situate themselves within networks where flows circulate, connecting different fields of cultural production (e.g., the scene and the field of advertising). For instance, Molloy and Larner, in the case of the New Zealand fashion market, argue that "mutually constitutive relationships between production, mediation and consumption are characteristic of the whole fields of creative industries" where "these activities and actors are creating the industry as much as the designers" (2010, 374).

Fans' practices with digital technologies in the creation and maintenance of music websites are the result of different types of knowledge, objects, emotions, and activities that are stabilized and assembled on websites and social networking profiles (Schatzki 2001, 2002). These practices allow music fans to configure and display a "digital habitus"—a disposition that structures ways of being and doing towards digital objects within fields—through the exchange of information in practice with ICTs (Bourdieu 1990; Entwistle 2009). In the making of music websites ICTs are mediated and assembled through a set of practices and discourses. Bourdieu's conceptualization suggests that "habitus" is an essential condition of a social setting, a field where individuals can relate to each other as in a music scene. In this sense, "the habitus structures ways of being and doing" (Entwistle 2009, 135). This presupposes a process of "cultivation" (Bourdieu 1986) through which individuals develop their habitus as a set of dispositions towards, for instance, artistic work such as music or digital technologies. This cultivation is the result of the investment of time in order to develop the dispositions required to understand the rules and values within a particular field, as in a music scene. In the case of music fans, this involves time invested listening to music, sharing music online with others, reading different websites about global music scenes, as well as going to gigs, but most importantly, spending a considerable amount of time in front of the computer.

Music fans can accumulate "digital capital" (Arriagada 2014) not only as skills in combining material arrangements for the production and circulation of meanings. They also manage a set of strategies as a result of those processes to occupy certain positions within fields and through the technological space they create by managing websites. Through their websites fans accumulate big audiences, many downloads, "clicks," and "likes" as a result of their abilities to make cultural distinctions around the scene's flows, and then put them into circulation through digital technologies. The websites and the digital positions these people occupy can then be objectified and converted into economic capital within different fields—e.g., advertising and music—but they are also direct representations of those fields. In this sense, websites are spaces for action and interaction between fans in association with other actors (e.g., musicians, people from the field of advertising), as well as flows and information and communication technologies (ICTs). In that field, music fans deploy a set of strategies and practices regarding ICTs, deploying a "digital habitus" in order to accumulate and display their digital capital.

SANTIAGO'S INDIE MUSIC SCENE

In February 2011, the Spanish newspaper *El País* published an article about the indie music scene in Santiago, which celebrated the creativity of Chile's cultural production, referring to it as a "paradise of pop." One explanation for this renaissance, according to interviewees, is Chile's "isolation" from the rest of the world. Yet, while geographical isolation may have partly contributed to the unique sound of the Santiago scene, interviewees also emphasized the importance of the boundary defying technology of the Internet. As the creator of one of Chile's most respected music websites observed, "Our purchasing power is not even half of what it is in Europe . . . That 70% of the Chilean population has an account on Facebook speaks volumes." He and a friend, both students of journalism, and obsessed with the slow, immersive genre of UK post-rock known as "shoegaze," created Super 45 (www.super45.net), posting music and album reviews of indie music bands from around the world, occasionally including news and reviews of Chilean bands. Last year Super 45 celebrated 18 years of activity. The *El País* article was an important, if belated, celebration of a thriving scene by the mainstream press, but more importantly, it was gesture of recognition to websites like Super 45.

In Chile, multinational record labels were crucial during the nineties, especially after the censorship that characterized the scene during Pinochet's dictatorship in the seventies and the end of the eighties (Jofre 2011). A properly independent music scene began to take shape towards the end of 1999, with the disappearance of the local branches of multinational record labels like EMI, SONY, and BMG, and the spread of the Internet access, MP3s, Napster, and file sharing (Jofre 2011). In this context, a host of producers, bands, and independent record labels flourished, using the Internet primarily for music distribution and strategies for production, commercialization, and consumption of music began to change.

The scene as we know it today emerged between 2002 and 2005, with the creation of the record labels Algo Records and Quemasucabeza. The former began publishing records from different rock bands, whose style made reference to the grunge and garage rock sound of nineties "alternative" rock from Seattle, Manchester, and New York. Quemasucabeza started publishing in 2003, but it was not until 2005, with two important records by Gepe (Gepinto 2005) and Javiera Mena (Esquemas Juveniles 2006), that the scene started to expand in earnest: Live performances increased, leading to more available venues, these situated in Santiago's downtown, especially in the northeast side. A ticket for those gigs might cost between 3.000 and 5.000 Chilean pesos (between $5 and $8USD) and the attendance varied (e.g., 20 to 250 people).

In the midst of all this activity, some labels developed relationships with mainstream outlets for the purposes of promotion, particularly Gepe and Javiera Mena. Santiago's indie music scene has been prolific, especially in the last three years. There is consistent growth in the number of records published by independent labels, varied in styles and artistic forms. However, in the last two years, an interesting process has transformed the scene, which centers on the relationship between the bands, fans, and established market agents. Because the scene is a pastiche of different styles and artists, which blends traditional and non-traditional music and modes of performance, it has attracted national and international media attention. Along with the *El País* article, *The New York Times* wrote about Santiago as the Number 1 place to visit in 2011, arguing that the city is an interesting cultural capital because of its innovative artists and musicians. Thus, coverage has attracted advertising agencies that, working on behalf of brands (Corona, Heineken, Puma, and Adidas amongst others), have begun organizing marketing events with musicians and labels (Algo Records, Cazador and Quemasuzabeza). The scene is, thus, in a state of transition. After moving away from major record labels and adopting an "indie" approach, it is once again embracing mainstream modes of production and consumption.

Santiago's indie music scene presents a hybrid identity as a result of the precarious nature of independent cultural production (e.g., flexible work, freelancing, unstable conditions). However, this does not necessarily affect its innovative and productive character as a cultural industry. For instance, actors involved in the scene combine multiple roles as musicians, producers, and managers of record labels, alongside more stable and formal paid jobs outside the scene. In terms of its aesthetic, Santiago's indie music scene gathers different genres of music, from folk to rock and electronic; and the indie character resides in its limited access to mainstream markets and audiences (Tironi 2009). The three main principles founding the scene are: 1) the hybridity of music creation—different styles are mixed—i.e., it is difficult to identify the musical identity with one style; 2) all musical projects expand and engage in non-conventional procedures for creation (field recordings, circuit bending, and instrument recycling), and diffusion (net labels, art performances);

and, 3) commercial marginalization that is observed in the limited access to mainstream, commercial markets, and audiences (Tironi 2009).

METHODS

This chapter is based on an eight-month ethnography conducted in Santiago in 2011. I followed the work of a group of 12 people (aged between 25 and 35) who create and maintain eight music websites about Santiago's indie music scene, as well as global music scenes. This included interviewing them and observing their practices and processes in the making of websites. It proposes a bottom-up approach to exploring the dynamics of cultural mediation and the role that forms of labor have in processes of cultural production, circulation, and consumption in the operation of a creative industry. The focus is on how these actors define what they do, organizing and mediating different types of local and global flows (e.g., informational and technological) through their uses of technology. An ethnographic approach to the study of music fans' practices involves an "intensive engagement with the everyday life of the inhabitants of the field site" (Hine 2000, 63). Similarly, through long-term observation it is possible to contextualize individual relationships with objects and their mutual constitution through their reflexivity and practices. Specifically, regarding the use of information and communication technologies in the making of websites, as Coleman suggests, an ethnographic approach helps to explore how "cultural identities, representations and imaginaries . . . are remade, subverted, communicated and circulated through individual and collective engagement with digital technologies" (Coleman 2010, 488).

In terms of their cultural capital, all of the research participants had completed secondary school and obtained university degrees. Typical qualifications were journalist (seven), multimedia communicator (two), translator (one), lawyer (one), and civil engineer (one). With two exceptions, they had all studied in private universities, which are the institutions responsible for the expansion of university access in the Chile (thus, where most of the middle-class obtain degrees). In the case of research participants, this does not necessarily mean that they are part of a small elite; by contrast, they are part of middle-class, bearing in mind that the majority of universities in the country are private. Only one person had received a postgraduate degree, (although not in Chile). It is interesting that in almost half the cases, they were the first in their family to obtain a university degree. In Chile, university degrees are obtained in four to six years compared to the three years that it takes to obtain a technical degree. In comparison to levels of education among the broader Chilean population, the research participants are above average.

In terms of their economic capital, most of the research participants have between one and four different paid jobs. In some cases, they have a full-time job contract in areas not related to the music scene, but most of them are working as freelancers. The average monthly income of the research participants was between 450.000 to 1.000.000 Chilean pesos ($800 to $1800 USD). Compared to other Chileans of the same age, this is above average. It is interesting that most of the research participants said it was because of their work in the making of the websites, particularly their knowledge of technology, that they entered the more formalized market space for employment (e.g., advertising companies, radio). Considering their ages, not all of them live independently of their parents.

THE PRACTICE OF MAKING THE WEBSITES

The websites are constructed and updated by their creators through different practices. These practices can be organized into two categories: 1) the site's design, and 2) the updating routines. The design of the website is an issue that is constantly explained by research participants in different conversations. It involves the organization of technical knowledge to set out the contents and taste classifications that are objectified in a particular design. This includes searching for other websites to obtain inspiration and to imagine the final result, the relation with technologies that are capable and "new" enough to be included on their own sites, the acquisition of the web URL through which people will access the site, and the constant process of trial and error to inspire confidence in the site. The updating routines of the websites involve practices through which individuals have access to different flows of information via the Internet, especially social networking sites such as Facebook and Twitter.

Music fans' practices of designing and updating websites are also constitutive and performative of their digital "habitus" and "capital." Different types of content are put into circulation on these websites, but also collected from various online sources; this content is crucial in the making of the fields where fans try to achieve positions of recognition. Fields are constructed in the form of a technological space through which individuals put into circulation flows of information and taste classification regarding music scenes and other issues in the same way as they are represented online. Music fans also establish networks of connection and circulation facilitated by a set of digital technologies in the making of their websites, as well as others such as Facebook and Twitter. Those networks are constituted by the different connections they establish with the audiences that visit their websites or follow their profiles on Facebook and Twitter, as well as people from different fields (for instance, advertising agencies). Through practices of designing, re-designing, and updating the websites, individuals use the space they are constantly creating to show their digital capital as cultural and technical expertise around cultural flows, but also as the result of the mediation practices of particular technologies.

The practice of designing the website is taken seriously by informants, and involves defining how, when, and what the site will include in terms of its structure and the information presented on it. This is always related to the technologies and applications that are available at different stages of the site's existence. For instance, some of the websites were created in the middle of the 2000s, with the basic applications that were available at that time. By looking at the different designs of their websites, respectively, research informants explain that the evolution of the site design occurs in parallel with the availability of applications. At the beginning, it was common for them to include newsletter subscriptions for their audiences in order to send them the latest news and content available on the sites. Thus, with the emergence of new applications like Flickr—that enable individuals to upload, store, and share their pictures, or Last.fm, which enables individuals to listen to music online, and increasing use by their audiences, a "box" with the application within the site were included. This also happened with other applications like Facebook or Twitter, which eventually became part of the site's design and structure. The complexity of the site's structure goes hand-in-hand with the development and emergence of new digital applications. In this sense, that complexity also assists individuals to improve their position within networks of circulation of content and flows online, to differentiate themselves from other websites that are doing the same thing, but most importantly to signify a level of sophistication regarding their relation with digital technologies. For instance, remembering the processes related to the design of the site, two informants, Alejandro and Alvaro, explain that one of the most important aspects of their site is the originality of its design. It is the result of a process of searching for ideas from other sites, but also of creating something new. For them it is not the same as having a design ("plantilla") provided by Blogger or WordPress.

In this sense, collecting ideas from other websites, particularly the ones that are part of the global music scene, is part of the fans' learning process. Bakardjieva's concept of "warm experts" (2005), that is, actors who help inexperienced people to connect to network technologies, takes a non-human form that are followed by individuals as references in terms of their design, technical structure, as well as content and information. The best example is the case of Pitchfork (pitchfork.com) which is a permanent reference in terms of its structure with which to present content, as well as its design component, but most importantly the technological applications that enable the presentation of the music (e.g., in the form of YouTube videos, using the application SoundCloud that reproduces audio files, or with Pitchfork, having its own music player enabling visitors to move between different web pages while listening to music). For instance one informant, Nicolas, aspires to have an exclusive application that reproduces music (like Pitchfork) for his webpage NNM.cl.

Choosing the Site's Domain

Website domains help individuals to construct cultural scales (Slater and Ariztia 2010) within local and global locations. Domains symbolically help individuals to situate themselves as part of national and global networks of cultural flows. In a sense, having a domain inserts the websites, as representations of the music scene, in wider networks of global music scenes. Informants explain that there is a transition from having a web address that is part of a platform (e.g., blogspot) so as to get the address with the Internet country code (in this case, '.cl' for Chile). However, for some informants there is still a difference between having a web address finished with the domain ".com," which is considered important in order to reach audiences beyond the boundaries of Chile. Regarding the acquisition of the web address, informants told different stories. For instance, Alejandro, Nicolas, Juan Pablo, and Felipe began their sites with the web address provided by the platform "blogspot." This means that to access the website it was necessary to write the name of the site and the domain "blogspot.com" (e.g., paniko.blogspot.com, 192.blogspot.com). It is common for fans to understand the evolution of their sites according to the web address they have. For Alejandro, the domain ".cl" was a birthday present from his parents, an important evolution for his site enabling the possibility of reaching wider audiences within the country. For Felipe, buying the ".cl" domain was a crucial point related to the continuity of his project. Having a blog rather than a website with its own domain or web address made it possible to keep the contents alive, without the possibility of being discharged by blogspot in this case (considering Felipe was uploading music albums without permission). Also, when the site started to receive revenue from advertising agencies, it became "necessary to obtain the. cl" domain.

Fans' discourses around the sites' domains are representations, but also a form through which they perform a sense of connection at a local and a global level, independently of the content of their websites, when most of them reproduce information from global music scenes (Garland 2009). Commonly, they establish a hierarchy related to their site's domains. For instance, at a lower level of importance in terms of recognition and connectivity, domains to create websites provided by free platforms (e.g., Blogger whose domain is, BlogSpot), are seen by informants as unsophisticated, considering that almost all of them began their sites with those domains. The domain ".cl" is located at an upper level according to their classifications and situates them and their sites in a national context, through which they can reach national audiences.

The Practices of Updating the Website: Discourses, Strategies, and Routines

Updating the websites is a key stage for music fans in the production of the field, a mediated online space constituted by different websites about music scenes (local and global). In the same way, individual practices help them to search for positions of recognition within the field they are creating. Updating the websites is the result of different practices related to content management. But most importantly, they represent a mark of distinction within the field music fans are constructing, constituted by their representations of music scenes and global trends via a set of digital skills and taste classification. This is translated into the frequency of updating and managing large amounts of data. All these practices reflect individuals' technical capacity to mediate technologies, as well as flows of information.

At the first level, music fans shared similar motivations for creating their own sites, just as they shared similar discourses, strategies, and routines as practices through which they produced and maintained them. This is reflected in the way they related to digital technologies in the making of the sites. However, at a second level, considering the similarities between their production practices, it is interesting to differentiate their activities and the particular goals that individuals consider relevant for the existence of their websites, especially in terms of the sites' design style and the different music styles they decided to include. For instance, some websites are more oriented towards "indie rock" music; others are oriented to mainstream rock. But at a third level, individual practices related to the sites' maintenance, through objectifications of taste classifications, differ with regard to their strategies to gain audiences in the form of "clicks" and "likes" on the sites' content. With their similarities and differences, these practices are the result of individual aspirations, shared knowledge, and dispositions about the use of digital technologies ("digital habitus"), and the beginning of their accumulation of "digital capital."

During the interviews and observation, it was common for informants to talk about the routines they undertake to update the websites. These routines involve spending a considerable amount of time in front of the computer surfing on the web, searching for interesting news and information related to the sites' topics. There are no fixed strategies or rules related to the sites' everyday updating, although they present new content daily. However, two geographically significant patterns emerge through observation of the daily maintenance of the websites. The first is related to the production of content based on other websites at a global level. That content is related to bands and published on websites, the most referenced by informants include Pitchfork, the site for the British magazine *New Musical Express* (NME), and the Spanish site Je Ne Sai Pop. If a new album by an international band is announced on those sites, the information is immediately translated and reproduced by informants' websites. It is common to observe the same information from global bands on the websites. For instance, when the French electronic music duo Daft Punk released their new single "Get Lucky," the song was immediately uploaded and commented upon on websites, as well as on the band's Twitter and Facebook accounts.

The second pattern is about the constant dissemination of information about local gigs in different places in Santiago and other regions of the country. Every day each website uploads details about gigs and concerts that are happening in different parts of the country, mostly in Santiago. Music fans constantly update the sites, something which is perceived to be "essential" by actors. Both routines are vital in order to achieve a sense of being permanently "up to date" regarding their topics of interest. In that context, digital technologies operate as a tool to facilitate access to those flows of information in the same way as they are tools to spread that information. In the latter case, digital technologies enable individuals to constantly be part of those flows, as well as being able to communicate those facts. But most importantly, updating the site represents individual capacity to differentiate themselves from other cultural mediators in the field they are creating. It represents being professional in the way they are involved and investing time on the site. As one informant, Juan Pablo, explains:

> If a site is not updated in a week, it is dead. How can you have nothing to post in a week? What do you do then? In that case, invest your time by doing something else.

Individual technical capacities to mediate technologies, as well as manage large amounts of data, are central elements in the development of a "digital habitus" and the accumulation of digital capital. They are always looking for new ideas and content from different websites in order to adapt it to the style of their sites. That means translating the content found on other websites, especially global ones, into the sites' written style and editorial line, but also producing their own content in the form of posts with interviews of musicians, music reviews of gigs and albums, as well as fashion trends. Observing informants' everyday practices updating the sites, it is common for them to talk about the information they have on their RSS feed. Accumulating information is the most important way of finding ideas and inspiration for their sites. It also shows their ability to manage content and taste classifications. Before uploading content onto their websites, the informants spend considerable amounts of time collecting and organizing information in the form of links and feeds. The practice of updating websites can be described as "content management," a combination of frequent updates with the organization and administration of sources and feeds.

A good example of the practices involved in updating the websites, and a way of differentiating themselves from other music fans and their websites, is how one informant, Max, describes the process. For him, there are no rules. However, with his friend Francisco, they used to attempt to upload at least three posts on the site daily. However, after trying this for a while, they decided to spend more time preparing posts. This is because they wish to differentiate themselves from other blogs and websites that are based on the same topics as Max's site (Pousta); at the same time, Max is learning to understand the interests of their audience. As he explains:

> After a couple of years writing posts on our site, we know our audience in a better way. All of the websites with similar "onda" (style)

> have the same information. In our case, we can't be leaders in men's fashion trends because in the U.S. there are websites that spend all the time doing that and they have all the access for doing it. We take that information, adapting it to Chile, with a slightly ironic stance, written according to Pousta's style. For instance, I always look at four blogs to see content. I read them and then start making connections and links. I see an article from France and then the same news from a Spanish site. Then I write in my head the post for my site. I always read my RSS, and then I send by e-mail the articles that I consider to be interesting. I spend hours doing that, especially on my iPad.

Thus, in addition to the daily routines necessary to produce content for their websites, individual uses of digital technologies are oriented to have access to networks of circulation of flows in the form of information and a sense of connection to other locations outside Chile and this practice is shared by fans.

CONCLUDING REMARKS: MUSIC FANS' PRACTICES IN THE MAKING OF A MEDIATED MUSIC SCENE

The practices of a group of music fans in the making of websites about Santiago's indie music scene are the result of different types of knowledge, objects, emotions, and activities that are stabilized and accumulated on websites. In this sense, the "digital habitus" of individuals—as dispositions that structure ways of being and doing towards digital objects—is developed through the exchange of information in those networks. It is also a form of shared competence (Shove et al. 2007), where an artifact is created through human action and a set of objects (e.g., computers, software, links). That competence is also the result of a network constituted by different combinations of objects and practices (e.g., conversations between actors about the contents of the sites, uses of digital technologies in order to produce the websites, and website design). Creating a website is the result of a distribution of competence between individuals and digital technologies, as well as interaction with their peers, the information available on other websites, and the uses that other people make of those technologies.

The chapter has described individual experiences and shown how using digital technologies based on the everyday making of their websites helps to situate them within a network of circulation of flows. In this sense, the practices related to the making and maintenance of websites help individuals to configure different uses of particular technologies. Those uses in the form of practices are objectified on the websites in their designs, as well as in the everyday maintenance (e.g., uploading content). In this sense, digital technologies operate as objects that facilitate individuals' positions within different networks based on practices through which they are mediated.

There is a sense of shared knowledge on the part of individuals regarding the use of digital technologies based on the practices performed in the making of the websites. However, that knowledge also involves a set of strategies displayed by music fans in order to show their technical abilities. It is in this context that the website and other online platforms operate as the field they are constructing to show their "digital habitus" and capital to distinguish between them to achieve positions of recognition within that digital field they are creating—a mediated music scene. Thus, the relationship music fans have with digital technologies does not operate as a result of values or dispositions that are fixed. On the contrary, their "digital habitus" is based on the practices they reproduce in different contexts regarding the making of their personal websites. Considering the hybrid and fluid character of Santiago's indie music scene in terms of the actors, places, and music styles that compose it, music websites produced by a group of fans operate as a virtual hub connecting local and global music scenes, as well as consumers and markets from different geographies.

REFERENCES

Appadurai, Arjun. *The Social Life of Things: Commodities in Cultural Perspective.* Cambridge: Cambridge University Press, 1986.

Arriagada, Arturo. "Cultural Mediators and the Everyday Making of Digital Capital." PhD Diss., The London School of Economics and Political Science, 2014.

Arriagada, Arturo, and Victor Cruz. "Music Fans as Mediators in the Age of Digital Reproduction." In *The Ashgate Research Companion to Fan Cultures,* edited by Duits, L., S. Reijnders, and K. Zwaan, 149–162. Surrey: Ashgate, 2014.

Bakardjieva, Maria. *Internet Society: The Internet in Everyday Life.* London: Sage, 2005.

Bourdieu, Pierre. "The Forms of Capital." In *Handbook of Theory and Research for the Sociology of Education*, edited by Richardson, J., 241–258. New York: Greenwood, 1986.

Bourdieu, Pierre. *The Logic of Practice.* London: Polity, 1990.

Coleman, Gabriella. "Ethnographic Approaches to Digital Media." *Annual Review of Anthropology* 39 (2010): 487–505.

Entwistle, Joanne. *The Aesthetic Economy of Fashion: Markets and Values in Clothing and Modelling.* Oxford: Berg, 2009.

Garland, Shannon. "The New, the Hip and the Far Away: Indie Media and Live Performance in New York City and Santiago, Chile." MSc Diss., Columbia University, 2009.

Hine, Christine. *Virtual Ethnography.* London: Sage, 2000.

Jofre, Alejandro. "Hazlo tu mismo: Aproximaciones a la escena musical independiente en Chile (2000–2009)." Undergraduate Diss., Universidad Diego Portales, 2011.

Molloy, Maureen, and Wendy Larner. "Who Needs Cultural Intermediaries Indeed? Gendered Networks in the Designer Fashion Industry." *Journal of Cultural Economy,* 3, no. 3 (2010): 361–377.

Schatzki, Theodor. "Introduction: Practice Theory." In *The Practice Turn in Contemporary Theory,* edited by Schatzki, T., K. Knorr-Cetina, and E. von Savigny, 10–23. London: Routledge, 2001.

Schatzki, Theodor. *The Site of the Social: A Philosophical Account of the Constitution of Social and Change*. University Park, PA: The Pennsylvania State University Press, 2002.

Shove, Elizabeth, and Matt Watson, Martin Hand, Jack Ingram M. *The Design of Everyday Life*. New York: Berg, 2007.

Slater, Don, and Tomas Ariztia. "Assembling Asturias: Scaling Devices and Cultural Leverage." In *Urban Assemblages How Actor-Network Theory Changes Urban Studies,* edited by Farías, I., and T. Bender, 91–108. London: Routledge, 2010.

Tironi, Manuel. "Gelleable Spaces, Eventful Geographies: The Case of Santiago's Experimental Music Scene."In *Urban Assemblages How Actor-Network Theory Changes Urban Studies,* edited by Farías, I., and T. Bender, 27–52. London: Routledge, 2009.

Tironi, Manuel. "Enacting Music Scenes: Mobility, Locality and Cultural Production." *Mobilities,* 7, no. 2 (2011): 185–210.

17 The Evolution of Music Tastemakers in the Digital Age

The Rise of Algorithms and the Response of Journalists

Bastian Lange

The decline of large corporations in the music industry—the "major labels"—as the dominant unit for the production of value-added processes is closely associated with the equally declining importance of traditional taste-making institutions such as radio, sales charts, and journalists (Bürkner et al. 2013; Coulson 2012; Hracs 2012; Leyshon 2009; Winter 2012). The status of music journalists as pivotal rating entities situated between music producers and fans has come under pressure from the increase in music listeners offering their assessments and ratings of musical pieces through writing for blogs (see Arriagada, this volume) and communicating on social networks as well as algorithms embedded in digital music platforms.

Recently, many music websites and digital platforms with social media functions have gained wider acknowledgement, representing the status of a more decentralized as well as personalized net-based collaborative recommendation system (Fahy and Nisbet 2011; Gillespie 2010). While popular music charts are compiled based on sales figures, reviews take place differently in social media networks (Winter 2012). Due to the expertise and interactive knowledge of a particular social "mass," a listening public with increasingly sophisticated musical taste has started to evaluate the mushrooming amount of available music (Tapscott and Williams 2008). This tells us how a new system might be able to provide an orientation framework made by users that can meet the needs of individuals' taste (Joosse and Hracs 2015; Lange and Bürkner 2013; Quan-Haase and Martin 2013).

THE ROLE OF BROKERS, INTERMEDIARIES AND CURATORS IN HYBRID CREATIVE MARKETS

In recent years, many music sites and digital shops with social media functions are relying less on professionally curated music suggestions and instead are offering the listener musical selections that are a result of Internet activity and collaboration. While sales figures are used as the benchmark for ratings in hit parades and charts, those awarded through social media networks represent the expression of knowledge held within a certain social "mass"—the crowd (Albarran 2013; see also Leyshon et al., this volume). Rating systems, drawing as they do on a vast reservoir of available songs, always promise to provide users with a form of roadmap of taste and style that accommodates their individual taste, while at the same time laying the foundation for the ranking of songs or their producers (musicians and bands, respectively). For many decades, the evaluation of songs was restricted mainly to professional music recommenders such as music journalists, radio presenters, and other professional organizers, programmers, festival directors, etc., who functioned as boundary spanners (Noble and Jones 2006) or cultural brokers (Welz 1996).

Existing digital evaluation systems—in the early years of the Internet as online forums, now nameless but omnipresent online assessment tools—are initially based on algorithms. They are preparing, sorting, evaluating, and selecting the spread and acceptance of automatically generated taste recommendations. As a result, a wide, nearly un-navigable flood of musical pieces with seemingly arbitrary ratings is offered. This presents challenges to listeners and the companies releasing the music. This flood also raises the question of how new and relevant music can be discovered and highlights a conflict between cognitive skills and professional expertise in respect to the growing use of socio-technical systems for sorting musical pieces. By extension, it raises the question of who or what is involved in the assessment of musical pieces?

The importance of brokers acting as tools of rating falls concomitantly as the status of large corporations in the music industry, the "major labels," declines (Hracs 2012). The term "curator" or "curatorship"—similar to broker and brokerage—alludes to an increasing discussion in economic geography and media studies about who provides meanings of taste, style, and general aesthetic knowledge that has substantial impact on peer and social groups, audiences, followers, and consumption (Gehl 2009; Hracs 2015; Joosse and Hracs 2015; Quan-Haase and Martin 2013).

Such knowledge and information-based intermediaries increasingly emerged in the gallery, art, and multimedia scene in different European metropolises, foremost in London in the 1990s (Grabher 2002, 2004). In structural terms, they are communicative providers of transfer services between the sub-systems of "business related services" and "creative scenes," apparently satisfying a necessary demand (Foster et al. 2011; Koppetsch and Burkart 2002, 532; Lange 2011; Macdonald and Williams 1993). Generally speaking, brokerage in this sense focuses on joining previously unconnected parties to facilitate coordination and collaboration (Obstfeld 2005). From an institutional perspective, Obstfeld (2005) refers to Burt (2005) when he states "brokerage employs a strategy of disunion whereby individuals reap benefits from preserving their unique ties to others and maintaining a separation among parties" (Lingo and O'Mahony 2010, 47).

Following the perspective of Ibara et al. (2005), this type of brokerage may enhance individual social capital but can be at odds with the creation of communal social capital. In the case of the music industry, radio DJs, journalists, and music critics generally dominated this intermediary function in the pre-digital era (Fahy and Nisbet 2011). Within this framework, traditional music communicators acted as filters, but also contextualizers of musical pieces, presenting the results of their work to the public. Today, however, a growing number of sophisticated digital evaluation systems provide extreme competition to these professionals.

These digital rating systems essentially draw on algorithms and prepare automatically generated taste recommendations created along a line of sorting, rating, and selection logics. This produces a vast amount of music rated in a way that consumers have a hard time discerning the relative value of the ratings and the labels releasing the music do not know who to work with when promoting their music. Joosse and Hracs argue "as more curators enter the marketplace to 'help' consumers, their conflicting voices may only be heard as a cacophony" (2015, 215).

This has created a conflict between professional expertise based on human cognitive skills, and the increasingly prevalent use of socio-technical non-human systems to sort musical pieces. It also indicates the on-going struggle when it comes to determining who the leading song-rating actors will be. The primary question in this context is which profession is equipped with the best interpretive prerogative to ensure quality standards in the expanding music landscape and to safeguard the authorship of musical pieces.

ALGORITHMS AND THE SEMANTIC WEB

New technologies and various types of devices have transformed the way music is consumed. Boosted by technological improvements in the field of digital networks, storage systems with increasing capacity, device portability, and other Internet services (including apps and other web tools), the size of personal music collections has grown immensely. The availability of vast reservoirs of music files raises the question of how a system of filtering and rating based on personal preferences can be applied to this volume of music.

A glance at the changes in behavior relating to purchases and consumption stands as confirmation: in its annual global report, SoundScan (2012) states, "Digital tracks reached an all-time high with 1.34 billion units sold in 2012, up 5.1% vs. 2011," while also noting that, "Digital album sales accounted for 37% of all album purchases in 2012 compared to 31% in 2011, 26% in 2010, 20% in 2009, 15% in 2008, 10% in 2007 and 5.5% in 2006." Through lowering entry barriers, digital technology allows more music to be made than ever before (Hracs 2012), while at the same time giving the consumer more ways than ever before to access it through streaming, downloading, piracy, etc. More music and access means a greater need for curators to help consumers.

Users now have access to digital music collections that are only navigable based on adequate and expert organization and categorization. In the present scenario where digital technology is allowing artists to add their music to the online world without going through formal channels for career development, how do artists that possess no revenue relevance for music companies and producers fit into these collections? Given that just 1 percent of artists accounted for between 80 and 90 percent of the annual revenues in the United States music market in 2012 (SoundScan 2012), how do music fans find the other artists?

New methods to access and retrieve data in this kind of digital collection have emerged in the development of sorting and ordering formats. Within this framework, the performer, title, and genre information may not be the only criteria by which music consumers are able to find the tracks they enjoy. A few superstars will remain retrievable, no matter what, but how are listeners meant to sift through the remaining 99 percent to discover pieces they may like? There is a fundamental interest within the music industry to provide listeners with technology that takes the vast quantity of music offered and filters it so listeners can discover new music and personalize future suggestions to match their tastes. In technical terms, however, how can this vast quantity of musical content be organized?

For several years, software developers and programmers have attempted to introduce rating algorithms that enable more precise predictions of which music the audience will seek. In the music industry, algorithms deliver search results that permit conclusions on what a user may listen to based on his or her postings, profile descriptions, and preferences, irrespective of how useful the recommendations intended for the user actually are. The rating of previous recommendations directly focus on the music listener and serve to provide substantial refinement to these recommendations. Hence, the rating does not center merely on the piece of music itself, but also on the consistency (or otherwise) with pre-existing ratings of this item of music and the recommendations expressed, compared relative to the majority opinion.

This establishes a non-central and network-like realm of rating which is causing the preferred values and recommendations issued by central institutions to lose much of their validity when it comes to taste preferences. These formerly preferred factors have been replaced with new rating and recommendation formats associated with the broad mass of music listeners. These formats are less interested in the "mainstream" taste and focus instead on more narrow, genre-specific listening and musical user profiles, while complex music recommendation systems facilitate the establishment of genre-specific user profiles structured in a compartmentalized form. An example of this new networking-driven technology enabling listener-based curation comes in the form of the "Semantic Web" concept.

SEMANTIC WEB

The semantic web is an extension of the web through standards by the World Wide Web Consortium (W3C). The standards support joint data formats and exchange protocols on the Web, most fundamentally the Resource Description Framework (RDF). The central societal idea is that the Semantic Web should allow a broad and joint interaction framework that enables all people to share data across application, enterprise, and community boundaries. The Semantic Web has advanced to become a frequently used technical term, referring in general to the on-going development of the World Wide Web and the Internet. Gradually emerging as an "Internet of Things and Ubiquitous Computing" (Bunz 2012), the high tech sector is focusing their efforts on equipping machines to process information collated by human beings. All of the information contained on the Internet and expressed in human language should be assigned a clear description of its significance (semantics) that can be interpreted and processed by computers. Machine implementation and actual handling of the data taken from the data network generated by human hand is only possible if machines are in a position to unequivocally allocate meaning. The Semantic Web goes beyond these combination options in that it attempts to link information on the level of its semantic content. Whereas for a long time only human beings were in a position to understand, interpret, and adequately contextualize unprocessed information contained on the World Wide Web, complex algorithms are now taking first steps in providing interpretations.

The structure of Internet pages does not indicate whether the information they contain is a snippet of text, a first name, a surname, the name of the city, the name of a company, or an address, and so machines are unable to process the content. The Semantic Web sets out to solve these problems. The data in a Semantic Web are structured selectively and prepared in a form that enables computers to process them in terms of their content meaning. Additionally, a Semantic Web permits computers (if the concept is put into practice) to use the manifold variety of individual items of information to generate new combinations of information.

FOAFING, FILTERING, AND NEIGHBORHOODS

Foafing—"friend of a friend (FOAF)", according to Celma et al. (2005), is one of the music recommendation systems that use Rich Site Summary (RSS) methods to offer streamlined music to suit the tastes of the user. This process entails collecting music-based information (e.g., a recently released album, news of relevance to a specific artist, or available audio files) using an RSS feed in XML language for content syndication—this establishes links between content on a variety of websites to create a topical complex. FOAF documents are used to define preferences. Hence, it is fair to say that foafing offers its users the option of creating FOAF profiles to extract music from extrapolated, descriptive, and context-based information (Celma et al. 2005).

Foafing creates the opportunity to recommend music to other listeners based on certain user settings and specific listening habits. One of the most important benefits in the creation of social communities is that a user can discover like-minded peers and their social networks can be organized around shared interests. The principle aim of Foafing is to allow people to recommend music to others (Celma et al. 2005). This creates a forum to rediscover music and to explore musical content based on corresponding user settings, a context-based information system (extracted from RSS Feeds used), and content-based descriptions (extracted automatically from the audio information). Foafing lets users receive the latest releases of musical pieces from places like iTunes, Amazon, and Yahoo Shopping, while also sourcing download offers from MP3 blogs, podcast sessions, and personalized playlists. It also presents a selection of concerts playing in the geographic proximity of the listener.

In addition to foafing, community-based approaches such as "Demographic Filtering" and "Collaborative Filtering" are important as they can be used to identify musical habits and preferences among users (Celma et al. 2005). The purpose of filtering is to use certain music preferences to establish social relationships between users based on their specific music habits. The histories of these relationships and user settings then generate the connections and preferences needed to offer predictions for other users. The concept of an "Item-Based Neighborhood" is very similar to filtering (Celma et al. 2005). A neighborhood considers similar ratings and then offers them to other equivalent profile matrixes. While this kind of web-based service is standard practice on social media platforms, it is fair to question just how suitable algorithms actually are for generating relevant contexts as an explicative framework to explore musical pieces beyond the simple act of listening.

The underlying assertion in the Semantic Web is that musical pieces have advanced to become an important instrument and medium to establish communication between Internet users who are interested in music. The purpose of the Semantic Web is to outline personal profiles based on machine-readable websites which themselves are able to establish connections between profiles. Foafing creates exemplary conventions and a digital language to describe website-based content and to inject this content into the communication on social networks. Filtering and neighborhood building takes this connection further in terms of online social network communities (Celma et al. 2005).

Efforts of this kind are only undertaken in the music industry with the aim of establishing streamlined recommendation systems: The underlying motivation is to create access to 95 percent of the available music—the so-called "long tail" (Anderson 2013) of largely unknown music producers. The baseline expectation is that the quality of this filtered information will improve dynamically thanks to user participation. Within this context, the algorithms are increasingly skilled in establishing generic context based on information relating to the musical pieces. This is the challenge facing traditional music journalists that have historically tapped into their cognitive, associative, and professional abilities to create a greater contextualization for musical pieces.

WHAT IS THE IMPACT OF BLOGGERS AND ALGORITHMS?

Digitization has enabled and encouraged a large number of music fans to join various digital services that provide access to an unprecedented volume of listening options. As a result, more people outside of the traditional role of music journalist, such as bloggers, have assumed the role of evaluating music in the online sphere. Although motivations vary with some people writing about music in the digital realm for fun, for positioning their social status and social capital, or for money, they all contribute to the wide range of musical sources established in the digital ether (Arriagada, this volume). Two examples of digital platforms offering curation and ratings from outside the world of traditional journalism outlets are the popular websites Pitchfork and Gorilla vs. Bear.

Although seemingly counterintuitive, digital technologies facilitating access to quasi-journalistic services have led to a situation in which "music journalism continues to be seen as a worthwhile field of professional activity" (Döhring 2011, 26). Indeed, Döhring states that the desire still exists "to live a life with 'music,' i.e., above all with musicians and free of social conventions" (2011, 26). By becoming close to musicians, music journalists, reviewers, and critics stand at a gateway between the music industry and the audience and, hence, possess a certain authoritative power in their rating of musical pieces.

Through this they acquire social influence, although in practice it may necessitate constantly renegotiating their interests between the standards of journalistic, professional distance, and the attendant stamp of quality on the one side with their individual preferences on the other. Only a very select group succeeds in producing artistic texts on music and styles that also satisfy high standards of journalism (e.g., Denk and Thülen 2012). Professionalism refers to occupation-related standards, identities, and allocation of roles found intrinsically associated with a form of gainful employment requiring a certain degree of expertise. The latter is acquired via specific courses of education.

Professionalization in terms of music journalism should be viewed as a process extending from the development of trust in individual experts to further-reaching qualification standards. The application of this understanding to the case of the music industry poses several questions. First, what are the specific processes of legitimization when it comes to individual and collective expertise? Second, what are the characteristics of trans-local standards in their relationship to localized expertise? Finally, what is the importance of the distance from the source of production of musical pieces?

The following discussion uses the three dimensions outlined above to show that professionalization in the music industry has become a paradox. The professional status of music journalists has come under substantial pressure and their position in the marketplace has been eroded. At the same time, the amount of music produced by local scenes that is readily available via online distribution suggests professionals may not be able to accurately cover it all, relying on bloggers and algorithms to fill the gap.

The vast increase in the number of those involved in Internet-based music rating paradoxically affects the status of music journalists. Although their purpose as professionals offering ratings and recommendations becomes more important as they are educated professionals well-versed in the topic at a time when there is an overwhelming amount of content, the context-generating power of the Semantic Web raises questions about the music journalists' professional status as individuals and social networks are empowered via personal tastes. In addition, the democratization of music production has led to an unexpectedly large number of semi-professional or independently produced musical pieces (Hracs, this volume). A radical shift in listening habits and consumer practices has also taken place (Pfadenhauer 2005).

The established compartmentalization and scene-dependence (Lange and Bürkner 2013) found in this kind of production context means that although reviewers operating on a local level are perfectly capable of assessing their local scene, they are ill-equipped to extrapolate this contextualization to trans-local rating structures. The local accumulation of expertise in the area of these raters—as the thesis states—can only be assessed in a restrictively uniform manner due to the local stylistic characteristics. Even if it is possible to identify certain standards within composition if one looks back to the epoch of classical music, the same standards appear somewhat unlikely as idiosyncratic local-regional styles and cultures of rating gradually emerge. This is reflected in the efforts undertaken by the majors to establish Local Divisions to identify specific local-regional styles. In other words, would it be possible to introduce a music magazine *Spex* in Shanghai or in the urban region around Istanbul?

If one follows the idea of local-regional styles, it becomes apparent that professional production contexts (in electronic music especially) are extremely compartmentalized, possess distinctly delineated styles, and come with aspects based on trust. Affiliation with a musical scene goes hand-in-hand with specific social manifestations such as trust, knowledge, and experience. Anyone seeking to make recommendations will, therefore, require the skill to establish social proximity to the contexts of production. Frequently, more advanced mediation and rating structures will only emerge from this kind of knowledge when coupled with a foundation of social trust. This is why independent critics and reviewers are permitted entry to the social birthing grounds of musical pieces production. In some cases this may even involve bands directly offering their products to the fans on the Internet.

The direct dissemination of musical pieces goes hand in hand with the exclusion and establishment of social distance toward critics and reviewers. These actors, in turn, are denied access to essential information and sources with which they are able to produce the context descriptions for these types of musical pieces for which their profession is claimed to possess the requisite qualification. Hence, social proximity and distance become pivotal determinants in the field of music reviewing and rating, and their existence lays the foundation for enabling the stamp of quality made by the music journalist.

In summary, professionalization is largely dependent on informal social relationships and network alliances. Firstly, they explain the emergence of new creative music milieus; secondly, however, they are directly opposed to the processes of professionalization itself. This means that the temporary organization of music projects with different production locations and a varying array of participants is more likely to restrict any sustainable pooling of experience, knowledge, and know-how between the music journalist and music producer. This situation also inhibits any long-term collaboration likely to produce greater quality, making professionalization entirely impossible. The paradox of professionalization in music journalism and the shifting geographic focus of the music industry from the national to the local covers the tense relationship between creative production and its quintessential need for autonomy on one hand, and the necessity for professionalization on the other. As a result, this chapter asserts that "Local Communities of Practice" advance to become relevant quality rating contexts for the global music landscape.

CONCLUSION

The status of music journalists as pivotal rating entities situated between music producers and fans is coming under increasing pressure. The deluge of specialized opinions, recommendations, and reviews emerging from the community of Internet users demonstrates the opportunity for listeners to position their opinions next to a choir of professional music journalists. In a concentrated form, the web contains a vast array of opinions and positions intended for a small group of readers found in forums, blogs, and online special interest areas—but this small group is rapidly becoming the mainstream as evidenced by the success of websites such as Pitchfork and Gorilla vs. Bear. Simultaneously, algorithms are acquiring an ever-greater capacity to include significance-generating contexts in the rating of musical pieces.

Ultimately, this diversification of sub-professional expertise fails to lend any impetus to professionalism in the music industry as the community of "democratic" opinion makers (listener or algorithm) is unable to contribute any stamp of quality, similar to that held by the profession of music journalists. In the future, more academic research should focus on the mutual interaction between human and non-human practices and their attempts to initiate guidance in a vast sphere of unknown musical pieces. What may result is a geographical perspective that analyzes in more depth the geographies of local-regional genres and the spatiality of social networks, events, and user-induced music orientation (Lange et al. 2014).

REFERENCES

Albarran, Alan B. *The Social Media Industries*. New York, NY: Routledge, 2013.

Anderson, Chris. *Makers. Das Internet der Dinge: die nächste industrielle Revolution*. München: Hanser, 2013.

Bunz, Mercedes. *Die stille Revolution : wie Algorithmen Wissen, Arbeit, Öffentlichkeit und Politik verändern, ohne dabei viel Lärm zu machen*. Orig.-Ausg., 1. Aufl.. ed. Edition Unseld. Berlin: Suhrkamp.

Bürkner, Hans-Joachim, Bastian Lange, and Elke Schüßler. "Perspektiven Auf Veränderte Wertschöpfungskonfigurationen in Der Musikwirtschaft." *Akustisches Kapital—Wertschöpfung in Der Musikindustrie*, edited by Bürkner, Hans-Joachim, Bastian Lange, and Elke Schüßler, 9–44. Bielefeld: Transcript, 2013.

Burt, Ronald S. *Structural Holes: The Social Structure of Competition*. Cambridge: Harvard University Press, 1992.

Burt, Ronald S. *Brokerage and Closure: An Introduction to Social Capital*. Oxford: Oxford University Press, 2005.

Celma, Oscar, Miquel Ramirez, and Perfecto Herrera. "Foafing the Music." London Queen University (http://www.foaf-project.org) 2005. Web. 01.07.2015 2015.

Coulson, Susan. "Collaborating in a Competitive World: Musicians' Working Lives and Understandings of Entrepreneurship." *Work, Employment and Society* 26 (2012): 246–261.

Denk, Felix, and Sven von Thülen. *Der Klang Der Familie: Berlin, Techno Und Die Wende*. Suhrkamp-Taschenbuch. 2. Aufl.. ed. Berlin: Suhrkamp, 2012.

Döhring, André. *Musikkommunikatoren: Berufsrollen, Organisationsstrukturen Und Handlungsspielräume Im Popmusikjournalismus*. Bielefeld: Transcript-Verlag, 2011.

Fahy, Declan, and Matthew Nisbet. "The Science Journalist Online: Shifting Roles and Emerging Practices." *Journalism* 12, no. 7 (2011): 778–793.

Foster, P., S.P. Borgatti, and C. Jones. "Gatekeeper Search and Selection Strategies: Relational and Network Governance in a Cultural Market." *Poetics* 39 (2011): 247–265.

Gehl, Robert. "Youtube as Archive: Who Will Curate This Digital Wunderkammer?" *International Journal of Cultural Studies* 12, no. 1 (2009): 43–60.

Gillespie, Tarleton "The Politics of 'Platforms'." *New Media and Society* 12, no. 3 (2010): 347–364.

Grabher, Gernot. "Cool Projects, Boring Institutions: Temporary Collaboration in Social Context." *Regional Studies* 36, no. 3 (2002): 205–214.

Grabher, Gernot. "Learning in Projects, Remembering in Networks?: Communality, Sociality, and Connectivity in Project Ecologies." *European Urban and Regional Studies* 11, no. 2 (2004): 103–123.

Hracs, Brian. "A Creative Industry in Transition: The Rise of Digitally Driven Independent Music Production." *Growth and Change* 43, no. 3 (2012): 442–661.

Hracs, Brian. "Cultural Intermediaries in the Digital Age: The Case of Independent Musicians and Managers in Toronto." *Regional Studies* 49, no. 3 (2015): 461–475.

Ibara, Herminia, Kilduff, Martin & Tsai, Wenpin. "Zooming In and Out: Connecting Individuals and Collectivities at the Frontier of Organizational Network Research", *Organization Science*, 16, no. 4 ((2005): 359–371.

Joosse, Sofie, and Brian Hracs. "Examining the Curation of Local Food in Sweden." *Geoforum* 64, August (2015): 205–216.

Koppetsch, Cornelia, and Günter Burkart. “Werbung Und Unternehmensberatung Als ‘Treuhänder’ Expressiver Werte? Talcott Parsons’ Professionssoziologie Und Die Neuen Ökonomischen Kulturvermittler.” *Berliner Journal für Soziologie* 12, no. 4 (2002): 531–550.

Lange, Bastian. “Accessing Markets in Creative Industries—Professionalisation and Social-Spatial Strategies of Culturepreneurs in Berlin.” *Entrepreneurship and Regional Development* 23, no. 3 (2011): 259–279.

Lange, Bastian, and Hans-Joachim Bürkner. “Value-Creation in the Creative Economy—the Case of Electronic Club Music in Germany.” *Economic Geography* 82, no. 2 (2013): 149–169.

Lange, Bastian, Dominic Power, and Lech Suwala. “Geographies of Field-Configuring Events.” *Zeitschrift für Wirtschaftsgeographie* 58, no. 4 (2014): 187–201.

Leyshon, Andrew. “The Software Slump?: Digital Music, the Democratisation of Technology, and the Decline of the Recording Studio Sector within the Musical Economy.” *Environment and Planning A* 41 (2009): 1309–1331.

Long Lingo, Elizabeth, and Siobhán O’Mahony. “Nexus Work: Brokerage on Creative Projects.” *Administrative Science Quarterly* 55, no. 1 (2010): 47–81.

Macdonald, Stuart, and Christine Williams. “Beyond the Boundary: An Information Perspective on the Role of the Gatekeeper in the Organization.” *Journal of Product Innovation Management* 10, no. 5 (1993): 417–427.

Noble, Gary, and Robert Jones. “The Role of Boundary-Spanning Managers in the Establishment of Public-Private Partnerships.” *Public Administration* 84, no. 4 (2006): 891–917.

Obstfeld, David. “Social Networks, the Tertius Iungens Orientation, and Involvement in Innovation.” *Administrative Science Quarterly* 50 (2005): 100–130.

Pfadenhauer, Michaela. “Ethnography of Scenes. Towards a Sociological Life-World Analysis of (Post-Traditional) Community-Building (31 Paragraphs).” *Forum Qualitative Sozialforschung/Forum: Qualitative Social Research (On-line Journal)*, Forum Qualitative Sozialforschung 6, no. (2005). Web. October 25, 2005.

Quan-Haase, Anabel, and Kim Martin. “Digital Curation and the Networked Audience of Urban Events: Expanding La Fiesta De Santo Tomás from the Physical to the Virtual Environment.” *International Communication Gazette* 75, no. 5–6 (2013): 521–537.

Soundscan. *The Nielsen Company & Billboard’s 2012 Music Industry Report.* Nielsen SoundScan. New York, 2012.

Tapscott, Don, and Anthony D. Williams. *Wikinomics: How Mass Collaboration Changes Everything,* Expanded ed. London: Atlantic Books, 2008.

Welz, Gisela. *Inszenierungen Kultureller Vielfalt: Frankfurt Am Main Und New York City.* Zeithorizonte 5. Berlin: Akademischer-Verlag, 1996.

Winter, Carsten. “How Media Prosumers Contribute to Social Innovation in Todays New Networked Music Culture and Economy.” *International Journal of Music Business Research* 1, no. 2 (2012): 46–73.

18 Leveraging Affect

Mobilizing Enthusiasm and the Co-Production of the Musical Economy

Andrew Leyshon, Nigel Thrift, Louise Crewe, Shaun French, and Pete Webb

The medical etymology of the word "crisis" refers to a turning point, at which the patient either gets better or worse, with the latter often leading to serious or even fatal outcomes. Translated into the economic sphere, crises can be longer lasting than is medically possible, so that the "economic body" can be in a state of crisis over extended periods, during which transformation and mutation may enable it to survive and recover. Since the late 1990s, the popular music industry has been an economic sector in a state of crisis because its principal means of revenue generation—the exploitation of intellectual property rights through the sale of recorded music—was undermined through the rise of file sharing enabled by new forms of computer-mediated coding and communications (Leyshon 2014).

As a result of this crisis, and as this volume shows, a series of mutations, transformations, and experiments have emerged within and beyond the industry as actors and institutions have sought to develop new means to enable the musical economy to reproduce itself. During the middle of the second decade of the twenty-first century, a number of high-profile artists undertook enterprises that might point to the new direction in which the musical economy is headed. For example, in September 2014, users of Apple's iTunes service discovered that the new album by the band U2 had been downloaded into their music collection at no financial costs as part of Apple's promotion of the iPhone 6. Although the music was given away freely, the cost was born by Apple's marketing division, as the band and its record company received an unspecified fee which, according to the *New York Times*, made up part of a $100 million dollar (USD) budget given over to the campaign (Sissario 2014). This form of promotional funding has become an additional and, in some cases, vital income stream for those artists who are prepared to link their music to other products or services as part of what are known as "brand partnerships" (Harris 2013). Yet, in this case, even if U2 had not been paid, there might have been a logic for them simply giving the music away, because since at least 2008 more revenue has been made from performing music in front of an audience than from selling recordings of it (Leyshon 2014; Wynn and Dominguez-Villegas, this volume). Indeed, at the time of writing, U2 hold the record for generating the largest gross income from a single tour (Leyshon 2014), so that the costs of recording their music and simply giving it way could have been justified as marketing for the band's live shows.

Illustrative of this shift towards performance are two further exemplars. The first is the three-week residency in London at the Hammersmith Apollo by Kate Bush between August and September 2014, which marked her first live performance for 35 years, and generated an estimated gross income of nearly £8 million (GBP), with tickets selling out within 15 minutes of going on sale. The second and related experiment was undertaken by the musician PJ Harvey in early 2015, who offered the public an opportunity to view the recording of her ninth album at London's Somerset House in a specially designed studio through one-way windows in viewing spaces. Although described as an art installation, the recording also proved highly popular as tickets for the recording sessions—four on weekdays and three on Saturdays—quickly sold out.

Meanwhile, the music industry has invested money in the hope that streaming services offer an alternative, sustainable business model where income can be generated from the intellectual property rights invested in sound recordings. Here consumers subscribe to an almost unlimited supply of recorded music, in return for a monthly fee and/or exposure to advertising (Arditi 2015; The Economist 2014). Such services, such as Spotify and Pandora, are seeking to extract rents from access to music through the curation of an ever-growing database of musical artifacts (see Lange, this volume). They do this not only by granting access to music, but also by sorting and sifting a universe of musical variation into packages or playlists that will appeal not only to known musical tastes and choices, but also, through the use of algorithms and detailed analyses of music at the most fragmentary level, creating new and unexpected connections between different recordings to keep users listening and paying their fees.

However, even these developments—branding, performance, and streaming—only really offer partial solutions to the problem of how the musical economy may reproduce itself given the loss of a stable market for intellectual property rights embedded in physical artifacts such as CDs (see Pratt, this volume). Brand partnerships, such as the deal between U2 and Apple, might provide artists with much needed income, although in many cases the artists would have to be at a certain level of development and with a significant enough audience for the sponsoring brand to wish to associate its products with their music. Meanwhile, many creative artists are cautious of linking their image to a brand over which they have no control. Performance helps artists if they can attract large enough audiences, although the market for live acts has filled up, meaning that this option is only really lucrative for those acts with both established and loyal fan bases that will regularly turn out to see their music played live and have other forms of income and/or very economical standards of living. As Hracs and Leslie (2014) have illustrated, while making a living from live performance is possible, it is a precarious and highly competitive mode of existence. Meanwhile, record companies see streaming as a means to recoup income lost through an earlier phase of digitalization, not least because it generated around $1 billionUSD in income for rights holders between 2009 and 2013 (Luckerson 2013). However, artists earn as little as $0.006 to $0.0084 (USD) per stream in royalties, so only those acts that generate very large volumes of streaming can ever hope to earn significant income this way.

None of these experiments, transformations, and mutations fully address the problems faced by new and existing artists from the more risk adverse approach adopted by record companies in response to the more precarious relationship between the funding of bands and the returns generated on this investment through sales and royalties. This has created something of a venture gap in the industry, where money to fund the emergence of new music is increasingly the responsibility of musicians in a way that it was not in the past. Partly in response to the more parsimonious position taken by record companies, there has emerged a greater awareness of alternative funding options open to artists, from traditional means such as seeking grants from charities and associations, or borrowing from friends and family, to newer developments such as commercial funding in the form of debt and investment (D'Amato 2014; Harris 2013). However, this chapter focuses upon a source of funding that seeks to leverage the power of affect and emotion through the phenomena of crowdfunding which, by targeting fans, has the potential to provide the investment needed to develop new music and establish musical careers but without the need to generate market standard returns on investment as demanded by more traditional funding routes.

The remainder of the chapter is organized as follows. In the second part we outline the promise and problems of the exploitation of fandom and enthusiasm within capitalism. In the third part we briefly review the academic literature on fans. The fourth part focuses on the rise of crowdsourcing as a way of mobilizing fan enthusiasm to fund new creative projects, with a particular focus on the music industry. The fifth part offers some conclusions to the argument pursued in the chapter.

LEVERAGING AFFECT, MOBILIZING FANDOM

"Imagine," suggest Blanchard and Bowles in their parable of business life, "a customer so pleased that he (sic) became a Raving Fan" (Blanchard and Bowles 1998, 10). Such imaginary consumer subjects made flesh would be highly desired by most businesses. Consumer discrimination, caution, and skepticism would be replaced by untrammelled enthusiasm, passion, and commitment. What business would not want customers to be avid followers and supporters of their products and services? The commercial success of ventures that trade directly in fandom—sports and entertainment, for example—illustrate the commercial possibilities of connecting products and services to powerful forces of fandom, adoration, and affect. Attempts to fuse the power of affect with consumption have spread widely across the capitalist system (Anderson 2014; Thrift 2005). However, converting consumers into passionate fans is not without its risks. When fans are enamored with their objects of affection, consumption may proceed briskly and unproblematically. But when fans become disenchanted, or worse, alienated, they can do more than merely stop consuming products and services; they can become "anti-fans," seeking to devalue the original brand, or even start their own media objects to follow and direct instead (Giuffre 2014).

This chapter discusses a relatively recent change in the contours of capitalism which has made the harnessing of fans to the interests of capitalism not just a business proposition but an integral part of *generating business propositions*. Driven by the networking capacity of the Internet, what were once seen as makeshift alliances and inspired improvisations are gradually settling in to a new pattern of producer-consumer relations that have the power to redefine what is understood as innovation and markets (see also Arriagada, this volume). This reworking is the result of a series of different processes that have evolved and coalesced to the point where they can be effective in producing a new phenomenon. This we call the production of Internet-enabled enthusiastic consumption, a new blurring between firms, consumers, and the creative process. Consumers are increasingly taking cues from one another rather than from conventional channels such as large corporations or media outlets, catalyzed in part through means of communication and consumption such as peer-to-peer (P2P) networks, web sites, blogs, and social networks. Producers of goods and services are also seeking out new mechanisms to harness the consumption knowledge of consumers through a wide array of brand placement and extension strategies such as ambient advertising, opt-in Internet sites, viral marketing campaigns, and the use of crowdfunding. We explore the contours of this phenomenon below through the specific example of fan communities. However, to begin, we identify at least five significant mechanisms that are bringing about such market shifts.

The first of the processes we identify is the increasing volume of "overflows" evident in modern firms; that is, activities and qualities of markets that escape the efforts by firms and other economic agents to contain them with prescribed frames of calculability (Barry and Slater 2002; Callon 1998; Callon et al. 2002; MacKenzie et al. 2007; Slater 2002). Firms now span more boundaries than previously, most especially as they have used outsourcing and similar strategies as means of allowing them to concentrate increasing attention on marketing and branding. The brand is increasingly the product that is consumed, the commodity itself being simply an appendix, a postscript to embody whatever story is being told (Lury 2004; Salzer-Morling and Strannegard 2004). This explains why, as outlined in the introduction, that some brands are keen to sponsor artists as it gives them scope to build music and its various cultural associations into the narrative of commodities. Significantly, too, the conventional distinctions between brand producer and consumer have become blurred, and brand theorists' long-held models of sender, message, and receiver have broken down in terms of both practical and theoretical resonance. Symbolic management is increasingly a core organizational competence across a whole range of sectors and consumers are rarely now the grateful receivers of pre-defined corporate messages. As symbolic management has become more important, the direct management of production has become less significant, which has increasingly been outsourced and devolved to other, typically smaller, companies within their "value chain." Within the music industry, record companies are content to allow other firms, such as management companies, to undertake development work, choosing instead to concentrate on the effective marketing of artists that have images and sounds stabilized elsewhere (Leyshon 2014).

The second process is that use of the Internet is now so commonplace that its associated practices have long sunk into the business background (Leyshon et al. 2005). This normalization of electronically-mediated forms of exchange has, in turn, brought about significant shifts in the ways in which business gets done. An online presence is crucial to organizational success and a key tactic in brand positioning (see: Arriagada, this volume; Johansson et al., this volume; Wynn and Dominguez-Villegas, this volume). Many important innovations in branding have developed on the Internet (Arvidsson 2005; Lury 2004), such as promotional clips too long for normal adverts but designed explicitly to be circulated virally among consumers through social media (Jenkins et al. 2013).

The third process is that the Internet has allowed new forms of business to come into existence to empower consumers. There are the examples of Craigslist and, in particular, eBay, that have brought a whole array of commodities to market that were hitherto invisible within contemporary spaces of exchange (White 2012). eBay has thus greatly extended the range and reach of commodification and has engendered a new regime of valorization, permitting businesses to emerge that previously would not have been viable for reasons of scale, scope or location (Zook 2005).

The fourth factor is the increasing importance of affective experience as a key component in the shaping of consumption (Pine and Gilmour 1999). The careful and increasingly knowing construction of affective experiences around commodities relies on bodies of knowledge that have evolved from the practical evolution of models based in advertising and market research, combined with various performative routines gleaned from a variety of theoretical sources by the cultural circuit of capital (Leyshon 2011; Thrift 2005). This development has particular resonance for the music industry, because the increasing ubiquity and availability of music, either through P2P networks or streaming, has made the problem of accessing music more tractable, and so relatively devalued. Rather, it is the affective experience of live performance, which is by definition unique and distinctive, that is increasingly valued and valorized (Leyshon 2014).

Fifth, and finally, we would point to the ways in which pervasive communications are transforming consumer practices (Rheingold 2002). Accelerating levels of consumer connectedness via electronic means, and in particular the growing ubiquity of Wi-Fi and smart phones, are combining to connect always-on consumers who may be always-on-the-move in new and potent ways. The ease by which both music and indeed artists can be accessed via downloads, streaming, or social media has not only contributed to the demise of traditional sites of consumption, such as record shops (see Sonnichsen, this volume), but also transformed the atomized, individual "sovereign" consumers into connected collectives of consumers which, we argue, is important in theorizing the fusion of production and consumption of value.

Taken together, this suite of processes empowers what were previously called "fans," allowing them much more range and influence on consumption than hitherto, and pulling them into the process of value creation itself. In turn, firms and producers have tried to structure their relationships with fan communities, both as a means of gaining access to consumers' enthusiasms and as a means of stimulating further innovation and obtaining funding. It is this interaction between fans and firms which is the main focus of the remainder of this chapter.

CONSUMING WITH ENTHUSIASM: FANS AS ECONOMIC SUBJECTS

Academic research on the economic and social role of fans has emerged from two separate but linked traditions. The first is cultural studies, and in particular work on sub-cultural formations, the emergence of which have often been linked to particular kinds of cultural production, traditionally music and fashion, in which the members of the sub-culture are often fans if not direct producers (Hebdidge 1979). The second tradition has been media studies and, in particular, work on audiences and their interaction with various media texts such as film, music, literature, and, especially, television (Abercrombie and Longhurst 1998).

Sandvoss (2005) identifies three main stages in the development of academic work on fans. The first was strongly influenced by the work of Stuart Hall on the production and consumption of texts and how they were encoded by producers and decoded by audiences. However, it "assumed a simple dichotomy of power, with producers on the one hand and fans on the other" and tended to celebrate the "fan's ability to evade [the] linear ideological influences" emanating from texts produced within cultural industries organized on capitalist lines (Sandvoss 2005, 154). This tendency to see fans as working-class agents of resistance challenging dominant structures of power was questioned by a second wave of fan studies influenced by Bourdieu's work on cultural capital. Fans often mobilized (sub) cultural capital to open up divides of power, discernment, and discrimination between audiences (Thornton 1995). These divides are often "constructed in opposition to class" (Sandvoss 2005, 39), so that, rather "than functioning as a practice of subversion, fandom, through the adaptation of existing hierarchies in a subcultural context, further cements the *status quo* by undermining the role of class as a vector of social change" (Sandvoss 2005, 156).

A third stage of fan research turned towards psychoanalysis and a focus on the relationship between fandom and identity to explain why fans make considerable emotional investments in the objects, subjects, and texts that they follow (Stacey 1994). The work of fandom is seen as a search for identity, a sense of self and social belonging under conditions of risk, fragmentation, and uncertainty. Fan communities can be seen as tribal collectives, affective assemblages of neo-tribes searching for shared sentiments, or at least approval of their assumed narrations of self (Hetherington 1998; Maffesoli 1996). The solidarity made possible by the Internet provides shared experience; validation is both sought and found. Labels, or groupings, become organizing factors in the lives of members, who seek support and affirmation by bonding with others of a similar kind. Moreover, in an ironic way, one could see fan communities as an illustration of Agamben's idea of communities that have moved both beyond identity and universality, communities which represent a bringing together of existences rather than essence (Agamben 1993).

The recognition of the importance of emotion and affect within the performance of fandom has led Sandvoss to define a fan as an individual who undertakes "the regular, emotionally involved consumption of a given popular narrative or text" (2005, 8). Abercrombie and Longhurst (1998, 121), meanwhile, define fans as a "skilled audience," but significantly argue that the competencies and skills of fans differ as do the actions that stem from their fandom. They argue that differences in the skills and competencies of fans constitute an "audience continuum"; thus, fans may be distinguished from general consumers but also, in turn, from what they describe as "cultists" and enthusiasts, representing a deepening of the "division of labor" of fandom (see Sandvoss [2005, 31], for a detailed distinction between these categories). Sandvoss argues "that [while] fandom at its core remains a form of spectatorship" (2005, 53), based on the fact that studies have revealed that "fans," as defined above, overwhelmingly outnumber the more active and engaged cultists or enthusiasts, the activities of the latter groups indicate that in some cases the emotional investment within the subjects of their fandom drives them to acts of textual production or other forms of active engagement. It is this tendency which we argue is increasingly being harnessed by economic agents to augment and refine their production of goods and services.

This interaction between producers and consumers through the intervention of fans (or more accurately, fan-enthusiasts) has long been recognized as significant within the cultural industries. Thus, most fan studies have focused on the regular and emotionally-invested consumption of texts such as television, films, music, sports, and literature. However, as Giuffre (2014) has argued, cultural studies of music fandom tends to be distinctive, in that it tends towards positive narratives which is a response to broader moral panics associated with certain musical forms and to a critique in the tradition of Adorno that sees popular music fans as dupes of base commerciality. Notwithstanding this, popular music fandom has produced work that provides insights into how organizations and institutions respond to the ways in which consumption more generally has become more culturally inflected, and developing their own set of fans, cultists and enthusiasts that can generate new sources of income or funding. For example, Guiney and Zhang (2012) have drawn attention to the ways in which the U.S. band The Grateful Dead mobilized the obsessive fandom of their audiences to pioneer a performance-based business model which encouraged fans to make their own copies of performances, organized and facilitated by the band itself which then circulated among fans as "bootleg" copies. They also made other concessions to fans, such as those with disabilities, by creating dedicated audience spaces at performances, which served to further infuse loyalty and devotion. While such acts may on the face of it be seen as limiting short-term income, by enabling non-copyright material to compete with recordings protected by IPR, or by reducing the amount of standing space at gigs to accommodate wheelchairs, for example, these short-term sacrifices were more than compensated by sales in ancillary markets, such as clothing and other merchandise, and by life-time "brand loyalty" (e.g., see Krugman 2008).

Indeed, and as we discuss below, it has been argued that many organizations have sought to mobilize the power of affect and emotional investment expended by fan communities in attempts to tap into the regular acts of consumption that they generate. It is to this tendency that we turn in the next section of the paper on crowdfunding. The following section of the chapter draws in part on Chapter 7 in Leyshon (2014).

TOWARDS THE CO-CREATION OF VALUE: THE RISE OF CROWDFUNDING

Crowdfunding seeks to align the interest of producers and consumers through a campaign to raise money to fund new ventures of various kinds. Crowdfunding has been defined as "an online collective action initiated by people or institutions to gather funds from a large number of contributors, usually using mediation of crowdfunding platforms to facilitate contact and flow of resources between parties" (Galuska and Bystrov 2014). Galuska and Bystrov (2014) estimate that are now over 2,600 crowdfunding platforms in existence. In the UK, which contains the world's most diverse ecology of crowdfunding platforms, the market has grown rapidly, from £267 million (GBP) in 2012, to £666 million (GBP) in 2013 and to £1.74 billion (GBP) in 2014 (Baeck et al. 2014).

Crowdfunding covers a spectrum of activity that at one extreme closely resembles traditional financial markets. Thus, it is possible to arrange personal and business loans, and even equity finance. The advantage that crowdfunding has over traditional forms of lending is that it is able to re-intermediate funds more cheaply than banks as platforms do not carry the same legacy costs of regulatory burden of traditional financial institutions (French and Leyshon 2004). However, as crowdfunding grows in importance so more of its activities are brought within the purview of financial regulators (Langley 2015). This analogue of the financial sector is by far the largest part of the market, accounting for over 98 percent of total lending. But in the smaller, other end of the crowdfunding spectrum, activities are able to unfold unhindered by the gaze of the regulator, for investments made here are both much smaller (around £6m in 2014 (Baeck et al. 2014) and not made for a financial return but as gifts and donations or in exchange for some kind of reward. It was this kind of transaction that evolved into crowdfunding, a means of funding creative and innovation-related projects by tapping into the enthusiasms and passions of motivated fans and enthusiasts (Bennett et al. 2014). In this respect, crowdfunding seeks to take advantage of the Internet's long tail (Anderson 2006), by aggregating geographically distributed sources of supply and demand to form markets with viable critical mass.

Crowdfunding has the potential to inculcate long-term relationships between borrowers and lenders/donators through the intermediation of the P2P platforms on which they are based. Borrowers have the opportunity to develop narrow but potentially temporally deep and repetitive sources of funding, particularly where lenders/donators provide money for motivations less to do with rate of return than social concern (e.g., green technology), interests or enthusiasms (e.g., cycle product innovation) or fandom and affect (e.g., musicians and artists). As such crowdfunding mobilizes what Michael Lewis (2001) has memorably described as "interest group" economics.

A range of crowdsourcing platforms have emerged to act as intermediaries between investors and borrowers to realize a range of projects that might not otherwise be funded through traditional financial intermediation. Within the music and entertainment field, a number of crowdfunding sites have come to prominence. Indeed, it was in this field that the principle of crowdfunding emerged, as in the late 1990s the out-of-favor neo-progressive rock band Marillion used an incipient online network of dedicated fans to raise $60,000 they needed to fund a U.S. tour. The band turned to their fans when they did not have the funds available to underwrite the costs themselves (Lewis 2001). Emboldened by this fundraising success, the band turned again to its fans to provide investment for a new record. Estimating that they needed an advance of £100,000 (GBP) to pay for recording costs, the band raised £200,000 (GBP) in weeks from 16,000 fans (Lewis 2001, 132).

The record industry's indifference towards Marillion in the late 1990s was soon extended to a host of other artists in an environment that made it difficult for recording companies to enforce the intellectual property rights contained within music. The loss of revenues reduced the capital record companies made available for musical creativity. In this milieu, crowdfunding platforms emerged as valued sources of new funding.

It took almost a decade for the ideas forged by the likes of Marillion to be formalized into crowdfunding platforms that would attract funds to support the musical economy. SellaBand was established in 2006, followed by Slicethepie (2007), Indiegogo (2008), and Pledge Music (2009). However, the best known crowdfunding platform in this field is Kickstarter, established in New York in 2009, and which expanded its operations into the UK in 2012. Kickstarter allows artists of all kinds to make appeals for money to fund their "projects," with the donor's reward being the successful completion of a project to which supporters were committed or at least interested in seeing bear fruit and even—although this is not obligatory—obtaining a copy of the output of the project or, in the case of performance art, for example, participation in it. An examination of the music section of Kickstarter quickly establishes that the activities for which artists seek funding are those formerly undertaken by record companies. These include the recording, mixing, and mastering of new songs, album artwork design, the manufacturing and printing of CDs, promotion and publicity, and website design. The amount of money requested varies, from relatively modest amounts to levels of investment that even record companies at the height of their financial powers may have hesitated to approve. For example, a former member of the band Dresden Dolls, Amanda Palmer, used Kickstarter to raise $100,000 (USD) to record her first solo album. The appeal period for all artists is strictly limited—if artists do not raise the target fund in a maximum of 90 days all investments are returned to supporters—Palmer managed to earn more than ten times her target figure, generating a total fund of $1.2 million (USD). The ability of Palmer to leverage the affect and loyalty of fans into investment capital was particularly impressive given that she was seen as a having only a relatively narrow market appeal. The money raised was used to record an album, which sold enough copies in its first week to make the *Billboard* top 10. In addition, Palmer hoped to bank $100,000 (USD) of the $1.2 million (USD) as pure profit (Lindvall 2012).

However, while this form of fundraising may enable some artists to circumvent the gatekeeping role of record companies, obtaining money this way is not without its own cost. The rewards that generate the highest investments tend to be those through which the artists give more of themselves through personal appearances and engagements, often in small-scale or relatively intimate settings. For example, two fans paid $10,000 for an "art-sitting" and dinner with Palmer (Lindvall 2012). Anecdotal evidence suggests that artists find these quite challenging, due to the high level of social and cultural capital required to manage them, and the potential unpredictability of the event. As Hracs and Leslie (2014) reveal in their study of independent musicians in Toronto, direct interaction with fans in person and even via social media requires considerable emotional labor as they seek to cultivate and build relationships that might be economically sustaining (Morris 2014). In this regard, such investments may be seen as more complicated exchanges that take on elements of the gift in as much as they have long-lasting social obligations and implications, and lack the degree of separation that traditionally accompanies transactions based on exchange.

CONCLUSIONS

It seems to us that there are two possible interpretations of these developments. The first, more positive gloss, is that they are part of a new technological democracy which allows for more public deliberation on products and services and, indeed, more input into their design, funding, and realization. Like democracy, this does not mean that everyone participates, or participates equally. Some consumers want to build, drive, and even fund the communities into which they are hooked and are orbiting around in tighter circuits and at faster speeds; this is the deep end of fandom. As we have noted, recent technological developments have enabled them to do this more fully. Indeed, as we have seen in some of the examples above, they have even moved into the funding and building of versions of products and services of which they are fans. Other consumers want a fleeting encounter according to the circumstances in which they find themselves.

Of course, a consumer community differs from a democracy because members must have a certain level of expertise to be able to participate fully. Whereas it is more or less possible to turn up and vote, it is not possible to simply become an expert programmer, make a film in digital format that can be downloaded from the Internet, or launch a crowdfunding campaign without having some—often considerable—level of expertise and resources of social and cultural capital (Davidson and Poor 2014). Therefore, while the field of open source or open innovation might appear to resemble a democracy, it has also been described as "a Darwinian meritocracy" which is "egalitarian at the contributor level" but "elitist when it comes to accepting innovations" (The Economist 2006), which is revealed by the often complex organizational structures underlying open source projects (Weber 2004) and also helps explain why only a few successful products and innovations have so far been winnowed out of a mass of collaborative projects. Nevertheless, according to Leadbeater and Miller (2004) the level of "amateur" expertise is in any case increasing in the population, to the extent that they identify a category which they describe as "pro-ams" (that is, professional-grade amateurs, who perform a range of activities to a very high standard, but who are not formally employed to do so). If this is indeed true, it will only hasten the level of participation in consumer communities, as well as making it much easier for firms and consumers to communicate about matters like design. The rise of crowdfunding, across a range of different areas and not just music and entertainment, opens up the possibility of a more democratic engagement with decisions about which kinds of projects might be funded, although this is of course controlled by the extent to which individuals have disposable income for such investment.

The second and less optimistic point of view to this is that all that is happening is that firms have found new models of drawing consumer knowledges and enthusiasms into their orbit from which they are able to derive a profit at remarkably little cost, or are able to raise venture capital without paying the going rate of interest or necessarily having to transfer an equity stake in their venture through donation and rewards-based crowdfunding. Further, they are also able to bolster their brands and reputations, which they police with the utmost vigor through copyright and other intellectual property rights. In the case of the music industry, it is possible to see crowdfunding as a costless incubator site for record companies, which provides a proof-of-concept test and brings new talent to the market, which record labels can then sign and channel recordings to streaming sites in which the record companies are heavily invested and divert very little money back to artists. In other words, the creative commons that some commentators want to see may be simply a new form of ownership, little more than the latest phase in the commodification of consumer desire. This is a way in which capitalism can extract value from resources that are more or less free and easily accessible; moreover, it is difficult to describe such value extraction as exploitation, if such resources are not only given freely but also with enthusiasm. Nevertheless, such exchanges can be seen as deeply asymmetric given the ways in which they enable firms to use such processes to harvest profits and accumulate capital. Moreover, it is also a process that is deeply socially divisive, for it is one to which participation is highly dependent upon high levels of cultural capital and no little degree of economic capital, given that there are economic costs in gaining access to the Internet.

Whatever the case, it seems certain that the co-creation of value represents a significant overflow and reframing of the market. This reframing has been generated by a powerful coalition of producers searching for extra profits, consumers searching to satisfy their desires, and the blandishments of the cultural circuit of capital. In other words, it comes from within the current market system rather than from without.

Moreover, this "trade in affect" is not without its dangers for producers: While fans might seem like ideal customers, as the regular, affect-driven consumption of their objects of fandom bleeds into the iterative consumption of goods and service in the market, fans can all too easily fall out of love with their objects of affection. As Sandvoss has observed, fans can express "fierce resistance . . . to transformations of their object of fandom" (2005, 162). Indeed, the act of falling out of love in response to such transformations can lead not to indifference but to outright hostility. Artists who fail to deliver on the rewards promised in their crowdfunding campaigns are particularly vulnerable to such backlashes.

The general developments outlined in this chapter indicate, we believe, movements towards what might be described as a general economic model of enthusiasm. This can be seen as a response to a motivation crisis in the core capitalist countries, as an attempt to overcome consumer cynicism caused by overexposure to marketing, and earlier attempts to understand and communicate with consumers. However, while crowdfunding helps structure a market for affect and fandom, it is unlikely that it is sufficient in overcoming the problems facing the musical economy. For one thing, as the novelty of crowdfunding fades and becomes a more ubiquitous way of raising funds, linked to marketing, then crowdfunding may enter the same cycle of demotivation and cynicism observed elsewhere. For another, the nature of crowdfunding is rapidly changing, and its growth is now largely driven by mainstream investment looking for higher than average returns on investment (Langley 2015). Although this investment is mainly being directed to crowdfunding platforms that replicate the financial system, rather than the rewards- and donation-based platforms that are focused on funding the creative industries, the incorporation of this alternative funding model into the mainstream with all the risks inherent within the financial system (Reinhart and Rogoff 2011), means that crowdfunding as a whole is exposed to the contagion of a broader financial crisis, and so a threat to its long-term future.

REFERENCES

Abercrombie, Nicholas, and Brian Longhurst. *Audiences*. London: Sage, 1998.

Agamden, Giorgio. *The Coming Community*. Minneapolis: University of Minnesota Press, 1993.

Anderson, Ben. *Encountering Affect: Capacities, Appartatuses, Conditions*. Farnham, Surrey: Ashgate, 2014.

Anderson, Chris. *The Long Tail: Why the Future of Business Is Selling Less of More*. New York: Hyperion, 2006.

Arditi, David. *Itake-Over: The Recording Industry in the Digital Era*. Lanham: Rowman & Littlefield, 2015.

Arvidsson, Adam. "Brands: A Critical Perspective." *Journal of Consumer Culture* 5, no. 2 (2005): 235–258.

Baeck, Peter, Liam Collins, and Bryan Zhang. *Understanding Alternative Finance: The UK Alternative Finance Report 2014*. London: Nesta, 2014.

Barry, Andrew, and Don Slater. "Introduction: The Technological Economy." *Economy and Society* 31, no. 2 (2002): 175–193.

Bennett, Lucy, Bertha Chin, and Bethan Jones. "Crowdfunding: A New Media & Society Special Issue." *New Media and Society* 17, no. 2 (2014): 141–148.

Blanchard, Kenneth, and Sheldon Bowles. *Raving Fans!: A Revolutionary Approach to Customer Service*. London: Harper Collins, 1998.

Callon, Michel. "Introduction: The Embeddedness of Economic Markets in Economics." In *Laws of the Markets*, edited by Callon, Michel, 1–57. Oxford: Blackwell, 1998.

Callon, Michel, C. Meadel, and V. Rabeharisoa. "The Economy of Qualities." *Economy and Society* 31, no. 2 (2002): 194–217.

D'Amato, Francesco. "Investors and Patrons, Gatekeepers and Social Capital: Representations and Experiences of Fan's Participation in Fan Funding." In *The Ashgate Research Companion to Fan Cultures*, edited by Duits, L., K. Zwaan, and S. Reijnders, 135–148. Farnham: Ashgate, 2014.

Davidson, Roei, and Nathaniel Poor. "The Barriers Facing Artists' Use of Crowdfunding Platforms: Personality, Emotional Labor, and Going to the Well One Too Many Times." *New Media and Society* 17 (2014): 289–307.

The Economist. "Open, but Not as Usual." *The Economist*, March 16, 2006.

The Economist. "Beliebing in Streaming." *The Economist*, March 22, 2014.

French, Shaun, and Andrew Leyshon. "The New, New Financial System? Towards a Conceptualization of Financial Reintermediation." *Review of International Political Economy* 11, no. 2 (May 2004): 263–288.

Galuszka, Patryk, and Victor Bystrov. "The Rise of Fanvestors: A Study of a Crowdfunding Community." *First Monday* 19, no. 5 (2014). http://firstmonday.org/ojs/index.php/fm/article/view/4117/072#author

Giuffre, Liz. "Music for (Something Other Than) Pleasure: Anti-fans and the Other Side of Popular Music Appeal." In *The Ashgate Research Companion to Fan Cultures*, edited by Duits, L., K. Zwaan, and S. Reijnders. Farnham: Ashgate, 2014.

Guiney, John A., and Congcong Zhang. "Community Building as Institutional Entrepreneurship: Exploring the Emergence of a Popular Music Community." *Entrepreneurial Executive* 17 (2012): 25–48.

Harris, Remi. *Easy Money? The Definitive Guide to Funding Music Projects*. London: MusicTank Publishing, 2013.

Hebdidge, D. *Subculture: The Meaning of Style*. London: Routledge, 1979.

Hetherington, K. *Expressions of Identity*. London: Sage, 1998.

Hracs, Brian J., and Deborah Leslie. "Aesthetic Labour in Creative Industries: The Case of Independent Musicians in Toronto, Canada." *Area* 46, no. 1 (2014): 66–73.

Jenkins, Henry, Sam Ford, and Joshua Green. *Spreadable Media: Creating Value and Meaning in a Networked Culture*. New York: New York University Press, 2013.

Krugman, Paul. "Bits, Bands and Book." *The New York Times*, June 6, 2008.

Langley, Paul. "The Marketization of Crowdfunding: A New Digital Financial Market Frontier." *Economic Geography* (forthcoming, 2016).

Leadbetter, Charles, and Miller, Paul. *Pro-Am: How Enthusiasts are Changing Our Economy and Society,* London: Demos, 2014.

Lewis, Michael. *The New New Thing: A Silicon Valley Story*. London: Coronet, 2001.

Lewis, Michael. *The Future Just Happened*. London: Hodder & Stoughton, 2001.

Leyshon, Andrew. "Towards an Non-Economic Economic Geography? From Black Boxes to the Cultural Circuit of Capital in Economic Geographies of Firms and Managers." In *The Sage Handbook of Economic Geography*, edited by Leyshon, A., R. Lee, L. McDowell, and P. Sunley, 383–97. Los Angeles, CA: Sage, 2011.

Leyshon, Andrew. *Reformatted: Code, Networks and the Transformation of the Music Industry*. Oxford: Oxford University Press, 2014.
Leyshon, Andrew, Shaun French, Nigel Thrift, Louise Crewe, and Pete Webb. "Accounting for E-Commerce: Abstractions, Virtualism and the Cultural Circuit of Capital." *Economy and Society* 34, no. 3 (Aug 2005): 428–450.
Lindvall, Helienne. "Amanda Palmer Raised $1.2m, but Is She Really 'the Future of Music'?." *The Guardian,* September 26, 2012. http://www.theguardian.com/media/2012/sep/26/amanda-palmer-future-of-music
Luckerson, Victor. "Here's How Much Money Top Musicians Are Making on Spotify." *Time*, December 3, 2013.
Lury, Celia. *Brands: The Logos of the Global Economy*. London: Routledge, 2004.
MacKenzie, Donald, Fabian Muniesa, and Lucia Siu, eds. *Do Economists Make Markets?* Princeton: Princeton University Press, 2007.
Maffesoli, Michel. *The Time of the Tribes*. London: Sage, 1996.
Morris, Jeremy Wade. "Artists as Entrepreneurs, Fans as Workers." *Popular Music and Society* 37, no. 3 (2014): 273–290.
Pine, B. Joseph, and James Gilmore. *Experience Economy: Work Is Theatre and Every Business a Stage*. Cambridge, MA: Harvard Business School Press, 1999.
Reinhart, Carmen M., and Kenneth Rogoff. *This Time Is Different: Eight Centuries of Financial Folly*. Princeton, NJ: Princeton University Press, 2011.
Rheingold, Howard. *Smart Mobs: The Next Social Revolution*. Cambridge, MS: Perseus Publishing, 2002.
Salzer-Morling, Miriam, and Lars Strannegard. "Silence of the Brands." *European Journal of Marketing* 38 (2004): 224–238.
Sandvoss, Cornel. *Fans: The Mirror of Consumption*. Cambridge: Polity, 2005.
Sisario, Ben. "For U2 and Apple, a Shrewd Marketing Partnership." *New York Times*, September 9, 2014.
Slater, D. "From Calculation to Alienation: Disentangling Economic Abstractions." *Economy and Society* 31, no. 2 (2002): 234–249.
Stacey, J. *Stargazing: Hollywood Cinema and Female Spectatorship*. London: Routledge, 1994.
Thornton, Sarah. *Club Cultures: Music, Media and Subcultural Capital*. Cambridge: Polity, 1995.
Thrift, Nigel. *Knowing Capitalism*. London: Sage, 2005.
Weber, S. *The Success of Open Source*. Cambridge, MA: Harvard University Press, 2004.
White, Michele. *Buy It Now: Lessons from Ebay*. Durham, NC: Duke University Press, 2012.
Zook, Matthew. *The Geography of the Internet Industry: Venture Capital, Dot-Coms and Local Knowledge*. Oxford: Blackwell, 2005.

Contributors

David Arditi (PhD, George Mason University) is Assistant Professor of Interdisciplinary Studies at the University of Texas at Arlington. His research explores the relationship between music and technology, and the way that relationship effects music, culture, and society. He is the author of *iTake-Over: The Recording Industry in the Digital Era.*

Arturo Arriagada is Assistant Professor in the School of Journalism at Universidad Adolfo Ibáñez (Chile). He holds a PhD in Sociology from the London School of Economics and Political Science. His research topics are the relation between audiences, digital technologies, and cultural industries; social media and political communication. He is currently working on two research projects, the social life of fashion bloggers and youth online sharing practices on Facebook.

Thomas L. Bell received his doctorate in geography from the University of Iowa and took an academic position in the Department of Geography at the University of Tennessee (1971–2009). He is currently Professor Emeritus from the department at Tennessee and Adjunct Professor in the Department of Geography and Geology at Western Kentucky University. Dr. Bell has published extensively in the areas of urban and economic geography and the geography of popular culture, especially music geography. He is the author or co-author of three textbooks in human and economic geography and the co-editor of a book (with Ola Johansson) about music geography, *Sound, Society and the Geography of Popular Music* (Ashgate 2009).

Amanda Brandellero is a postdoctoral researcher in the Department of Sociology at the University of Amsterdam. Her research examines how cultural forms travel across different spatial contexts. Amanda has published on the subject of migrant musicians and world music production and the dynamics of globalization in international music charts. She is currently researching the globalization of the market for contemporary art through a case study of art production in São Paulo and Rio de Janeiro in Brazil.

Hans-Joachim Bürkner is a professor of economic and social geography at the University of Potsdam and senior researcher at the Leibniz Institute for Regional Development and Structural Planning, Erkner, Germany. He has been involved in studies on value creation in local scene-based music production and the reorientation of artists, producers, and independent labels enforced by digitization and globalization. Recent articles and an edited volume focus on the significance of digitization for the strategies of local stakeholders, on changing value configurations and production strategies in electronic dance music, and on the relevance of various capital forms (including Sonic Capital) for meeting the challenges of market disruption.

Louise Crewe is Professor of Economic Geography at the University of Nottingham. She is the author of *The Geographies of Fashion* (Bloomsbury, 2016) and of *Second Hand Cultures* (Berg, 2003) with Nicky Gregson.

Rodrigo Dominguez-Villegas is a graduate student at the University of Massachusetts-Amherst and an independent consultant for the Migration Policy Institute.

Shaun French is Associate Professor in Economic Geography at the University of Nottingham. He is editor of *Key Methods in Geography* (second edition) (Sage, 2010) with Nick Clifford and Gill Valentine.

Alexandre Frenette specializes in the study of work, creative industries, and youth labor markets. He earned his PhD in sociology at the Graduate Center, City University of New York (CUNY) in 2014 and is currently a Postdoctoral Scholar at Arizona State University's Herberger Institute for Design and the Arts. Using the music industry as a case study, he is currently working on a monograph about the challenges and the promise of internships as part of higher education, tentatively titled *The Intern Economy: Laboring to Learn in the Music Industry*.

Margaret M. Gripshover is an associate professor of geography in the Department of Geography and Geology at Western Kentucky University. She received her doctorate in geography from the University of Tennessee, Knoxville. Her research is centered at the intersection of cultural, economic, and historical geography. She has published articles and book chapters on topics including cultural landscapes, urban geography, diffusion of innovations, as well as geographic aspects of baseball and horse racing. Dr. Gripshover's regional specializations are in the American South and Midwest.

Joni R. Haijen is coordinator of the Centre for Urban Studies at the University of Amsterdam. Her research focuses on uncovering the ways in which macro-economic changes in the creative industry impact on the local situation of indie artists. She has conducted ethnographic research on the socio-economic position of indie musicians in the Dutch hip-hop scene. In addition, she has assisted in several research projects on the cultural, economic, and geographical dynamics of the commodification of music in the cultural industries. She is currently editing a book titled *Amsterdam Artists. (0)20 Portraits.*

Brian J. Hracs is a lecturer in human geography at the University of Southampton. His research examines how digital technologies and global competition are reshaping the marketplace for music and other cultural products. Brian has published music-related articles on topics such as the "MP3-Crisis," the employment experiences of independent musicians, the flows of musical talent, and the commercial strategies musicians use to "stand out in the crowd." He is currently researching the processes and spatial dynamics of "curation" through a study of record shops in Stockholm, London, and Toronto.

Johan Jansson is associate professor at the Department of Social and Economic Geography, Uppsala University and affiliated with CIND (Centre for Research on Innovation and Industrial Dynamics). Jansson has a PhD in Human Geography and his research interests are generally directed towards the field of economic geography, with a theoretical focus on agglomerations, local-global linkages, knowledge flows, creative (urban) milieus, quality, entrepreneurship, curation, and branding. Empirically, his focus is different cultural industries (e.g., design, music, arts), the Internet industry, industrial districts, urban and regional development. Jansson has published several articles, books, book chapters, and reports on these topics.

Ola Johansson received his PhD at the University of Tennessee in 2004. He is now associate professor of geography at the University of Pittsburgh at Johnstown. Ola is the co-editor of the book *Sound, Society, and the Geography of Popular Music* (Ashgate 2009). He has published music-related articles on topics such as touring, scenes, music and national identity, music and urban development, and hybridity in music. As a recent guest scholar at Linnaeus University, Ola has researched Swedish popular music. When not thinking about music, Ola is also an urban geographer.

Robert C. Kloosterman is Professor of Economic Geography and Planning at the University of Amsterdam. He is head of the research group Geographies of Globalization. Part of his research activities are focused on cultural industries, including music. He has published on the rise of African-American music in the United States, Morrissey, the clustering of music in urban environments, and Kraftwerk.

Bastian Lange is an urban and economic geographer specializing on the creative industries and questions of governance and regional development. He has been Guest Professor at the Humboldt University in Berlin (2011–2012) and responsible for several research projects funded by the federal ministry of research and education. His academic work focuses on questions of cultural entrepreneurship, value configuration in creative industries, and urban development. He is particularly interested in socio-economic transformation processes within the creative knowledge age, refining them into a useable form for the fields of politics, business, and creative scenes.

Andrew Leyshon is Professor of Economic Geography at the University of Nottingham. His most recent book is *Reformatted: code, networks and the transformation of the music industry* (Oxford University Press, 2014). He is currently editing a book on the financial system entitled *Money and Finance after the Crisis* (Wiley) with Brett Christophers and Geoff Mann.

Jimi Nilsson is a PhD student in Economic Geography at the School of Business, Economics and Law at the Gothenburg University, Sweden. Jimi's research is focused on how technological development in the music industry has affected the geographies of creative and non-creative work for Swedish musicians. He has examined the reorganization of the permanent and temporary spaces of music work and creativity, and the role played by such spaces for Swedish musicians' working lives and artist careers.

Andy C. Pratt is Professor of Cultural Economy, Director of the Centre for Culture and Creative Industries at City University London, UK, and Research Director of AHRC Creative Economy Hub: Creative Works London. His work is concerned with the organization of work in the cultural economy and its consequences for those workers and wider society. He is concerned with socio-economic interactions and the role of proximity, networks, and institutions; his work is international in scope. As well as researching and writing about policy, he has advised various UN agencies (UNESCO, ILO, UNCTAD, WIPO), and many cities globally, on cultural economy policy-making.

Michael Seman is a senior research associate at the University of North Texas Economics Research Group. He received his doctorate in urban planning and public policy from the University of Texas at Arlington and his work primarily examines the intersection of the creative economy, entrepreneurship, and economic development on the urban landscape. Michael is currently writing a book about music scenes and how they can transform cities for the University of Texas Press. His work can be found in many academic journals and he also writes for Portland State University's Artisan Economy Initiative and *The Atlantic: CityLab*.

Tyler Sonnichsen is a PhD student and graduate teaching associate in the Department of Geography at the University of Tennessee in Knoxville, Tennessee. He is interested in cultural and urban geography with a focus on media, representation, and public memory. Tyler is currently investigating how underground musical networks influence international perception of urban landscapes in the United States. He earned his MA in Geography from California State University, Long Beach, and his BS in Television-Radio-Film from Syracuse University.

Laura Speers is a Teaching Fellow in the Department of Culture, Media and Cultural Industries at King's College London. She was previously Postdoctoral Associate (Knowledge Exchange and Postgraduate Training) for the Faculty of Humanities and Social Sciences at Queen Mary University of London. Her PhD, undertaken at King's College London, explored hip-hop authenticity and identity politics in the context of the London scene. Laura's research interests include creativity and cultural labor, popular culture, and social change.

Nigel Thrift is Executive Director of the Schwarzman Scholars, an international leadership program based in Beijing. Prior to that he was Vice Chancellor at the University of Warwick. His most recent books are Globalization in Practice (Oxford University Press, 2014 co-edited with Adam Tickell, Steve Woolgar and William Rupp) and Arts of the Political: New Openings for the Left (Duke University Press, 2013) with Ash Amin.

Tarek E. Virani is a post-doctoral research associate at Queen Mary University of London. He has contributed to research that examines various elements of: music scenes and cultural infrastructure, the role of knowledge in the cultural economy, cultural policy, creative and cultural hubs, artistic knowledge within locally bounded artistic communities, musical education, working historical geographies of cities, and interdisciplinary collaborations between higher education and the cultural economy. He is currently working on a number of projects that examine specific parts of the cultural economy within the city of London. Tarek is also an active musician and producer, releasing material regularly.

Allan Watson is Senior Lecturer in Human Geography at the Staffordshire University, UK, and an Associate Director of the Globalization and World Cities (GaWC) research network. Allan's research interests center on the economic geography of the global music industry, and includes work on global urban networks of music production, and on work and emotional labor in the recording studio sector. Allan is author of *Cultural Production in and Beyond the Recording Studio* (Routledge, 2014) and co-editor of *Creative Cities Policy: Invisible Agents and Hidden Protagonists* (Routledge, 2015). He is currently undertaking research examining the economic geography of the music economy of North West England.

Pete Webb is Senior Lecturer in Sociology and Programme Director at the University of the West of England. He is the author of *Exploring the Networked Worlds of Popular Music: Milieu Cultures (*Routledge, 2010) and *Key Themes in Popular Music Studies (*Palgrave, 2012).

Jonathan R. Wynn is Assistant Professor of Sociology at the University of Massachusetts-Amherst, a member of the Placemaking Leadership Council, and author of *The Tour Guide: Walking and Talking New York* (2011) and *Music/City: American Festivals and Placemaking in Austin, Nashville, and Newport* (2015).

Index

U.C.B.
LIBRARY